The Economics of Crowdfunding

For academics, practitioners, and government policymakers, this book provides a sophisticated, comprehensive analysis of this new and important means of capital aggregation across for-profit and nonprofit sectors worldwide.

Michael Klausner,
Nancy and Charles Munger Professor of Business and Professor of Law, Stanford University

This is an excellent book, a must-read, for anyone interested in the broad phenomenon of crowdfunding.

Mingfeng Lin,
Associate Professor of Management Information Systems, University of Arizona

It is important that we recognize and respond to the opportunities and challenges arising from innovative methods of financing, such as crowdfunding. This book provides a review of the experience to date, covering important issues such as signaling, fraud, and regulatory models. The insights here are relevant to academics, entrepreneurs, investors, and policymakers.

Maureen Jensen,
Chair and CEO of the Ontario Securities Commission

Douglas Cumming • Lars Hornuf
Editors

The Economics of Crowdfunding

Startups, Portals and Investor Behavior

palgrave
macmillan

Editors
Douglas Cumming
Schulich School of Business
York University, Toronto, Canada

Lars Hornuf
Faculty of Business Studies and Economics
University of Bremen
Bremen, Germany

Max Planck Institute for Innovation and Competition
Munich, Germany

Center of Finance, University of Regensburg
Regensburg, Germany

CESifo
Munich, Germany

ISBN 978-3-319-88181-2 ISBN 978-3-319-66119-3 (eBook)
https://doi.org/10.1007/978-3-319-66119-3

Softcover re-print of the Hardcover 1st edition 2018

Cover illustration: venimo / Alamy Stock Photo

Printed on acid-free paper

This Palgrave Macmillan imprint is published by Springer Nature
The registered company is Springer International Publishing AG
The registered company address is: Gewerbestrasse 11, 6330 Cham, Switzerland

To Dylan and Sasha Cumming, and Maria Christina Müller.

Foreword

The "crowd" has attracted considerable attention from many academic fields. For good reason, crowd-based processes have gained more and more practical relevance, for instance in problem-solving or in finance. In this book volume on the economics of crowdfunding, Douglas Cumming and Lars Hornuf have gathered an impressive group of contributors exploring various facets of the phenomenon.

The definition of crowdfunding is comprehensive: Cumming and Hornuf include reward-based and donation-based crowdfunding, equity crowdfunding (crowdinvesting), and marketplace (peer-to-peer) lending within the scope of the investigations presented here. Given the early stage of the evolution of these processes, going for breadth is a compelling choice.

The chapters in this volume cover a wide set of topics. In Chap. 1, the editors provide an insightful overview of the literature regarding donation- and reward-based crowdfunding, crowdinvesting, and crowdlending models. The first part of the book then turns to the role of crowdfunding for small companies and start-ups. Leboeuf and Schwienbacher discuss in Chap. 2 the role of crowdfunding as a novel financing tool for small enterprises and explore which types of firms are most likely to benefit from widely available crowdfunding. Vismara (Chap. 3) addresses informational inefficiencies in crowdfunding markets and identifies various forms of signals as possible solutions to these problems. Lambert, Ralcheva, and Roosenboom (Chap. 4) take a close look at the relationship between the entrepreneur who seeks to obtain financing and the crowd, and at the informational asymmetries that may ultimately limit the efficacy of crowdfunding. Hainz (Chap. 5) then turns to cases of fraudulent behavior in the context of crowdfunding. Coming to grips with such cases and possible underlying incentives for fraud will be an important factor in strengthening crowdfunding as a new financing tool.

Market structure aspects are studied by Fenwick, McCahery, and Vermeulen in Chap. 6, while Mollick studies the impact of reward-based crowdfunding on entrepreneurship in Chap. 7, employing surveys of Kickstarter funders. The backers of projects are also at the focus of Chap. 8 where Bayus and Kuppuswamy analyze dynamics over the project funding cycle.

The final three chapters cover regulatory aspects of crowdfunding. Bradford (Chap. 9) presents an analysis of regulation in the USA, while Klöhn (Chap. 10) explores the European regulatory environment. Amour and Enriques (Chap. 11) compare regulation in the USA and the UK. Given that countries are by now almost competing to set attractive boundary conditions for financing via the crowd, these country-level and comparative assessments should be highly relevant to policy makers and researchers alike.

For any academic or practitioner who wants to have a quick and thorough start into the fascinating and complex economics of crowdfunding, this volume is an excellent point of departure. The collection of articles tackles the phenomenon of crowdfunding comprehensively. Final answers as to how important crowdfunding will be as a novel financing instrument in the future will still have to be explored. Presently, the contributions assembled here cover major research questions, summarize the existing literature, and offer first insights regarding regulatory responses. The editors and the authors have undertaken an important step toward a better understanding of a fascinating and multifaceted phenomenon.

Max Planck Institute for Innovation and Competition, Munich, Germany

Dietmar Harhoff
July 2017

Preface

This book studies crowdfunding as a new financing tool in the entrepreneurial finance ecosystem. The analyses in the book serve multiple purposes. From an academic perspective, the book attempts to give a topical overview over the recent scholarly literature on crowdfunding. While five years ago, very few academics started to shift their attention toward this new topic, by the end of the decade almost no finance and certainly no entrepreneurial finance conference goes without research findings in crowdfunding. Even entire conferences have been dedicated to crowdfunding. On February 8, 2013, the *Crowdinvesting Symposium* took place for the first time at LMU Munich and on October 17, 2013, the *Berkeley Crowdfunding Symposium* discussed the latest research on crowdfunding. Journals like *Entrepreneurship Theory and Practice* as well as *Small Business Economics* have dedicated special issues to crowdfunding. From a practitioners' perspective, this book summarizes what works in crowdfunding and what does not. Portal owners and entrepreneurs looking for funding might use the insights provided here to structure their campaigns effectively. Investors learn from empirical studies about their own behavior and potentially avoid making costly mistakes. Finally, from a policy-maker perspective, the book provides evidence whether crowdfunding should be fostered or prohibited as a new financing tool. To address these questions in a rigorous and state-of-the-art manner, we have gathered some of the most well-known scholars in the field.

The book tackles four broad topics. The first three are economic in nature and investigate what we have learned so far about start-ups, portals, as well as backers and investors in the crowdfunding realm. These topics are covered by 19 outstanding management, finance, and economics scholars. Thereafter, based on the economic evidence, four outstanding legal scholars have investigated how crowdfunding is currently regulated and potentially ought to be regulated in the future. Their focus is on the USA, the European Union, as well as individual member states such as the UK and Germany.

Moreover, to make the book more readable and consistent, we decided on the following simple terminologies. Crowdfunding encompasses four major business models. The *donation-based crowdfunding* model involves, for example, the funding of philanthropic and research projects. Under this model, backers donate money to support a project without expecting compensation. This differs under the *reward-based crowdfunding* model in which backers are promised tangible or intangible perks, such as a supporter T-shirt or having their name posted on the campaign website. At times, the reward-based model of crowdfunding may resemble a pre-purchase, such as when backers fund a product or service they wish to consume and which is still to be developed by the entrepreneur. Under these models, the crowd is referred to as *backers*, because they do not invest but donate their funds or pre-purchase a product or service. Popular examples are video games (e.g., Star Citizen) or the Pebble smartwatch. Portals include, for example, Crowdfunder.co.uk, Indiegogo, Kickstarter, and Startnext.

Crowdinvesting—which is also referred to as investment-based crowdfunding, securities crowdfunding, or equity crowdfunding—is a subcategory of crowdfunding and refers to an alternative form of external finance for firms in countries that permit the solicitation of the general public. The solicitation often takes place without or with a "light" version of a securities prospectus (e.g., JOBS Act Title III in the USA or the Small Investor Protection Act in Germany). The crowd participates in the uncertain future cash flows of a firm via equity, mezzanine, or debt finance. The crowd is referred to as *investors*, as they make a financial decision and do not consume a product. Portals include, for example, Companisto, Crowdcube, Republic, Seedrs, Seedmatch, and WiSeed.

Crowdlending is another subcategory of crowdfunding where loans are extended to an individual or firm at a fixed interest rate. The crowd is referred to as *lenders*. Unlike in the crowdinvesting domain, repayment by the borrowers starts immediately. Portals include, for example, LendingClub, FundingCircle, and Auxmoney.

Toronto, Canada
Bremen, Germany

Douglas Cumming
Lars Hornuf

Acknowledgments

This book evolved as part of the research project "Crowdinvesting in Germany, England and the USA: Regulatory Perspectives and Welfare Implications of a New Financing Scheme," which was supported by the German Research Foundation (*Deutsche Forschungsgemeinschaft*) under the grant number HO 5296/1-1. Lars Hornuf would also like to thank Gerrit Engelmann for his excellent support in formatting the book consistently. Douglas Cumming gratefully acknowledges the Social Sciences and Humanities Research Council of Canada for financial support.

Contents

List of Figures

List of Tables

1

Introduction

Douglas Cumming and Lars Hornuf

Crowdfunding has experienced tremendous growth and developed into a global multibillion-dollar business over the course of the last five years. The most successful segment of the nascent market is crowdlending, which is also referred to as peer-to-peer lending or marketplace lending, and had an estimated global market volume of USD 25 billion in 2015 (Massolution 2016). Although more recent figures on the overall market volume are not yet available, market growth has most likely continued during the years 2016 and 2017. The portal Lending Club alone reported to have funded loans worth USD 31 billion by the end of 2017. The other market segments are considerably smaller and are comparable in

D. Cumming
Schulich School of Business, York University, Toronto, ON, Canada

L. Hornuf (✉)
Business Studies & Economics, University of Bremen, Bremen, Germany

Max Planck Institute for Innovation and Competition, Munich, Germany

Center of Finance, University of Regensburg, Regensburg, Germany

CESifo, Munich, Germany

D. Cumming, L. Hornuf (eds.), *The Economics of Crowdfunding*,
https://doi.org/10.1007/978-3-319-66119-3_1

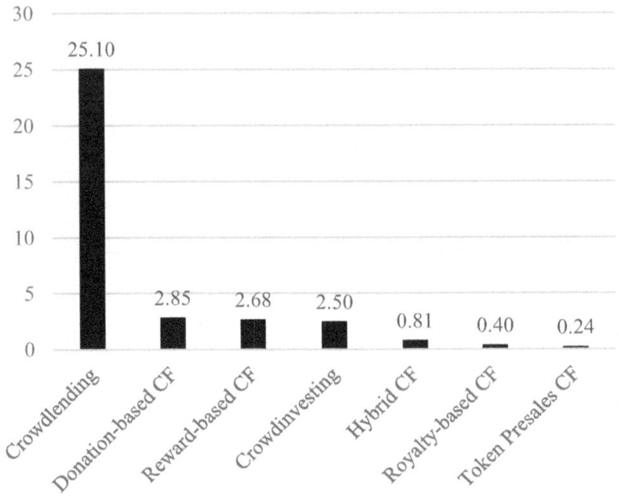

Fig. 1.1 Global crowdfunding market by segment volume, USD billions in 2015

size. According to Massolution (2016), donation-based crowdfunding reached a global volume of USD 2.85 billion, reward-based crowdfunding USD 2.68 billion, and crowdinvesting USD 2.50 billion in 2015. New segments such as royalty-based crowdfunding, hybrid forms of crowdfunding, and token presales or Initial Coin Offerings exhibit relatively small market volumes (Fig. 1.1).

Depending on the jurisdiction under which platforms are operating, their business models often cut out traditional financial intermediaries. On the upside, this might reduce transaction costs and make financial services more cost-efficient. Furthermore, crowdlending portals may be well equipped to develop credit risk models that are geared to high-risk loans. They may thus provide a better assessment of high-risk customers than traditional financial intermediaries that used to refuse certain individuals and businesses access to mainstream financial services. Put differently, crowdfunding portals have identified the inability of traditional banks to extend loans as a business opportunity and consequently seek to fill the existing funding gaps. At the same time, many crowdfunding markets lack financial intermediaries that screen and monitor borrowers. Portals have regularly no skin in the game and consequently have little incentives to consider the performance of their investors. Under the new US crowdinvesting rules, the funding portals and their directors are even prohibited to have any financial interest in the issuer. From a macroeconomic and systemic risk perspective, this might be a desirable setting, as no crowdfunding platform can become too big to fail.

Moreover, all crowdfunding platforms cater per definition to two-sided markets. This means that platforms need not only attract borrowers, start-ups, or charity beneficiaries but also individuals who are willing to donate or put their money into a risky investment. Thus, if platforms intend to operate in the market over a considerable period of time, they should, in line with Rochet and Tirole (2003), have good incentives to serve the interest of all market participants including the investors. Whether the owners and managers of a crowdfunding platform intend to operate a long-term business or rather engage in fly-by-night operations is ultimately an empirical question. However, some caution is warranted. Over the course of one and a half years, the Chinese crowdlending platform Ezubao, for example, had attracted a total of USD 7.6 billion from around 900,000 investors. In January 2016, it became obvious that the portal operated a Ponzi scheme and senior executives had spent considerable amounts of investors' money on private expenses, making very little real investments.

Platforms are not the only market players that engage in fraud. Several project creators in reward-based crowdfunding have been identified as being scams (Cumming et al. 2016). For example, the Kobe beef jerky campaign was just about being completed, when Kickstarter stopped the USD 120,309 going to the fraudsters' bank account. Whether the crowd is well positioned to identify scams is not clear. Mollick and Nanda (2015) find, for a sample of theater projects, that the financing decisions of the crowd and professional funders are quite consistent and that there is no difference in the quality of projects that receive funding by the crowd and those funded by professionals. On the other hand, crowdfunding platforms lack some of the features that Surowiecki (2004) identified as being important for the 'wisdom of the crowd' to emerge. Although the crowd might be a diversified enough group to distinguish valuable projects and scams, the decision-making process of backers and investors on the various Internet platforms is hardly independent and might also be driven be irrational herding. Some early contributions from the crowdlending realm indicate that investors can, however, also engage in strategic and rational herding (Herzenstein et al. 2011a).

If operations did not already fall under existing securities or banking laws, policy makers have so far taken a wait-and-see approach or implemented a light form of regulation that is to be adapted once regulators have learned more about the functioning of crowdfunding markets. The reason for the reluctant approach of many regulators is that they also understand the potential of serving underbanked individuals and small businesses that are at the core of economic growth. Large groups of the population might for the first time receive funding that was not available to them but should have been from an economic efficiency standpoint. Furthermore, crowdfunding also has a democratizing element in the sense that investors get access to a new asset class that was not available to them before.

In recent years, the academic literature has also shown a growing interest in crowdfunding. Some segments have received attention earlier than others, which was mostly due to data availability and the relevance of the respective crowdfunding segments. As noted in the *Preface* of this book, crowdfunding consists of four different business models. The funding of philanthropic and research projects is known as the *donation-based crowdfunding* model, where *backers* donate money to a project without subsequently receiving a monetary compensation. Still, backers may derive utility from the act of donation, for which Andreoni (1989) coined the term warm-glow effect. In an early study, Saxton and Wang (2014) analyzed data from Facebook Causes. They evidence that in the Internet traditional economic explanations are less important for charity-giving decisions than social network effect explanations are. Moreover, they revealed that health-related causes were most appealing to donors. Crowdfunding platforms that return donations in the event of not meeting capital goals tend to lead to larger contributions in total according to simulations (Wash and Solomon 2014) and empirical evidence (Cumming et al. 2015). Further, donors often invest very early or very late in crowdfunding and projects are more likely to be completely funded if donors invest early (Solomon et al. 2015).

Under the *reward-based crowdfunding* model, *backers* are promised a product or a perk. In a seminal article, Mollick (2014) examined the delivery rate in reward-based crowdfunding campaigns. Using data from Kickstarter, he found that most project creators intend delivering the product they promised, but many deliver it with a considerable delay. *Crowdinvesting*, which is also referred to as investment-based crowdfunding, securities crowdfunding, or equity crowdfunding, is an Internet-based form of external finance for firms. Solicitation of *investors* often takes place without or with a 'light' version of a securities prospectus. Investors participate in the uncertain future cash flows of a firm via equity, mezzanine, or debt finance. In one of the first articles on the topic, Ahlers et al. (2015) examine the effectiveness of signals that start-ups use to induce investors. They find that retaining equity and providing more detailed information about risks are interpreted as effective signals by the crowd. In another seminar article, Agrawal et al. (2015) find that local funders are less responsive to information about the cumulative funds raised during a crowdinvesting campaign. They further evidence that this effect is largely driven by investors during the early phase of the campaign who have an offline social relationship with the creator.

Crowdlending is another form of crowdfunding where loans are extended to an individual or firm at a fixed interest rate. Under this model, the crowd may adequately be referred to as *lenders*. Unlike in the other crowdfunding models, repayment often starts immediately. In one of the first articles, Lin et al. (2013) find that female borrowers secure financing more often than men. Moreover, Herzenstein et al. (2011b) show that a detailed loan description positively affects the probability of financing. Recently, Iyer et al. (2015) have highlighted that soft factors together with the rating category of the loan enable lenders to infer approximately one-third of the variation in the creditworthiness indicated in the borrower's credit score. While a complete overview of the literature on crowdlending goes beyond the scope of this introduction, a worthwhile summary of the most important articles for the different crowdfunding segments is provided by Dorfleitner et al. (2017, 85ff.).

While this book gives an overview of the current state of crowdfunding research and partly develops it further, we also want to provide a glimpse on what we believe are future research topics. First, while rigorous research has developed in all segments of crowdfunding, little research exists that takes a comparative stance. For example, one might ask whether firms fare better when they are funding new projects through reward-based crowdfunding, crowdinvesting, or crowdlending. On the other side of the coin, it is not yet clear whether it is more efficient for backers to invest in a firm, to extend a loan, or to receive a product that can later potentially be resold or consumed. Second, while scholarly literature has looked at funding success, not much is known about the ultimate success of a venture. Future research might thus ask whether crowdfunding creates sustainable firms and what the relevant success factors are to that respect. Third, little is known about the motives of backers and investors. While pure or impure altruism most likely plays a role in donation-based crowdfunding, the warm-glow effect might to some extent even exist in crowdinvesting and crowdlending. Given that some investors might systematically lose money from these investments and still decide to support this type of ventures for non-monetary reasons, it raises interesting policy questions that ought to be answered in the future. The authors in this book already answer some of them.

References

Agrawal, Ajay, Christian Catalini, and Avi Goldfarb. 2015. Crowdfunding, Geography, Social Networks, and the Timing of Decision. *Journal of Economics and Management Strategy* 24: 253–274.

Ahlers, Gerrit K., Douglas Cumming, Christina Günther, and Denis Schweizer. 2015. Signaling in Equity Crowdfunding. *Entrepreneurship Theory and Practice* 39: 955–980.

Andreoni, James. 1989. Giving with Impure Altruism: Applications to Charity and Ricardian Equivalence. *Journal of Political Economy* 97: 1447–1458.

Cumming, Douglas J., Lars Hornuf, Moein Karami, and Denis Schweizer. 2016. Disentangling Crowdfunding from Fraudfunding. *Social Science Research Network*. https://ssrn.com/abstract=2828919. Accessed 20 Feb 2017.

Cumming, Douglas J., Gaël Lefoeuf, and Armin Schweinbacher. 2015. Crowdfunding Models: Keep-It-All vs. All-or-Nothing. *Social Science Research Network*. https://papers.ssrn.com/abstract=2447567. Accessed 20 Feb 2017.

Dorfleitner, Gregor, Lars Hornuf, Matthias Schmitt, and Martina Weber. 2017. *FinTech in Germany*. Heidelberg: Springer.

Herzenstein, Michal, Utpal M. Dholakia, and Rick L. Andrews. 2011a. Strategic Herding Behavior in Peer-to-Peer Loan Auctions. *Journal of Interactive Marketing* 25: 27–36.

Herzenstein, Michal, Scott Sonenshein, and Utpal M. Dholakia. 2011b. Tell Me a Good Story and I May Lend You Money: The Role of Narratives in Peer-to-Peer Lending Decisions. *Journal of Marketing Research* 48: 138–149.

Iyer, Rajkamal, Asim Ijaz Khwaja, Erzo F.P. Luttmer, and Kelly Shue. 2015. Screening Peers Softly: Inferring the Quality of Small Borrowers. *Management Science* 62: 1554–1577.

Lin, Mingfeng, Nagpurnanand R. Prabhala, and Siva Viswanathan. 2013. Judging Borrowers by the Company They Keep: Friendship Networks and Information Asymmetry in Online Peer-to-Peer Lending. *Management Science* 59: 17–35.

Massolution. 2016. 2015CF. The Crowdfund Industry Report. http://reports.crowdsourcing.org/index.php?route=product/product&product_id=54. Accessed 7 Mar 2017.

Mollick, Ethan R. 2014. The Dynamics of Crowdfunding: Determinants of Success and Failure. *Journal of Business Venturing* 29: 1–16. https://doi.org/10.2139/ssrn.2088298.

Mollick, Ethan R., and Ramana Nanda. 2015. Wisdom or Madness? Comparing Crowds with Expert Evaluation in Funding the Arts. *Management Science* 62: 1533–1553.

Rochet, Jean-Charles, and Jean Tirole. 2003. Platform Competition in Two-Sided Markets. *Journal of the European Economic Association* 1: 990–1029.

Saxton, Gregory D., and Lili Wang. 2014. The Social Network Effect: The Determinants of Giving Through Social Media. *Nonprofit and Voluntary Sector Quarterly* 43 (5): 850–868.

Solomon, Jacob, Wenjuan Ma, and Rick Wash. 2015. *Don't Wait!: How Timing Affects Coordination of Crowdfunding Donations*. Paper presented at Proceedings of the 18th ACM Conference on Computer Supported Cooperative Work (547–556), New York, USA.

Surowiecki, James. 2004. *The Wisdom of Crowds: Why the Many Are Smarter than the Few and How Collective Wisdom Shapes Business, Economics, Societies, and Nations*. New York: Anchor Books.

Wash, Rick, and Solomon, Jacob. 2014. *Coordinating Donors on Crowdfunding Websites*. Paper presented at Proceedings of the 17th ACM Conference on Computer Supported Cooperative Work and Social Computing (38–48), New York, USA.

Douglas Cumming is Professor of Finance and Entrepreneurship and the Ontario Research Chair at the Schulich School of Business, York University. He has published over 150 articles in leading refereed academic journals in finance, management, and law and economics. He is the incoming editor-in-chief of the *Journal of Corporate Finance* (January 2018), and a co-editor of *Annals of Corporate Governance, Finance Research Letters, and Entrepreneurship Theory and Practice*. He is the author and editor of over a dozen books. Cumming's work has been reviewed in numerous media outlets, including *The Economist*, the Wall Street Journal, *The New York Times*, and *The New Yorker*.

Lars Hornuf is Professor of Finance at the University of Bremen. He was a visiting scholar at University of California, Berkeley; Stanford University; Duke University; and Georgetown University. From 2014 to 2017, Hornuf held a grant from the German Research Foundation on 'Crowdinvesting in Germany, England and the USA: Regulatory Perspectives and Welfare Implications of a New Financing Scheme'. In 2016, he wrote two expert reports for the Federal Ministry of Finance on the German FinTech market and the Small Investor Protection Act. Hornuf's work has been covered in newspapers like *The Economist* and *Foreign Policy*.

Part I

Startups

2

Crowdfunding as a New Financing Tool

Gaël Leboeuf and Armin Schwienbacher

2.1 Introduction

The lack of access to finance is well recognized as being one of the main difficulties for many start-ups, especially risky and innovative ones (Carpenter and Petersen 2002). While much of this difficulty stems from the severe information asymmetries and agency costs that many start-ups face, others may be due to the lack of fit with the investors' investment objectives. When external finance is required, selecting the right form of finance is crucial for successfully developing an entrepreneurial activity, and this choice involves different trade-offs, owing to different pros and cons for each type of financing source (Cosh et al. 2009). For example, in general, start-ups with an intermediate level of growth prospects are not eligible for venture capital finance, as managers seek investments in risky

---

G. Leboeuf
Univ Lyon, Université Lumière Lyon2, Coactis EA4161, Lyon, France

A. Schwienbacher (✉)
Department of Finance and Accounting, SKEMA Business School, Euralille, France

D. Cumming, L. Hornuf (eds.), *The Economics of Crowdfunding*,
https://doi.org/10.1007/978-3-319-66119-3_2

but high-growth companies. These start-ups may then receive funding from business angels or friends and family. Similarly, while most traditional start-ups rely on bank loans (Robb and Robinson 2014), candidates for bank loans need to provide collateral and sufficient cash flows to sustain interest payments, two elements that research and development (R&D)-intensive start-ups typically do not have.

The digital revolution, combined with social media and structured crowdfunding platforms that act as intermediaries between fund seekers (entrepreneurs) and small fund providers (the crowd), offers new opportunities to raise capital to develop a company or launch a project, and sometimes even to finance risky R&D expenditures in existing entrepreneurial companies (Belleflamme et al. 2014; Mollick 2014). Internet-based crowdfunding now allows even small entrepreneurs to raise funds from a large crowd, as communication costs have virtually disappeared with the Internet. In countries with a lack of sufficient seed and start-up capital such as angel finance and friends and family, crowdfunding has the potential to help fill the funding gap because it allows nonqualified individuals to also invest in innovative start-ups (Hornuf and Schwienbacher 2017). In the case of reward-based crowdfunding, the amount of funds collected during the campaign may further offer valuable feedback on the market prospects of the product being produced by the entrepreneur (Chemla and Tinn 2016; Schwienbacher 2014).

While research on crowdfunding still offers a largely incomplete picture of the phenomenon, existing studies indicate that crowdfunders participate for very different reasons and that these reasons also vary across the different types of crowdfunding. Moreover, entrepreneurs launching a crowdfunding campaign may self-select to do so, as crowdfunding may not be the best choice for all entrepreneurs. Therefore, in this chapter we argue that while crowdfunding may fill a funding gap, specific types of entrepreneurs are more likely to benefit, as they are better able to match crowdfunders' preferences for participating in a crowdfunding campaign and reap the benefits of crowd participation.

In this chapter, we first discuss how crowdfunding fits into the traditional financing cycle of small businesses and start-ups. We then raise the question as to whether crowdfunding solves a specific funding gap, a necessary condition to justify crowdfunding as a viable source of entrepreneurial finance in the long run. Finally, we elaborate on the type of entrepreneurial activities and entrepreneurs who are more likely to benefit from crowdfunding. Many of these issues are covered in more detail in subsequent chapters.

2.2 The New Financing Cycle

Start-ups get financed under what is commonly described as the so-called financial growth-cycle paradigm, proposed by Berger and Udell (1998). This paradigm largely considers a linear relationship between sources of funding and stages of development, in which the type of funding is a function of the start-up's stage of development. In this framework, each funding source is characterized by its relative capacity to deal with information asymmetries and moral hazard and, most crucially, by its funding capacity in terms of size. Start-ups at their initial stage may rely on friends and family, bootstrap finance, and business angels, all of which may provide limited amounts of capital. For larger amounts, venture capital funds may be tapped, as they often make staged investments of several millions of dollars or euros. Much larger and more developed companies may go public through an initial public offering as a means to raise money on a regulated, public stock market. These firms, however, are already at a more mature stage, with lower technological and market risks, and thus are prone to less information asymmetry problems. Bank finance may be available for any amount (Schwienbacher 2013) but is not suitable for start-ups exhibiting high levels of information asymmetry or moral hazard problems or start-ups with a lack of collateral and insufficient revenues to support interest payments.

A first-order question is where crowdfunding is situated in this framework. We suggest that the answer depends largely on the type of crowdfunding considered. Reward-based crowdfunding more closely resembles supplier finance, while crowdlending resembles bank finance, an equity-based crowdfunding angel (Hornuf and Schwienbacher 2016), and, to a lesser extent, venture capital finance (and perhaps even an initial public offering on smaller stock market segments, such as the Marché Libre in Paris or the Alternative Investment Market in London, though only for some outliers for the time being). Indeed, recently, some start-ups have raised several millions of euros on equity-crowdfunding platforms in

Germany, making it a potentially credible alternative to venture capital (Hornuf and Schwienbacher 2017). Donation-based crowdfunding may at times resemble bootstrap finance, insofar as bootstrap finance sometimes involves relying on "free" resources. Considering these distinctions, crowdfunding typically fits with early stage and expansion-stage finance in terms of stage of development.

Still, crowdfunding needs to fill a funding gap to be a viable source of funding (for a general discussion on funding gaps in the context of entrepreneurial finance, see Cressy 2002). If it only substitutes for another source such that it merely crowds out the existing source without offering some specific benefits (either lower transaction costs or reduced contractual inefficiency), its economic value is limited. Research, however, suggests that this is not the case. While crowdfunding may generate its own transaction costs and risks (Griffin 2013; Hazen 2012; Hildebrand et al. 2016; Mollick 2013), it may provide efficient funding for some types of entrepreneurial initiatives. One possible source of gains is the extra information obtained in reward-based crowdfunding campaigns on possible demand for the product (Chemla and Tinn 2016; Schwienbacher 2014). In this type of crowdfunding, the entrepreneur typically produces the product as a reward so that it resembles "prepurchasing." Then, the crowdfunding campaign gives a better view of market demand, similar to a market analysis—except that, here, individuals do not simply claim to be willing to buy the product but already prepurchase it, making it a more credible source of information than a simple market analysis. Moreover, under an all-or-nothing funding model, risk may be reduced for the entrepreneur, because the threshold level for undertaking the project provides a call option to the entrepreneur, who will then not undertake the project if demand does not cover costs (Cumming et al. 2016). This model reduces operational risk of the project because no financial resources have been engaged yet; they are only engaged if enough demand is secured during the reward-based crowdfunding campaign. Relatedly, Hakenes and Schlegel (2014) show that in equity-based crowdfunding, investors are willing to reveal private information about their interest to invest if the campaign is run under the all-or-nothing funding model, as then they are guaranteed that their commitment will be canceled in case of lack of sufficient interest by other potential investors. The generation of valuable information through the aggregation of individual preferences is often referred to as a manifestation of "wisdom of crowds," which leads to information that cannot become available with traditional sources of finance.

Crowdfunding may further help entrepreneurs access venture capital funds. Recent studies show that successful crowdfunding campaigns tend to attract follow-up funding more easily in the form of venture capital. In the subsample of projects that raised more than USD 100,000 on Kickstarter or Indiegogo, Shafi and Colombo (2016) find that these entrepreneurs were significantly more likely to raise venture capital. This means that crowdfunding is a valuable first step in attracting the attention of larger investors, if necessary.

A final reason for the possible viability of crowdfunding as a distinct source of entrepreneurial funding involves the lack of seed capital available in the economy, as often argued in Europe, due to the lack of angel finance. In this case, crowdfunding may help reduce the gap between available seed capital and availability of valuable investment opportunities. Hornuf and Schwienbacher (2017) argue that this point makes equity-based crowdfunding even more important in Europe than in the United States. Considering these different arguments, it seems plausible that crowdfunding is helping fill a funding gap.

2.3 The Crowd as Financier

In this section, we take a closer look at the crowd as fund provider. The crowd represents a pool of potential funders, each with a different profile and expectations but sharing the same willingness to finance a project or an entrepreneur. While some members may be part of a specific community of fans sharing common interests and preferences (especially for art and music projects), most often these individuals do not know one another. In what follows, we discuss some profiles of crowdfunders for the different crowdfunding types (donation-/reward-based crowdfunding, crowdinvesting, and crowdlending) and their motivation to participate in crowdfunding campaigns. Then, we discuss mechanisms offered by crowdfunding to investors to evaluate their decision to back a project or a proposed investment opportunity, including risk sharing, herding behavior, and informational cascade.

2.3.1 Profiles and Motivations of Crowdfunders

The main objective of an entrepreneur who relies on crowdfunding is to raise capital from a large number of small investors. While donation- and reward-based crowdfunding can only rely on nonprofessional participants (fans, donors, or consumers), crowdinvesting and crowdlending offer promises of possible capital gains and dividends (for equity) or interest payments (for loans), thus enabling professional investors to participate as well.

An important distinction between professional and nonprofessional participants is that the main goal of nonprofessional participants is not purely based on profits (Bretschneider et al. 2014; Cumming and Johan 2013). For example, the backers of a Kickstarter campaign may contribute to prepurchase an object (a consumption decision), to help a known entrepreneur (support of an entrepreneurial initiative), to support a cause they believe in (charity), or to obtain recognition by being part of a group. Conversely, professional investors need to generate profits from their investing activities, especially if they manage capital for clients, even if they may follow other goals such as promoting socially responsible investments and economic development. These latter goals will generally be of second order, however.

It is important to distinguish between donation- or reward-based crowdfunding and crowdinvesting and crowdlending. In donation-based crowdfunding, backers do not receive any reward from their contribution. In reward-based crowdfunding, backers may be eligible to receive a reward, depending on the promises made by the entrepreneur and the amount pledged during the campaign. Entrepreneurs offer greater rewards for higher contributions. In contrast, in crowdlending and crowdinvesting, entrepreneurs offer crowdfunders the possibility to earn financial returns and, thus, to become an investor. The possibility to earn financial returns is more likely to attract more traditional investors, including professional investors; for example, AngelList offers a program for professional investors, while Lending Club recently started with a pension fund. Table 2.1 illustrates the main motivations crowdfunders pursue based on their profile (professional or nonprofessional investors) and on the type of crowdfunding (donation-/reward-based

Table 2.1 Differences in motivation between professional and nonprofessional investors

	Donation- and reward-based crowdfunding	Crowdlending and crowdinvesting
Professional investors	–	Financial returns (with or without secondary objectives, such as supporting entrepreneurial activities, networking, and portfolio diversification)
Nonprofessional investors	Reward, warm glow, altruism, recognition, reciprocity, identification	Financial returns, supporting entrepreneurial activities, fun to invest/participate, recognition, reciprocity, identification

Note: Adapted from Bretschneider et al. (2014), Cumming and Johan (2013)

crowdfunding or crowdinvesting/crowdlending). While professional investors tend to limit contributions to profit-generating crowdfunding types (crowdlending and crowdinvesting), we find nonprofessional participants in both categories (profit-generating and donation-/reward-based). Although we know that warm glow, altruism, recognition, reciprocity, and identification have an impact on the decision to participate, the main motivation of investors is compensation in the form of either expected final returns or the promised reward (Cholakova and Clarysse 2015).

The overall number of backers may also affect the ultimate level of benefits accruing to individual backers. Belleflamme et al. (2015) discuss the different ways that network effects may affect the overall utility from participating in a crowdfunding campaign. Such network effects may occur between groups (cross-group effects between entrepreneurs and crowdfunders) and within a single group (within-group effects between entrepreneurs themselves or crowdfunders themselves). In the first case, a network effect may arise across projects of a same category, as more crowdfunders on the platform may attract more entrepreneurs (more crowdfunders means greater funding capacity overall), which in turn may attract even more crowdfunders (more entrepreneurs means a greater variety of projects). The second case considers network effects within the group of crowdfunders. Two opposing effects may occur. On the one hand, more crowdfunders may make it more attractive for other individuals to join the platform because projects are more likely to be funded and, thus, successful; on the other hand, more crowdfunders can mean more competition for a limited number of rewards or securities. This negative impact is most likely to be severe in crowdinvesting, in which a limited number of securities are sold. Whether network effects have a positive or negative impact on group participation depends on the type of platform and its structure.

Next, it is possible to distinguish profiles of investors/backers according to their behavior in and active contribution to the project. Lin et al. (2014) classify crowdfunders into four groups: active backers, trend followers, altruistic backers, and the crowd. Active backers are those who invest early during the campaign in many projects and are less sensitive to the number of backers who have already invested in a project. Trend followers invest later in projects and are more sensitive to the number of backers who have already committed; they wait to see how funding dynamics evolve. Altruistic backers invest for reasons other than investment success; thus, they are the typical backers in donation-based crowdfunding. Finally, the broader crowd encompasses backers with no typical behavior of the three former groups.

It is also worth noting the presence of another class of backers: peers. Indeed, many entrepreneurs in crowdfunding campaigns are also backers in other projects (Zvilichovsky et al. 2015). When supporting projects of others before starting their own campaign, entrepreneurs increase their chances to succeed. Through reciprocity, entrepreneurs are likely to receive pledges for their own project from other entrepreneurs they helped before starting.

2.3.2 Risk/Return Balance and Assessment of Investment Opportunities

Although the backers may be motivated by various reasons and the amount involved may be rather low in crowdfunding, the crowd remains responsive to the relationship between risk and success (or return) of the project. Cumming et al. (2016) show that the crowd responds to both the level of the funding goal and the funding model used. By funding model, the authors are referring to the two important models "all-or-nothing" and "keep-it-all." They investigate the context of Indiegogo, an international crowdfunding website on which entrepreneurs can choose between the two models. If a project requires a higher goal, the crowd could view the project as having larger fixed costs and thus having a lower chance to gather the amount required. In the same way, if an entrepreneur chooses the keep-it-all funding model, the project can be underfunded (as the entrepreneur receives the money even if the funding goal is not achieved), and the risk borne by backers is higher from the increased risk of never receiving the reward or any return on their investment.

Moreover, the crowd has other mechanisms to assess the quality (and the likelihood of success) of a crowdfunded project. As with any traditional investment, crowdfunders have access to the basic information provided directly by the entrepreneur on the crowdfunding platform (e.g., business plan, legal information). Depending on the platform, the information may be closely audited and formatted or, in contrast, exhibit great heterogeneity among projects. Still, Mollick (2013) finds that the crowd evaluates the quality of a project by using the same signals as venture capitalists. In addition, despite the persistence of traditional biases in investment decisions such as the home bias (Hornuf and Schmitt 2016; Lin and Viswanathan 2015), crowdfunding allows a significant reduction in gender and geographic bias (Agrawal et al. 2011; Mollick and Robb 2016). Compared with traditional venture capital financing, the geographic distribution is larger in crowdfunding (less limited to some specific areas such as the Silicon Valley), and recent studies show more women leading crowdfunding campaigns. Moreover, the crowd is able to evaluate the project quality at least as accurately as experts, with the advantage of providing good evaluation of the target market because, most of the time, members of the crowd are not only investors but also the final users (Mollick 2013).

As participation of others is often visible in real time during the crowdfunding campaign, a backer considering participating can estimate the willingness of others to support the same project. Alternatively, for crowdfunding platforms trying to reduce herding behavior by hiding previous participations, comments and/or testimonials are a good indicator of crowd support. This leads to specific dynamics during the campaign in which the contribution of one individual is determined by the behavior of others. In this context, two effects may affect the decision to pledge: the number of previous backers and their reputation. First, the number of backers provides a good signal of the support gained from the crowd. According to Kuppuswamy and Bayus (2017), the crowd will be more prone to participate if the number of previous backers at the time of investment is already high. Second, some backers may decide to disclose their identity, while others keep their pledge anonymous. If an opinion leader or an informed backer decides to disclose his or her pledge, he or she will act as a certifier and attract other backers, in turn increasing the probability of campaign success (Parker 2014; Ralcheva and Roosenboom 2016). By aggregating both standard financial information and soft information about borrower quality, Iyer et al. (2015) show that the crowd can assess the risk of a project and predict failure at least as accurately as a traditional bank scoring system.

2.4 The Entrepreneur as Fundraiser

Most of the big successes in crowdfunding are closely linked to high-tech firms. Three-dimensional printers, virtual reality glasses, and smart watches are the most famous crowdfunded projects. Nevertheless, crowdfunding has existed for a long time, and nonprofit organizations were the first to use it as a financing source. With their reliance on altruism, charity, or warm glow, tapping a large crowd was the best way to collect significant amounts of money to finance their activities. When Internet-based crowdfunding began appearing at the end of 2000 as a result of the digital revolution, the first firms to use it were overwhelmingly cultural firms (e.g., film, music, games), which were then directly followed by design and technological projects. Today, crowdfunding has become an option for every kind of start-up. When a project may have global impact, some platforms offer a worldwide audience. For local projects, other platforms are available and target a specific country (or even a specific region) or industry (platforms specialized in music, clean technology, real estate, and even restaurant).

The first goal for an entrepreneur using crowdfunding is to raise funding, but other motivations may also be at play (Gerber et al. 2012). For example, by using reward-based crowdfunding, an entrepreneur can raise funding but also test the market for the future product. A lack of support for the project may indicate a too narrow market for the final product. Another advantage of a crowdfunding campaign is the ability to use a cheaper marketing campaign. By taking advantage of the platform's popularity and traffic, a new product will have an initial audience and will benefit from a word-of-mouth effect to reach the most likely customers.

Another motivation is the willingness to replicate the successful experience of others (Gerber et al. 2012). However, using an Internet platform to present a project publicly may also have some drawbacks. During a traditional funding process involving banks, angel investors, or venture capital funds, an entrepreneur can easily try to find other investors (e.g., another bank or venture capital fund) in case the first attempt fails. For example, if a bank rejects a loan request, the entrepreneur can approach another bank. Restricted by the confidentiality of bank businesses, this second bank will not know about the first rejection or the changes the entrepreneur made to his or her project presentation (business plan) in response to the received feedback from the first attempt. In the case of venture capital and angel finance, entrepreneurs typically contact many investors at the same time to attract attention from a few of them. In crowdfunding, entrepreneurs almost never get a second chance to make a first good impression. The Internet is decentralized by nature, and any information becomes rapidly replicated on many other websites, even if this information originates from a single source. When something becomes public on the Internet, it is very difficult to remove all traces of that information. This rule also applies to crowdfunding campaigns. First, many crowdfunding platforms keep track of previous campaigns launched and often allow access to the presentation page of all previous projects, even failed ones. Second, even when the platform removes (or limits access to) the information about a past failed attempt, plugging the name of the project leader into a search engine will sometimes bring to the surface many external sources of information that may disclose the entrepreneur's history. Though requiring some effort on the part of the investor/backer, the reputation of the entrepreneur leading the project may play an important role in a second campaign success. For these reasons, entrepreneurs who experience a first success are more likely to launch second campaigns. These findings are also in line with theories on entrepreneurial self-confidence (Bandura 1982; Hayward et al. 2010). After a first success, the self-confidence of the entrepreneur will increase, and he or she will more likely reenter with a new project. However, an entrepreneur who undergoes a first failure will lose self-confidence and be less likely to undertake a second crowdfunding campaign. Nevertheless, recent studies show that the campaigns launched by entrepreneurs with a first success tend to underperform the first campaign by attracting fewer backers and collecting less money (Leboeuf 2016; Yang and Hahn 2015). These studies argue that when the first campaign is successful, people assume that many of the interested backers have already participated in the new venture. However, when an entrepreneur launches a second campaign shortly after the first, new participants (i.e., other than those who participated in the first campaign already) may represent a smaller fraction of the backers. Thus, the surprise effect becomes less pronounced, making any "hype" related to the second campaign less likely.

For the entrepreneur with a first failed crowdfunding experience, the stigma of failure (Landier 2006) plays a central role in how the nonprofessional crowd will assess the opportunity to invest in a crowdfunding campaign. Even if the number of backers and the amount pledged are higher than those during the first attempt, and even if the entrepreneurs try to mimic successful campaigns in terms of characteristics (e.g., size, funding model, campaign duration) and disclosure (e.g., length of text, number of pictures provided), the probability of success of the second campaign will be lower than any first campaign (Leboeuf 2016). Most of the time, these efforts are insufficient to overcome the negative reputation gained from the first failure.

A vibrant stream of research on the entrepreneurial perspective of crowdfunding investigates the extent to which entrepreneurs rely on their relatives, close friends, and social networks, often labeled as "social capital" and proxied by the number of LinkedIn and Facebook connections of the entrepreneur. These studies show that the success of a crowdfunding campaign strongly relies on the entrepreneur's capability of mobilizing his or her social capital (Agrawal et al. 2011, 2015; Colombo et al.

2015; Mollick 2013; Vismara 2016). Moreover, this stream of literature shows that the entrepreneur's willingness to keep the crowd updated by posting new comments and updates during the campaign helps raise more funds (Ahlers et al. 2015; Block et al. 2017). Thus, good preparation and continuous involvement during the campaign are crucial.

2.5 Concluding Remarks

In this chapter, we demonstrate that crowdfunding is a legitimate funding source for different types of entrepreneurs and that it fills a funding gap, ranging from seed capital to later-stage funding, depending on the type of crowdfunding considered. Moreover, this new form of funding is able to attract nontraditional investors thanks to its specific properties and mechanisms. A greater number of people may be more easily tempted to participate because of the small amounts involved for each backer, though this may also lead to herding behavior and self-implication due to the disintermediated nature of crowdfunding.

However, crowdfunding still needs to demonstrate strengths to become a sustainable funding model for entrepreneurs. First, it needs to increase the trustworthiness for investors (Cumming and Johan 2013) by reducing information asymmetry in the mechanisms of the various types of crowdfunding (to avoid investor concerns about where their money goes, under which legal form, liquidity issues that may arise, and so on) and by tackling the risks of fraud (false projects, wrong usage of the funds received by the entrepreneur) (James 2013). Second, the platforms need to keep in mind that they face nontraditional investors and that perhaps they should not engage in too much due diligence when the crowd is perfectly capable of assessing the value of a project (Mollick and Nanda 2015). That is, platforms need to prevent the risks of fraud but not the project's market risks.

Crowdfunding is now at a specific point in time in terms of development. During its first decade, crowdfunding experienced tremendous growth and developed under light regulation (leading to a high degree of freedom of actions and active experimentation). In addition, the crowdfunding market is still highly decentralized across many platforms and many mechanisms. This form of decentralized development is similar to the situation the Internet faced upon its establishment some decades ago. Today, however, the Internet is mostly centered on big players (often called GAFAM, or Google, Apple, Facebook, Amazon.com, and Microsoft) that control much of the market and are suspected of reducing freedom (e.g., Google filters search results, Facebook censors some messages posted by users, Apple is highly restrictive of application developers, and Microsoft licenses prohibit some usages of its own software). A threat to crowdfunding as it is known today is the overregulation of the market and the overconcentration of platforms that will begin appearing as the market starts consolidating. An increase of regulations will mechanically enhance participants' protection; however, by tightening the restrictions imposed on investor profiles, overregulation may lead to a negative effect on investors' freedom. Concentration, for its part, will lower transaction costs at the price of reducing options for entrepreneurs to tap the right crowd. Fewer platforms mean fewer choices for specialized or local platforms. The next big challenge for crowdfunding will be to find a suitable equilibrium as it begins consolidating as a market.

References

Agrawal, Ajay K., Christian Catalini, and Avi Goldfarb. 2011. The Geography of Crowdfunding. *National Bureau of Economic Research*. http://www.nber.org/papers/w16820.pdf. Accessed 17 Mar 2017.

———. 2015. Crowdfunding: Geography, Social Networks, and the Timing of Investment Decisions. *Journal of Economics & Management Strategy* 24: 253–274.

Ahlers, Gerrit K.C., Douglas J. Cumming, Christina Gunther, and Denis Schweizer. 2015. Signaling in Equity Crowdfunding. *Entrepreneurship Theory and Practice* 39: 955–980.

Bandura, Albert. 1982. Self-Efficacy Mechanism in Human Agency. *American Psychologist* 37: 122–147.

Belleflamme, Paul, Thomas Lambert, and Armin Schwienbacher. 2014. Crowdfunding: Tapping the Right Crowd. *Journal of Business Venturing* 29: 585–609.

Belleflamme, Paul, Nessrine Omrani, and Martin Peitz. 2015. The Economics of Crowdfunding Platforms. *Information Economics and Policy* 33: 11–28.

Berger, Allen N., and Gregory F. Udell. 1998. The Economics of Small Business Finance: The Roles of Private Equity and Debt Markets in the Financial Growth Cycle. *Journal of Banking and Finance* 22: 613–673.

Block, Jörn, Lars Hornuf, and Alexandra Moritz. 2017. Which Updates During an Equity Crowdfunding Campaign Increase Crowd Participation? *Small Business Economics*. Forthcoming.

Bretschneider, Ulrich, Katharina Knaub, and Enrico Wieck. 2014. Motivations for Crowdfunding: What Drives the Crowd to Invest in Start-ups? Paper presented at European Conference on Information Systems *(ECIS)*, Tel Aviv, Israel, June 9–11.

Carpenter, Robert E., and Bruce C. Petersen. 2002. Is the Growth of Small Firms Constrained by Internal Finance? *Review of Economics and Statistics* 84: 298–309.

Chemla, Gilles, and Katrin Tinn. 2016. Learning Through Crowdfunding. *Social Science Research Network*. https://papers.ssrn.com/abstract=2804541. Accessed 17 Mar 2017.

Cholakova, Magdalena, and Bart Clarysse. 2015. Does the Possibility to Make Equity Investments in Crowdfunding Projects Crowd Out Reward-Based Investments? *Entrepreneurship Theory and Practice* 39: 145–172.

Colombo, Massimo G., Chiara Franzoni, and Cristina Rossi-Lamastra. 2015. Internal Social Capital and the Attraction of Early Contributions in Crowdfunding. *Entrepreneurship Theory and Practice* 39: 75–100.

Cosh, Andy, Douglas J. Cumming, and Alan Hughes. 2009. Outside Entrepreneurial Capital. *Economic Journal* 119: 1494–1533.

Cressy, Robert. 2002. Funding Gaps: A Symposium. *Economic Journal* 112: F1–F16.

Cumming, Douglas J., and Sofia A. Johan. 2013. Demand Driven Securities Regulation: Evidence from Crowdfunding. *Venture Capital: An International Journal of Entrepreneurial Finance* 15: 361–379.

Cumming, Douglas, Gaël Leboeuf, and Armin Schwienbacher. 2016. Crowdfunding Models: Keep-It-All versus All-Or-Nothing. *Social Science Research Network*. https://papers.ssrn.com/abstract=2447567. Accessed 28 Feb 2017.

Gerber, Elizabeth, Julie Hui, and Pei-Yi Kuo. 2012. *Crowdfunding: Why People are Motivated to Post and Fund Projects on Crowdfunding Platforms*. Paper presented at ACM Conference on Computer Supported Cooperative Work, February 11–15.

Griffin, Zachary J. 2013. Crowdfunding: Fleecing the American Masses. *Case W. Reserve Journal of Law, Technology & the Internet* 4: 375.

Hakenes, Hendrik, and Friederike Schlegel. 2014. Exploiting the Financial Wisdom of the Crowd—Crowdfunding as a Tool to Aggregate Vague Information. *Social Science Research Network*. https://papers.ssrn.com/abstract=2475025. Accessed 28 Feb 2017.

Hayward, Mathew L.A., William R. Forster, Saras D. Sarasvathy, and Barbara L. Fredrickson. 2010. Beyond Hubris: How Highly Confident Entrepreneurs Rebound to Venture Again. *Journal of Business Venturing* 25: 569–578.

Hazen, Thomas L. 2012. Crowdfunding or Fraudfunding? Social Networks and the Securities Laws—Why the Specially Tailored Exemption Must Be Conditioned on Meaningful Disclosure. *North Carolina Law Review* 90: 1735–1807.

Hildebrand, Thomas, Manju Puri, and Jörg Rocholl. 2016. Adverse Incentives in Crowdfunding. *Management Science* 63: 587–608.

Hornuf, Lars, and Matthias Schmitt. 2016. *Does a Local Bias Exist in Equity Crowdfunding? The Impact of Investor Types and Portal Design*. Max Planck Institute for Innovation & Competition Research Paper No. 16-07.

Hornuf, Lars, and Armin Schwienbacher. 2016. Crowdinvesting—Angel Investing for the Masses? In *Handbook of Research on Venture Capital: Volume 3. Business Angels*, ed. Hans Landström and Colin Mason, 381–397. Cheltenham, UK: Edward Elgar.

———. 2017. Should Securities Regulation Promote Equity Crowdfunding? *Small Business Economics* 49: 579–593.

Iyer, Rajkamal, Asim I. Khwaja, Erzo F.P. Luttmer, and Kelly Shue. 2015. Screening Peers Softly: Inferring the Quality of Small Borrowers. *Management Science* 62: 1554–1577.

James, Thomas G. 2013. Far from the Maddening Crowd: Does the Jobs Act Provide Meaningful Redress to Small Investors for Securities Fraud in Connection with Crowdfunding Operations. *Boston College Law Review* 54: Art.7.

Kuppuswamy, Venkat, and Barry L. Bayus. 2017. Does My Contribution to Your Crowdfunding Project Matter? *Journal of Business Venturing* 32: 72–89.

Landier, Augustin. 2006. Entrepreneurship and the Stigma of Failure. *Social Science Research Network*. https://papers.ssrn.com/abstract=850446. Accessed 28 Feb 2017.

Leboeuf, Gaël. 2016. Does the Crowd Forgive? *Social Science Research Network*. https://papers.ssrn.com/abstract=2788483. Accessed 28 Feb 2017.

Lin, Mingfeng, and Siva Viswanathan. 2015. Home Bias in Online Investments: An Empirical Study of an Online Crowdfunding Market. *Management Science* 62: 1393–1414.

Lin, Yan, Wai F. Boh, and Kim H. Goh. 2014. How Different are Crowdfunders? Examining Archetypes of Crowdfunders and Their Choice of Projects. *Academy of Management Proceedings*: 1–13309.

Mollick, Ethan R. 2013. Swept Away by the Crowd? Crowdfunding, Venture Capital, and the Selection of Entrepreneurs. *Social Science Research Network*. https://papers.ssrn.com/abstract=2239204. Accessed 28 Feb 2017.

———. 2014. The Dynamics of Crowdfunding: An Exploratory Study. *Journal of Business Venturing* 29: 1–16.

Mollick, Ethan R., and Ramana Nanda. 2015. Wisdom or Madness? Comparing Crowds with Expert Evaluation in Funding the Arts. *Management Science* 62: 1533–1553.

Mollick, Ethan R., and Alicia Robb. 2016. Democratizing Innovation and Capital Access: The Role of Crowdfunding. *California Management Review* 58: 72–87.

Parker, Simon C. 2014. Crowdfunding, Cascades and Informed Investors. *Economics Letters* 125: 432–435.

Ralcheva, Aleksandrina, and Peter Roosenboom. 2016. On the Road to Success in Equity Crowdfunding. *Social Science Research Network*. https://papers.ssrn.com/abstract=2727742. Accessed 28 Feb 2017.

Robb, Alicia M., and David T. Robinson. 2014. The Capital Structure Decisions of New Firms. *Review of Financial Studies* 27: 153–179.

Schwienbacher, Armin. 2013. Financing the Business. In *The Routledge Companion to Entrepreneurship*, ed. Ted Baker and Friederieke Welter, 193–206. Abingdon, Oxon: Routledge.

———. 2014. Entrepreneurial Risk-Taking in Crowdfunding Campaigns. *Social Science Research Network*. https://papers.ssrn.com/abstract=2506355. Accessed 28 Feb 2017.

Shafi, Kourosh, and Massimo G. Colombo. 2016. Does Reward-Based Crowdfunding Help Firms Obtain Venture Capital and Angel Finance? *Social Science Research Network*. https://papers.ssrn.com/abstract=2785538. Accessed 28 Feb 2017.

Vismara, Silvio. 2016. Equity Retention and Social Network Theory in Equity Crowdfunding. *Small Business Economics* 46: 579–590.

Yang, Lusi, and Jungpil Hahn. 2015. *Learning from Prior Experience: An Empirical Study of Serial Entrepreneurs in IT-enabled Crowdfunding*. Paper presented at International Conference on Information Systems (ICIS), Fort Worth, TX. Conference paper available at http://aisel.aisnet.org/icis2015/proceedings/HumanBehaviorIS/21/

Zvilichovsky, David, Yael Inbar, and Ohad Barzilay. 2015. Playing Both Sides of the Market: Success and Reciprocity on Crowdfunding Platforms. *Social Science Research Network*. https://papers.ssrn.com/abstract=2304101. Accessed 28 Feb 2017.

Gaël Leboeuf is Assistant Professor of Finance at the Université Lumière Lyon 2. He holds a Ph.D. in Corporate Finance from SKEMA Business School and Lille University. After eight years in the retail banking industry, he graduated from Lille University in 2013 with a master's degree in International Financial Analysis and is working on reward-based crowdfunding research questions. He is also a long-time defender of the open-source movement.

Armin Schwienbacher is Professor of Finance at SKEMA Business School since 2010. He previously worked at the Université Lille 2 (France), Louvain School of Management (Université catholique de Louvain, Belgium), and Universiteit van Amsterdam (the Netherlands), and as a guest lecturer at Duisenberg School of Finance (the Netherlands), Rotterdam School of Management (the Netherlands), and the European School of Management and Technology (Germany). He was a visiting scholar at the Haas School of Business (UC Berkeley, USA) in 2001–2002 and a visiting professor at Schulich School of Business (York University, Canada) in 2014–2015. Schwienbacher regularly teaches courses in corporate finance and entrepreneurial finance. He is the Director of the Ph.D. Program in Finance and Accounting at SKEMA Business School.

3

Signaling to Overcome Inefficiencies in Crowdfunding Markets

Silvio Vismara

3.1 Introduction

George Akerlof, Michael Spence, and Joseph Stiglitz received the 2001 Nobel Prize in Economics for their work in information economics (Akerlof 1970). Previously, most economic studies simply ignored information asymmetries and assumed that markets would behave substantively the same as markets with perfect information (Stiglitz 2000, 2002). The signaling theory (Spence 1973, 2002) is perhaps the most widely used approach to study markets with incomplete and asymmetrically distributed information in finance, entrepreneurship, and management (Bergh et al. 2014; Connelly et al. 2011). Essentially, proponents send signals, or observable actions that provide information about unobservable attributes and likely outcomes, to reduce the gap between stakeholders' knowledge of them and their enterprise.

S. Vismara (✉)
Department of Economics and Technology Management, University of Bergamo, Bergamo, Italy

D. Cumming, L. Hornuf (eds.), *The Economics of Crowdfunding*,
https://doi.org/10.1007/978-3-319-66119-3_3

This theory is particularly adaptive to the study of crowdfunding markets. The signal's effectiveness also depends on the characteristics of the receiver, and specifically its costs of accessing and processing information. Crowdfunding decreases the costs of access to information, but targets receivers (i.e., the "crowd") with presumably high information-processing costs. Crowdfunding platforms allow fundraising from a pool of online backers, and must cope with collective action problems, as crowd-funders have neither the ability nor the incentive to devote substantial resources to due diligence. This might be so because they have invested meager amounts, making due diligence economically inefficient. Moreover, it might be individually efficient for crowd-funders to conduct due diligence if they invest higher amounts and consequently expect higher returns. However, they still cannot coordinate who pays for the due diligence due to collective action problems, or they simply have incentives for a free ride. This may generate a reluctance to invest in crowdfunding projects, with potential investors willing to do so only if compensated by a discount, which could eventually produce an Akerlof-type market failure, resulting in vanishing markets because the only equilibrium price would be zero. It is particularly important for the future of these markets to demonstrate signals' validity, as once receivers have received a signal and have used it to successfully make an informed choice, they are more likely to attend to similar signals in the future.

In this chapter, I first briefly position a study of signals in crowdfunding within the broader literature on signaling in entrepreneurial finance. Second, I deliver a theoretical discussion and define signals in crowdfunding, including examples of penalty and handicap signals, and differentiate them from passive characteristics and cheap talk. I propose a taxonomy of signals that matches the senders—namely, such organizations as firms and nongovernmental organizations (NGOs), and individuals, both proponents and fellow crowd-funders—and receivers, such as backers, lenders, and investors. Existing studies are classified in this taxonomy based on the definitions of reward- and donation-based crowdfunding, crowd-investing, and crowd-lending (Chap. 1). Third, I provide a review of the few studies on signal certification and post-signal performance, and suggest that such studies are central in identifying effective signals. I conclude by identifying future research directions.

3.2 Signaling in Entrepreneurial Finance

In a Modigliani–Miller world without informational asymmetries, tax bankruptcies, or agency costs, capital structure is irrelevant to a firm's total value. However, capital structure matters in the real world, and companies in need of new financing face an important question regarding how to overcome information asymmetries with potential backers. Self-financing is a source of entrepreneurial capital that is less subject to problems caused by information asymmetries, as entrepreneurs contribute their own money. However, the ability to rapidly grow will be constrained with these limited resources if external sources of capital are not used. When a firm determines a need for external funds, it must then gain access to capital markets.

The existence of asymmetric information in capital markets means that external investors might not adequately assess their investment projects. This effect is most important in the case of a small and innovative business, due to a lack of reliable information about its actual status and performance. It is indeed difficult to provide convincing signals regarding an innovation project's quality, although this is a key growth determinant in any new technology-based firm. Many discussions have revolved around the unsuitability of debt for early stage financing (Stiglitz and Weiss 1981). Debt holders bear a downside risk, but do not share the upside of successful innovation. Further, debt-financing prospects are limited for start-ups, as most of their resources are intangible and tend to have limited salvage value because of their highly specific nature (Hubbard 1998).

For these reasons, most entrepreneurial finance literature focuses on external equity (Carpenter and Petersen 2002). This represents a bias, as evidence indeed exists that even early stage entrepreneurial firms rely extensively on bank debt (Cassia and Vismara 2009; Robb and Robinson 2014; Hanssens et al. 2016). Broadly, start-ups raise funds from multiple sources (Hanssens et al. 2015), and central to the present study, new forms of debt capital are quickly developing for entrepreneurial firms; one such form is the mini-bond. It is currently unclear whether the trading of mini-bonds will primarily occur in traditional, regulated markets (e.g., ExtraMOT in Italy) or new crowdfunding platforms (e.g., Crowdcube in the United Kingdom). Cumming and Vismara (2016) note that it is unclear as to what will happen when or if interest rates increase, making traditional bank lending less appealing than at present. Another form of debt capital for entrepreneurial firms includes crowdlending, a debt-based transaction between individuals and existing businesses (mostly small firms), with many individual lenders contributing to one loan. The study of these financing mechanisms offers a promising way to contribute to entrepreneurial finance literature.

Information asymmetry, and its related adverse selection problems in an entrepreneurial setting, is particularly pronounced due to the difficulty that entrepreneurs face in conveying their new ventures' quality to firm outsiders, resulting in potentially severe agency issues and moral hazard problems. Young technology firms' dilemma involves potential investors' problems in evaluating the focal firm's prospects, as the cost of exchange increases when a firm cannot be reliably evaluated (Williamson 1985). Many public policies have limited such problems by adopting an explicit goal to develop risk capital markets for small firms. For instance, several stock exchanges have established market segments dedicated to small firms with lower listing barriers (Vismara et al. 2012). Crowdfunding markets are, to some extent, another extreme of loosely regulated public markets.

3.3 Signals in Crowdfunding

Problems in information asymmetries are more severe in crowdfunding than in other entrepreneurial finance markets. Projects on the capital demand side are typically proposed by first-time entrepreneurs, which might actually be favorable, as this might confirm that this new activity acts to close funding gaps. Individuals with previously no access to financial resources can now gain access for the first time. To this extent, crowdfunding may help democratize entrepreneurial finance. On the capital supply side, crowd-funders are less equipped to overcome information asymmetry, as they lack the experience and capability to evaluate different opportunities, as well as the incentives to do so, due to fixed costs that limit the opportunities to perform *ex ante* due diligence and *ex post* monitoring. Signals play a crucial role in such a context.

Signals are an economic actor's activities—not passive characteristics—that positively relate to an unobserved attribute that an exchange partner values, and whose cost inversely relates to the quality of the sender (i.e., some signalers are in better positions than others to absorb associated costs).[1] Differential costs provide the basis for a selection process whereby receivers can use the signal to select a sender from among a larger set of signalers. Effective signals are those that create a separating equilibrium, in which low-quality firms find it more costly or risky to signal than high-quality firms. A costly signal, but one that is not differentially so for imitative signalers, does not create a separating equilibrium. When signaling costs are the same for different quality groups, this generates a pooling equilibrium, by which receivers are left unsure as to which signals to believe; one cannot prevent low-quality providers from imitating the signals of high-quality providers under such conditions. To be effective, dishonest signals should not pay off.

The same rationale applies to risk, which is the danger of being caught for false signaling. To be effective, the risk must be stronger for lower-quality senders. Penalty costs are a form of negative feedback that could serve as a substitute for signal costs. Signal costs differ in that they occur by implementing the signal, whereas penalty costs occur only from false signaling. Ownership stakes offer a conventional example. Retained equity is typically interpreted as a signal of entrepreneurial intentions, and strongly correlates with the probability of success in an initial or follow-on offer in stock markets (Leland and Pyle 1977). Consistent with corporate finance literature, if growth is the primary goal of crowdfunders committed to long-term goals, then they should be expected to retain control of a firm after an offering. As confirmation of this information's importance, the percentage of equity offered is clearly reported on the home page of projects posted on crowdfunding platforms. Ahlers et al. (2015) and Vismara (2016) demonstrate that previous results from different financial settings hold in equity crowdfunding, in that a larger percentage of equity offered by founders reduces the probability of equity crowdfunding campaigns' success.

A related type of signal, based on bonding mechanisms, is handicap signaling. For example, lockup clauses are used in initial public offerings (IPOs), which produce liquidity costs for the firm's original shareholders. Insiders in high-quality firms are more willing to "lock in" to the firm's ownership, thereby signaling their commitment. The handicap is more burdensome in low-quality firms, thus creating a separating equilibrium. A similar bonding option comes from the structure of tax incentives in the United Kingdom. Benefit occurs in an enterprise investment scheme (EIS) when shares are held for at least three years from the date of issue; otherwise, the tax relief will be withdrawn. Opting for such a mechanism provides a form of *a priori* confirmation, whereby the signaler will self-damage if the signal proves to be false.

Stiglitz (2000) highlights two broad information types in which asymmetry is particularly important: information about quality and information about intent. High-quality firms intend to act in a manner that receivers desire, while low-quality firms do not. However, intentions are credible signals only when they are binding, and repercussions occur if the signal's senders do not follow through on their intended behavior. As signalers and receivers have partially competing interests, lower-quality signalers have an incentive to deliver false signals to entice receivers to select them. Examples of such "cheap talk" come from the IPO markets (Farrell and Rabin 1996; Almazan et al. 2008). It is unsurprising that IPO prospectuses are enticing, as these are created with a perspective toward promoting newly listed ventures. Entrepreneurs and hired intermediaries are indeed keen to create prospectuses that illuminate their firms.[2] With few exceptions, all companies going public declare that they raise capital to pursue positive net present value (NPV) projects (Paleari et al. 2008). Unfortunately, many of them use IPO proceeds to repay debt and rebalance their capital structures. A similar example of cheap talk in crowdfunding could include the exit intentions (e.g., IPO acquisitions) that proponents declare at listing, which will not suffer costs in the case of different post-campaign behavior.

Table 3.1 illustrates a taxonomy of signals that matches the senders—such organizations as firms and NGOs, and individuals, both proponents and fellow crowd-funders—and receivers, such as backers, lenders, and investors. Subsequently, existing studies are classified in this taxonomy

Table 3.1 Taxonomy of signals in crowdfunding

		Crowdfunding	Crowd-lending	Crowd-investing
Receiver/sender		Backers	Lenders	Investors
Organizations	NGOs	?	NO	NO
	Firms	Burtch et al. (2013), Burtch et al. (2014), Ordanini et al. (2011),	Lin et al. (2013)	Ahlers et al. (2015), Ralcheva and Roosenboom (2016), Vismara (2016)
Individuals	Proponents	Mollick (2014), Kuppuswamy and Bayus (2014)	Hildebrand et al. (2016)	NO
	Crowd-funders	Burtch et al. (2013), Colombo et al. (2015), Kuppuswamy and Bayus (2014)	Collier and Hampshire (2010), Yum et al. (2012)	Moritz et al. (2015), Hornuf and Schwienbacher (2017), Vismara (2017)

along the definitions of reward- and donation-based crowdfunding, crowd-investing, and crowd-lending (Chap. 1). The proponent in crowd-investing is by definition a company, but reward- and donation-based campaigns are mostly launched by individuals. The governance and organizational implications of the capital-raising process through crowdfunding arguably differ (Cumming et al. 2016b).

It can be noted before proceeding that signals benefit the sender by reducing information asymmetries with the receiver; however, signals may also provide intrinsic, substantive value. It is beyond the scope of this chapter to quantify and discern the purely information-based certification effect from signals' intrinsic, substantive values (Colombo et al. 2016).[3]

Finally, while signaling theory provides the best theoretical lens through which to study crowdfunding of the motivations discussed in this chapter, other theories may complement our understanding of these markets. Bergh et al. (2014) propose that sense-making (Weick 1995) and the information-processing theory (Thomas and McDaniel 1990) have the advantage of using a behavioral perspective that could overcome the signaling theory's rational-actor assumption. These two concepts could help decipher why a signal assumes different meanings among receivers, or how different signals interact.

3.3.1 Signals from Proponents to Crowd-Funders

This section reviews various papers that focus on the determinants of crowdfunding campaigns' success, as summarized in Table 3.2. Some of these studies explicitly focus on signals, while others more broadly describe the factors associated with crowdfunding campaigns' increased chances of success. Studies on donation- or reward-based crowdfunding argue that motivations other than potential monetary returns are important for funders. Research on donation-based crowdfunding communities draws from extensive literature on charitable giving (e.g., Burtch et al. 2014) and public goods (e.g., Burtch et al. 2013; Kuppuswamy and Bayus 2014). This literature examines principles that are unlikely to apply to investors in financial markets, such as crowd-investing or crowd-lending. Cholakova and Clarysse (2015) and Vismara (2016) coherently discover that offering rewards to investors does not increase crowd-investing campaigns' probability of success.

Different motivations to bid are likely to require different signals. Mollick (2014) used a sample of reward-based projects posted on Kickstarter to demonstrate that a founder's number of social network connections positively associates with the capital raised for a project. Belleflamme et al. (2014) documented that entrepreneurs use their social networks and established platforms on the Internet to directly interact with the crowd. Colombo et al. (2015) examined the same platform to discover that the founder's social capital plays a crucial role in attracting backers in a campaign's early days, which consequently mediates the offer's success. Social capital's role in donation-based crowdfunding has also been confirmed (Ordanini et al. 2011). However, research is still lacking on the role of entrepreneurs' social capital in a crowd-investing context.

Table 3.2 Empirical evidence from crowdfunding studies

Signal/type of crowdfunding	Crowdfunding (donations)	Crowdfunding (rewards)	Crowd-investing
Early investments	A high number of contributions in the early days of offering increases the probability of crowdfunding campaigns' success (Burtch et al. 2013)	A high number of contributions in the early days of offering increases the probability of crowdfunding campaigns' success (Colombo et al. 2015)	Early contributions are fundamental in increasing success of funding; positive correlation (Vismara 2017)
Other investors	Prior investors negatively affect later participants; likely connected to the idea of self-relevance (Burtch et al. 2013)	Raising substantial amounts of capital in the early days of a campaign is a predictor of success in a "success breeds success" self-reinforcing pattern (Colombo et al. 2015)	Contributions in the early days of offering are fundamental in attracting other investors (Vismara 2017)
Venture quality	?	Social capital and preparedness are associated with an increased chance of project success, suggesting that quality signals play a role in project outcomes (Mollick 2014)	A positive correlation exists between venture quality (specifically, human and intellectual capital) and success (Ahlers et al. 2015). Consistent evidence exists for the strong positive impact of intellectual property rights protections in equity crowdfunding's success (Ralcheva and Roosenboom 2016)

(*continued*)

Table 3.2 (continued)

Signal/type of crowdfunding	Crowdfunding (donations)	Crowdfunding (rewards)	Crowd-investing
Social capital	?	Both personal social contacts and those built within crowdfunding communities may be vehicles to attract seed financing (Colombo et al. 2015). Between two founders that linked their Facebook profiles, the one with more Facebook friends has a higher probability of success; nevertheless, having no Facebook account is better than having few online connections (Mollick 2014)	Public profile investors attract other investors (Vismara 2017). A founder's greater number of social connections will increase the probability of an equity crowdfunding campaign's success (Vismara 2016)
Top Management Team (TMT) size	?	?	The number of TMT members positively relates to campaign outcome, reflecting perception by outside investors as a positive signal of a firm's ability to cope with market uncertainty (Ahlers et al. 2015; Vismara 2017)

(*continued*)

Table 3.2 (continued)

Signal/type of crowdfunding	Crowdfunding (donations)	Crowdfunding (rewards)	Crowd-investing
Geography	?	Geography may play an important role in crowdfunding efforts' success (Mollick 2014). Investment patterns over time are independent of the geographic distance between the entrepreneur and investor, even if the role of family and friends is quite important in early stages. It can be considered that this study has been made on a crowdfunding platform for musical artists, or in a particular environment (Agrawal et al. 2011)	A location in a larger city positively impacts funding success (Ralcheva and Roosenboom 2016). The geographic distance between the start-up and investors, as well as learning effects and sniping, do not affect the backers' willingness to pay (Hornuf and Neuenkirch 2017)
Campaign duration	A charitable-giving project is more influential the longer it lasts (Burtch et al. 2013)	Duration decreases the chances of success, possibly because longer durations are a sign of a lack of confidence (Mollick 2014)	A negative correlation exists between duration and success, possibly because duration is fixed and can only change during the campaign; it can be shorter if it is already successful, or it can be extended in some cases (Vismara 2017)

(*continued*)

Table 3.2 (continued)

Signal/type of crowdfunding	Crowdfunding (donations)	Crowdfunding (rewards)	Crowd-investing
Number of investors	?	Correlation of 0.10 (with $p < 0.05$) between the number of backers and a crowdfunding campaign's success (Mollick 2014)	The number of investors should correlate with an equity crowdfunding campaign's probability of success (Ahlers et al. 2015). The mean of the number of investors is much higher for successful projects (Ralcheva and Roosenboom 2016)
Target size	?	Increasing goal size is negatively associated with success (Mollick 2014)	The mean target amounts of successful projects are significantly higher than unsuccessful ones (Ralcheva and Roosenboom 2016). Campaign characteristics play a meaningful role in backers' willingness to pay. Both the funding goal and pre-valuation serve as signals for potentially lucrative investments, as an increase in these variables is associated with a higher premium (Hornuf and Neuenkirch 2017)
Awards, grants, or patents	?	?	The most economically significant impact to reach success, according to our specifications, is associated with previously winning a grant or an award (Ralcheva and Roosenboom 2016). No evidence exists for grants/awards' positive impact, possibly due to the sample size (Ahlers et al. 2015). Vismara (2017) discovers an impact for patents held at listing

(continued)

Table 3.2 (continued)

Signal/type of crowdfunding	Crowdfunding (donations)	Crowdfunding (rewards)	Crowd-investing
Presentation and updates	?	Such signals as videos and frequent updates are associated with greater success, and spelling errors reduce the chance of success (Mollick 2014)	Posting an update significantly and positively affects the number of investments made by the crowd and the investment amount collected by the start-up. This effect does not occur immediately in its entirety; rather, it lags behind the update by a few days. The positive effect increases with the number of words in the update. Regarding the update's content, a positive effect can be attributed to updates about new funding and business developments, as well as updates on promotional campaigns operated by the start-up (Block et al. 2017). Investors making investment decisions consider information updates on a portal website, other investors' comments, and more sophisticated investors' investment decisions. They refrain from investing when observing withdrawals (Hornuf and Schwienbacher 2017)

(continued)

Table 3.2 (continued)

Signal/type of crowdfunding	Crowdfunding (donations)	Crowdfunding (rewards)	Crowd-investing
Privacy	?	Reducing access to information controls induces a net increase in fundraising, yet this outcome results from two competing influences: treatment increases the willingness to engage with the platform (a 4.9% increase in the probability of contribution) and simultaneously decreases the average contribution (a USD 5.81 decline) (Burtch et al. 2014)	?
Nonfinancial motives	?	The results indicate that nonfinancial motives play no significant role, both in the decision to pledge and to invest in the project for product-based campaigns (Cholakova and Clarysse 2015)	The results indicate that nonfinancial motives play no significant role, both in the decision to pledge and to invest in the project for product-based campaigns (Cholakova and Clarysse 2015)

(*continued*)

Table 3.2 (continued)

Signal/type of crowdfunding	Crowdfunding (donations)	Crowdfunding (rewards)	Crowd-investing
Due diligence	The data further indicate that the application of due diligence generally has a strong, positive influence on the fundraising success rate and amount in the platform, controlling for all services a platform offers (Cumming et al. 2017)	The data further indicate that the application of due diligence generally has a strong, positive influence on the fundraising success rate and amount in the platform, controlling for all services a platform offers (Cumming et al. 2017)	The data further indicate that the application of due diligence generally has a strong, positive influence on the fundraising success rate and amount in the platform, controlling for all services a platform offers (Cumming et al. 2017)
Equity retention	/	/	A larger percentage of equity offered by founders will reduce the probability of equity crowdfunding campaign success (Ahlers et al. 2015; Vismara 2016)

Ahlers et al. (2015) used a sample of 104 projects from the Australian Small Scale Offerings Board (ASSOB), a business-matching platform, to identify which characteristics of the business (e.g., risk factors or pre-planned exit intentions) and of its top management team (e.g., its size or level of education) affect the probability of a proposal's success. The use of insider equity is a widely explored version of this signaling type in strategy literature. Insiders affirm their strategies' potential in the stock market via their own investments; financial commitment reflects their private knowledge, and their willingness to assume risk serves as a bond to suffer personal loss if the firm does not perform well. Thus, managerial ownership serves as an important signal, wherein a separating equilibrium is created not by differential signal costs, but by differential penalty costs; Ahlers et al. (2015) and Vismara (2016) discover supportive evidence. Finally, other possible signals currently under research or to be investigated include quality and the length of the text describing the project, video, quality of reward, and pictures.

3.3.2 Other Types of Signals

The previous section addressed signals from proponents to crowd-funders. Another way to create a separating equilibrium would be to involve a third party in the signaling process that is willing to assume the costs of signaling. Sociological evidence (Podolny 1993) notes that reputable actors enhance the prestige through which one is viewed; similarly, third-party endorsements have been studied as signals of a firm's quality to uninformed external investors. The underlying idea includes prestigious players that highly value their reputations, and will carefully guard against tarnishing it. The third party in this case bears the signaling costs, as it is their reputational capital at stake.

Affiliation with a prestigious underwriter or venture capitalist has been shown to be associated with better firm performance in an IPO context (Beatty and Ritter 1986; Carter and Manaster 1990; Carter et al. 1998; Megginson and Weiss 1991; Migliorati and Vismara 2014). The IPO literature has also considered other financial intermediaries involved in going public, such as top-quality auditors (Beatty 1989), universities (Bonardo et al. 2011), and rating agencies (Khurshed et al. 2014), but has discovered that they are less effective certification mechanisms. Crowdfunding investors cannot rely on reports issued by financial analysts or on such formal intermediaries as IPO underwriters. One possible exception includes certifications by pre-crowdfunding investors. Ralcheva and Roosenboom (2016) find that offerings in Crowdcube backed by venture capitalists have a higher probability of success, but it is difficult to discern whether the substantial benefit delivered by such an affiliation increases the chance per se, or if this occurs due to a reduction in information asymmetries. Further, it is indiscernible whether the affiliation with a venture capitalist is the firm's action or characteristic.

Signals delivered by other investors become essential with a lack of third-party endorsement. Their bids are clearly observable, or highly visible to potential investors, and costly; if investors bid for low-quality projects, they earn low or no returns. As information cascades (Bikhchandani et al. 1992) among investors play a prominent role in finance (Welch 1992), they are likely to do so in crowdfunding. IPOs with a high level of institutional demand in the first days of bookbuilding also see high levels of bids from retail investors in the later days (Khurshed et al. 2014).

Regardless of whether regulatory differences across platforms are signals, or the countries themselves, entrepreneurs select where to list as a signal. For instance, the platform structure may denote a "keep-it-all" versus "all-or-nothing" choice as a signal. Two papers use the similarities and differences between German crowdfunding platforms to deliver new insights: in an exploratory study of 23 interviews in Germany, Moritz et al. (2015) report that investors' decision-making processes in crowdinvesting are influenced by other market participants. Most new ventures posted on the Companisto platform use prior investors' statements as external credentials in the ventures' presentation videos. Hornuf and Neuenkirch (2017) analyze the pricing of cash flow rights in start-up companies using a unique data set of 44 crowd-investing campaigns on Innovestment. In contrast with all other European crowd-investing portals, Innovestment operates a multi-unit, second-price auction in which backers themselves can specify the price of an investment ticket. They exploit this unique auction mechanism to analyze backers' willingness to pay for cash flow rights, and discover that campaign characteristics, investor sophistication, progress in funding, herding, and stock market volatility influence backers' willingness to pay in an economically meaningful manner, while geographic distance, learning effects, and sniping at an auction's end have no effect.

Vismara (2017) contributes to this nascent literature by extending the study from signals sent by project proponents, to encompass the signaling dynamics between investors. Some of these studies predict previous bids' positive effect on the campaigns' outcome. Reciprocity, a shared identity, the desire to support a cause, and social image are their primary motivations. In contrast, if individuals primarily care about the end result (i.e., the provision of goods), they are less likely to help in the actual or perceived presence of other supporters. Theory predicts that pure altruism leads to crowding out, with each new contribution decreasing the appeal of subsequent contributions. Hence, the likelihood of bidding would negatively relate to the number of previous backers. Depending on the perspective and empirical setting, some non-crowd-investing studies discover a positive linear effect of other community members' funding decisions on individual contributions (e.g., Colombo et al. 2015), while others discover a negative effect (e.g., Burtch et al. 2013, 2015) or a non-linear relationship (e.g., Kuppuswamy and Bayus 2014). In their work, Kuppuswamy and Bayus (2014) use a sample of Kickstarter projects to reveal that a project's additional backer support negatively relates to its past backer support, but this effect subsides as the project-funding cycle approaches its closing date.

Hornuf and Schwienbacher (2016) derive an additional key difference between reward-based crowdfunding and crowd-investing. While proponents in the former raise as much as possible, crowd-investing involves a maximum number of shares that entrepreneurs are willing to sell. They also note that the funding goal itself might be a signal sent by the founder.

3.4 Signal Confirmation and Post-Signal Performance

Most crowdfunding studies have investigated signals as determinants of campaigns' success. The next step involves demonstrating why it is optimal for high-quality firms to signal, and why low-quality firms would not. A confirmation mechanism enables a determination of whether the beliefs in the signal are indeed realized for both the signal sender and receiver. Further, a signal's value is confirmed if the senders subsequently outperform their peers who did not send the signal. Beliefs, in other words, must be confirmed by subsequent experience (Spence 2002). A test for separating equilibrium consecutively requires moving beyond the receiver's reaction to a signal, as well as studying whether the expectation associated with a signal's presence is confirmed, with post-signal findings (Colombo et al. 2016). These arguments can also be found in the theoretical literature on signaling theory and market equilibria. For example, Cadsby et al. (1990) note how high-quality firms can exploit the opportunity to use a signal to break a pooling equilibrium and generate a separating equilibrium in financial markets. In this section, I first discuss the theories proposed to explain the IPOs' long-term performance, and then summarize the few papers on the long-term performance of firms that raised funds via crowdfunding.

Companies tend to perform below the market's benchmark during the first few years after an IPO. This anomaly was first identified by Ritter (1991), and numerous international studies have thus far conducted consequent research. Literature, starting with Jain and Kini (1994), has most recently even pointed to post-issue underperformance, in terms of operating measures. The explanations proposed for this phenomenon revolve around three primary theories (Khurshed et al. 2003): (1) market timing; (2) window dressing; and (3) asymmetric information.

The first explains underperformance in terms of a timing decision in entering the market, whether exogenous or endogenous to the floated company. One exogenous reason involves the "window of opportunity" theory (Loughran and Ritter 1995), which states that companies go public or generally raise equity capital not when the growth prospects are good and financing is required, but when the control shareholder finds it optimal. The incentive to go public is particularly strong in periods in which a specific sector indicates large market ratios. For instance, consider the Internet bubble in the late 1990s, or the recent consideration reserved for the energy share market. Market timing may otherwise endogenously originate in the issuing company so it is inclined to go public at a time of maximum performance, namely, when it can exploit the market's favorable valuation.

The window-dressing theory is similarly based on this consideration, in that, before the IPO, companies are subject to strong incentives to "embellish" their balance sheets. These firms may evoke "creative" accounting in the form of earnings management, which leads to greater pre-IPO profitability that cannot be maintained post-issue. This results in deteriorating post-issue operational performance due to a simple mean reversion effect (Fama 1998).

A third reason for long-term underperformance arises from the asymmetric information theory, which discusses the opportunism (moral hazards) derived from changes in ownership structure at the time of IPO. Indeed, the decision to go public increases agency costs by dispersing the share ownership. Therefore, this changes the relationship between the principal (shareholders) and agent (manager). This decline in performance could be caused by both an *ex ante* adverse selection effect by companies that decide to go public (Leland and Pyle 1977) and *ex post* opportunistic behavior (Jensen and Meckling 1976), such as the company management's pursuit of private benefits once public (perquisite consumption).

Some papers have investigated crowdfunding after campaigns have closed. Mollick's (2014) study of Kickstarter finds that less than 5% of projects fail to deliver their products, and 75% deliver with a delay. Small projects are more likely to fail in delivering rewards, while the proponent's characteristics do not affect the probability of a project's success. Cumming et al. (2016a) offer examples of documented cases of fraudulent behavior in reward-based crowdfunding in the United States.

By providing a first market assessment of the project and evidence of connection with active supporters, firms are expected to benefit from a successful crowdfunding campaign, not only with the product, but also in the financial market. However, the only available study thus far on the "success after the success" in (reward-based) crowdfunding is that by Mollick and Kuppuswamy (2014).[4]

Signori and Vismara (2016) first quantify the return on investments in equity crowdfunding. The authors use an augmented dataset with combined information from Crowdcube, Crunchbase, and the Companies House to study a population of 212 successfully funded initial equity offerings on the crowdfunding platform Crowdcube from their 2011 inception to 2015. This study reveals that 10% of these firms failed, while 30% pursued one or more seasoned equity offerings, either in the form of private equity injection (10%), follow-on offerings in the same platform (22%), or as targets in a merger or acquisition (1%). The expected annualized return for an initial crowdfunding investor is 8.8%, implying an annual value creation of GBP 25 million. Among the determinants of post-campaign outcomes, the presence of nonexecutives, patents, and tax incentives are associated with seasoned offerings, while none of the companies initially backed by professional investors have subsequently failed.

One way to identify whether equity crowdfunding closes an important funding gap is to look at insolvency rates; if these are comparatively high, this might provide evidence that these firms should not have initially received funding. Hornuf and Schmitt (2016) discover that, on average, firms started crowd-investing campaigns three years after their establishment. The authors further note that equity crowd-funded campaigns have somewhat higher survival rates in the United Kingdom than in Germany. Nevertheless, 70% of the German campaigns funded between September 1, 2011, and December 31, 2015, were still operating as active businesses four years after the campaign ended.

I conclude this review on post-campaign outcomes with a few suggested research directions. Can we differentiate whether signals refer to campaign success (i.e., successful funding) and venture success (i.e., a successful exit with no insolvency)? What is crowdfunding's impact on different performance indicators, such as exits, employment, patents, angel or VC finance, or sales growth, among others?

3.5 Conclusions

The cornerstone of entrepreneurial finance is that properly functioning financial systems can reduce the information and transaction costs in a world in which writing, issuing, and enforcing contracts consumes resources; information is asymmetric; and its acquisition is costly. Recent financial innovations, such as crowdfunding markets, promise to be a step in this direction, and signaling theory provides a privileged angle by which to investigate these markets. The present manuscript has proposed a taxonomy of signals in crowdfunding that will hopefully guide future research on this topic. Specifically, I again stress that among the future directions identified in this study, an analysis of post-signal performance is central not only to the correct use of signaling theory, but to the future of crowdfunding markets. As crowdfunding's ultimate goal is to build an enduring business, a successful campaign is therefore a beginning, and not an end.

Notes

1. In this section, I adopt a strict definition of "signal" coherent with Spence's original economic model. Literature has used less strict definitions, and has also included an actor's inherent characteristics. When I review the current literature on signaling in crowdfunding in the next section, I will specifically identify how individual papers address signals.
2. I discuss the window-dressing theory later, in the section on signal confirmation and post-signal performance, in which I draw conclusions on the parallelism between crowdfunding offerings and initial public offerings by discussing the evidence and theories on IPOs' long-term performance. I provide a definition and examples of cheap talk in this section that conform to Stiglitz's original economic model; literature has used less strict definitions. When I review the current literature on signaling in crowdfunding in the following sections, I will specifically identify how individual papers address signals.
3. Additionally, some papers take a comparative perspective across platforms (Cumming and Zhang 2016; Cumming et al. 2017), or focus on specific topics, such as gender issues (Mohammadi and Shafi 2017; Vismara et al. 2017).
4. A survey of 158 successfully funded Kickstarter projects reveals that approximately 18% of the respondents raised outside risk capital in the forms of venture capital (VC) or business angel (BA) investing, while 8% through additional reward-based crowdfunding campaigns. The proponents' specific industry experience and the presence of "a substantially complete business plan before fundraising" are the main predictors of outside funding (Mollick and Kuppuswamy 2014, 12).

References

Agrawal, Ajay K., Christian Catalini, and Avi Goldfarb. 2011. The Geography of Crowdfunding. *National Bureau of Economic Research*. http://www.nber.org/papers/w16820. Accessed 20 Feb 2017.

Ahlers, Gerrit K., Douglas Cumming, Christina Günther, and Denis Schweizer. 2015. Signaling in Equity Crowdfunding. *Entrepreneurship: Theory and Practice* 39: 955–980.

Akerlof, George A. 1970. The Market for Lemons: Quality Uncertainty and the Market Mechanism. *Quarterly Journal of Economics* 84: 488–500.

Almazan, Andres, Sanjay Banerji, and Adolfo de Motta. 2008. Attracting Attention: Cheap Managerial Talk and Costly Market Monitoring. *Journal of Finance* 63: 1399–1436.

Beatty, Randolph P. 1989. Auditor Reputation and the Pricing of Initial Public Offerings. *Accounting Review* 64: 693–709.

Beatty, Randolph P., and Jay R. Ritter. 1986. Investment Banking, Reputation and the Underpricing of Initial Public Offerings. *Journal of Financial Economics* 15: 213–232.

Belleflamme, Paul, Thomas Lambert, and Armin Schwienbacher. 2014. Crowdfunding: Tapping the Right Crowd. *Journal of Business Venturing* 29: 585–609.

Bergh, Donald D., Brian L. Connelly, David J. Ketchen, and Lu M. Shannon. 2014. Signaling Theory and Equilibrium in Strategic Management Research: An Assessment and Research Agenda. *Journal of Management Studies 51*: 1334–1360.

Bikhchandani, Sushil, David Hirshleifer, and Ivo Welch. 1992. A Theory of Fads, Fashion, Custom, and Cultural Change as Informational Cascades. *Journal of Political Economy* 100: 992–1026.

Block, Jörn, Lars Hornuf, and Alexandra Moritz. 2017. Which Updates During an Equity Crowdfunding Campaign Increase Crowd Participation? *Small Business Economics*. Forthcoming.

Bonardo, Damiano, Stefano Paleari, and Silvio Vismara. 2011. Valuing University-Based Firms: The Effects of Academic Affiliation on IPO Performance. *Entrepreneurship Theory and Practice* 35: 755–776.

Burtch, Gordon, Anindya Ghose, and Sunil Wattal. 2013. An Empirical Examination of the Antecedents and Consequences of Contribution Patterns in Crowd-Funded Markets. *Information Systems Research* 24: 499–519.

———. 2014. Cultural Differences and Geography as Determinants of Online Pro-Social Lending. *MIS Quarterly* 38: 773–794.

———. 2015. The Hidden Cost of Accommodating Crowdfunder Privacy Preferences: A Randomized Field Experiment. *Management Science* 61: 949–962.

Cadsby, Charles B., Murray Frank, and Vojislav Maksimovic. 1990. Pooling, Separating, and Semiseparating Equilibria in Financial Markets: Some Experimental Evidence. *Review of Financial Studies* 3: 315–342.

Carpenter, Robert E., and Bruce C. Petersen. 2002. Capital Market Imperfections, High-Tech Investment, and New Equity Financing. *Economic Journal* 112: 54–72.

Carter, Richard B., Frederick H. Dark, and Ajai K. Singh. 1998. Underwriter Reputation, Initial Returns, and the Long-Run Performance of IPO Stocks. *Journal of Finance* 53: 285–311.
Carter, Richard, and Steven Manaster. 1990. Initial Public Offerings and Underwriter Reputation. *Journal of Finance* 45: 1045–1067.
Cassia, Lucio, and Silvio Vismara. 2009. Suppliers as Fund Suppliers: Firms' Trade Credit and the Local Level of Development of the Banking System in Europe. *Investment Management and Financial Innovations* 6: 46–58.
Cholakova, Magdalena, and Bart Clarysse. 2015. Does the Possibility to Make Equity Investments in Crowdfunding Projects Crowd Out Reward-Based Investments? *Entrepreneurship Theory and Practice* 39: 145–172.
Colombo, Massimo G., Chiara Franzoni, and Cristina Rossi-Lamastra. 2015. Internal Social Capital and the Attraction of Early Contributions in Crowdfunding. *Entrepreneurship Theory and Practice* 39: 75–102.
Colombo, Massimo G., Michele Meoli, and Silvio Vismara. 2016. Signalling in Science-Based IPOs: The Combined Effect of Affiliation with Prestigious Universities, Underwriters, and Venture Capitalists. *Social Science Research Network*. https://ssrn.com/abstract=2801556. Accessed 20 Feb 2017.
Collier, Benjamin C., and Robert Hampshire. 2010. *Sending Mixed Signals: Multilevel Reputation Effects in Peer-To-Peer Lending Markets*. Paper presented at Proceedings of the 2010 ACM Conference on Computer Supported Cooperative Work (197–206), Savannah, USA.
Connelly, Brian L., S. Trevis Certo, R. Duane Ireland, and Christopher R. Reutzel. 2011. Signaling Theory: A Review and Assessment. *Journal of Management* 37: 39–51.
Cumming, Douglas J., Lars Hornuf, Moein Karami, and Denis Schweizer. 2016a. Disentangling Crowdfunding from Fraudfunding. *Max Planck Institute for Innovation and Competition Research Paper*, No. 16-09. https://ssrn.com/abstract=2828919. Accessed 28 Feb 2017.
Cumming, Douglas J., Michelle Meoli, and Silvio Vismara. 2016b. *Investors' Choice Between Cash and Voting Rights: Evidence from Dual-Class Equity Crowdfunding*. Working Paper, University of Bergamo.
Cumming, Douglas J., Alice Rossi, and Silvio Vismara. 2017. *What Do Crowdfunding Platforms Do? A Comparison Between Investment-Based Platforms in Europe*. Working Paper, University of Bergamo.
Cumming, Douglas J., and Silvio Vismara. 2016. A Research Journey Into Entrepreneurial Finance. In *The Routledge Companion to makers of modern entrepreneurship*, ed. D.B. Audretsch and E.E. Lehmann, 64–73. London, UK: Routledge.

Cumming, Douglas J., and Yelin Zhang. 2016. Are Crowdfunding Platforms Active and Effective Intermediaries? *Social Science Research Network*. https://ssrn.com/abstract=2882026. Accessed 20 Feb 2017.

Fama, Eugene F. 1998. Market Efficiency, Long-Term Returns, and Behavioral Finance. *Journal of Financial Economics* 49: 283–306.

Farrell, Joseph, and Matthew Rabin. 1996. Cheap Talk. *Journal of Economic Perspectives* 10: 103–118.

Hanssens, Jürgen, Marc Deloof, and Tom Vanacker. 2015. Underexplored Issues in Entrepreneurial Finance. In *The Concise Guide to Entrepreneurship, Technology and Innovation*, ed. D.B. Audretsch, C.S. Hayter, and A.N. Link, 219–222. New York, NY: Edward Elgar.

———. 2016. The Evolution of Debt Policies: New Evidence from Business Startups. *Journal of Banking and Finance* 65: 120–133.

Hildebrand, Thomas, Manju Puri, and Jörg Rocholl. 2016. Adverse Incentives in Crowdfunding. *Management Science* 63 (3): 587–608.

Hornuf, Lars, and Matthias Neuenkirch. 2017. Pricing Shares in Equity Crowdfunding. *Small Business Economics* 48: 795–811.

Hornuf, Lars, and Matthias Schmitt. 2016. Success and Failure in Equity Crowdfunding. *CESifo DICE Report* 14: 16–22.

Hornuf, Lars, and Armin Schwienbacher. 2016. Crowdinvesting—Angel Investing for the Masses? In *Handbook of Research on Venture Capital: Volume 3. Business Angels*, ed. H. Landström and C. Mason, 381–397. Cheltenham, UK: Edward Elgar.

Hubbard, R. Glenn. 1998. Capital Market Imperfections and Investment. *Journal of Economic Literature* 36: 193–225.

Jain, Bharat A., and Omesh Kini. 1994. The Post-Issue Operating Performance of IPO Firms. *Journal of Finance* 49: 1699–1726.

Jensen, Michael C., and William H. Meckling. 1976. Theory of the Firm. Managerial Behavior, Agency Costs and Ownership Structures. *Journal of Financial Economics* 3: 305–360.

Khurshed, Arif, Stefano Paleari, Alok Pandè, and Silvio Vismara. 2014. Transparent Bookbuilding, Certification and Initial Public Offerings. *Journal of Financial Markets* 19: 154–159.

Khurshed, Arif, Stefano Paleari, and Silvio Vismara. 2003. The Operating Performance of Initial Public Offerings: The UK Experience. *Social Science Research Network*. https://ssrn.com/abstract=439240. Accessed 20 Feb 2017.

Kuppuswamy, Venkat, and Barry L. Bayus. 2014. Crowdfunding Creative Ideas: The Dynamics of Project Backers in Kickstarter. *Social Science Research Network*. https://ssrn.com/abstract=2234765. Accessed 20 Feb 2017.

Leland, Hayne E., and David H. Pyle. 1977. Informational Asymmetries, Financial Structure, and Financial Intermediation. *Journal of Finance* 32: 371–387.

Lin, Mingfeng, Nagpurnanand R. Prabhala, and Siva Viswanathan. 2013. Judging Borrowers by the Company They Keep: Friendship Networks and Information Asymmetry in Online Peer-to-Peer Lending. *Management Science* 59: 17–35.

Loughran, Tim, and Jay R. Ritter. 1995. The New Issues Puzzle. *Journal of Finance* 50: 23–51.

Megginson, William L., and Kathleen A. Weiss. 1991. Venture Capitalist Certification in IPOs. *Journal of Finance* 46: 879–903.

Migliorati, Katrin, and Silvio Vismara. 2014. Ranking Underwriters of European IPOs. *European Financial Management* 20: 891–925.

Mohammadi, Ali, and Kourosh Shafi. 2017. Gender Differences in the Contribution Patterns of Equity-Crowdfunding Investors. *Small Business Economics.* Forthcoming.

Mollick, Ethan. 2014. The Dynamics of Crowdfunding: An Exploratory Study. *Journal of Business Venturing* 29: 1–16.

Mollick, Ethan, and Venkat Kuppuswamy. 2014. After the Campaign: Outcomes of Crowdfunding. *Social Science Research Network.* https://ssrn.com/abstract=2376997. Accessed 20 Feb 2017.

Moritz, Alexandra, Jörn Block, and Eva Lutz. 2015. Investor Communication in Equity-Based Crowdfunding: A Qualitative-Empirical Study. *Qualitative Research in Financial Markets* 7: 309–342.

Ordanini, Andrea, Lucia Miceli, Marta Pizzetti, and Anantharanthan Parasuraman. 2011. Crowd-Funding: Transforming Customers Into Investors Through Innovative Service Platforms. *Journal of Service Management* 22: 443–470.

Paleari, Stefano, Enrico Pellizzoni, and Silvio Vismara. 2008. The Going Public Decision: Evidence from the IPOs in Italy and in the UK. *International Journal of Applied Decision Sciences* 1: 131–152.

Podolny, Joel M. 1993. A Status-Based Model of Market Competition. *American Journal of Sociology* 98: 829–872.

Ralcheva, Aleksandrina, and Peter Roosenboom. 2016. On the Road to Success in Equity Crowdfunding. *Social Science Research Network.* https://ssrn.com/abstract=2727742. Accessed 20 Feb 2017.

Ritter, Jay R. 1991. The Long-Run Performance of Initial Public Offerings. *Journal of Finance* 46: 3–27.

Robb, Alicia M., and David T. Robinson. 2014. The Capital Structure Decisions of New Firms. *Review of Financial Studies* 27: 153–179.

Signori, Andrea, and Silvio Vismara. 2016. Returns on Investments in Equity Crowdfunding. *Social Science Research Network*. https://ssrn.com/abstract=2765488. Accessed 20 Feb 2017.

Spence, Michael. 1973. Job Market Signaling. *Quarterly Journal of Economics* 87: 355–379.

———. 2002. Signaling in Retrospect and the Informational Structure of Markets. *American Economic Review* 92: 434–459.

Stiglitz, Joseph E. 2000. The Contributions of the Economics of Information to Twentieth Century Economics. *Quarterly Journal of Economics* 115: 1441–1478.

———. 2002. Information and the Change in the Paradigm in Economics. *American Economic Review* 92: 460–501.

Stiglitz, Joseph E., and Andrew Weiss. 1981. Credit Rationing in Markets with Imperfect Information. *American Economic Review* 71: 393–410.

Thomas, James B., and Reuben R. McDaniel. 1990. Interpreting Strategic Issues: Effects of Strategy and the Information Processing Structure of Top Management Teams. *Academy of Management Journal* 33: 286–306.

Vismara, Silvio. 2016. Equity Retention and Social Network Theory in Equity Crowdfunding. *Small Business Economics* 46: 579–590.

———. 2017. Information Cascades Among Investors in Equity Crowdfunding. *Entrepreneurship Theory and Practice*. Forthcoming.

Vismara, Silvio, Davide Benaroio, and Federica Carne. 2017. Gender in Entrepreneurial Finance: Matching Investors and Entrepreneurs in Equity Crowdfunding. In *Gender and Entrepreneurial Activity*, ed. Albert Link. Cheltenham: Edward Elgar.

Vismara, Silvio, Stefano Paleari, and Jay R. Ritter. 2012. Europe's Second Markets for Small Companies. *European Financial Management* 18: 352–388.

Weick, Karl E. 1995. *Sensemaking in Organizations*. Thousand Oaks, CA: SAGE Publications.

Welch, Ivo. 1992. Sequential Sales, Learning, and Cascades. *Journal of Finance* 47: 695–732.

Williamson, Oliver E. 1985. *Economic Institutions of Capitalism*. New York: Free Press.

Yum, Haewon, Byungtae Lee, and Myungsin Chae. 2012. From the Wisdom of Crowds to My Own Judgment in Microfinance Through Online Peer-to-Peer Lending Platforms. *Electronic Commerce Research and Applications* 11: 469–483.

Silvio Vismara is Professor of Entrepreneurial Finance at the University of Bergamo, Italy; an adjunct professor at the University of Augsburg, Germany; and a research fellow at Indiana University, USA. He is the associate editor of *Small Business Economics* and of the *Financial Review*, and a member of the editorial review board of *Entrepreneurship Theory and Practice* and *Journal of Technology Transfer*. His research on initial public offerings (IPOs) and crowdfunding has been covered by *The Economist*, *Financial Times*, and *Investors' Chronicle*. He is a scientific consultant for the Italian Stock Exchange.

4

The Crowd–Entrepreneur Relationship in Start-Up Financing

Thomas Lambert, Aleksandrina Ralcheva, and Peter Roosenboom

4.1 Introduction

After raising USD 2.4 million from a crowdfunding campaign on Kickstarter in 2012, Oculus VR, LLC, a California-based manufacturer of a virtual reality headset, generated large media attention when only two years later it got taken over by Facebook for USD 2 billion in cash and stock.[1] Many of the original backers were not only surprised but also disappointed by this outcome. The Oculus Rift enthusiasts, who backed the project on Kickstarter, expected "something else" from their participation in the crowdfunding campaign, as testified by this backer: "Maybe I was naive [about Oculus]. I thought it was more just like someone doing it for a hobby and just wanted to do something fun for the community. I didn't know it was going to turn into a USD 2 billion deal."[2] On Kickstarter, one of the biggest pre-ordering/reward-based crowdfunding portals, backers are not entitled to the company's revenues

T. Lambert (✉) • A. Ralcheva • P. Roosenboom
Rotterdam School of Management, Erasmus University Rotterdam, Rotterdam, The Netherlands

D. Cumming, L. Hornuf (eds.), *The Economics of Crowdfunding*,
https://doi.org/10.1007/978-3-319-66119-3_4

or profits. Nevertheless, many of the Oculus supporters felt "betrayed." In this case, participation in a *crowdinvesting* campaign, in which entrepreneurs sell shares of their start-up companies to investors through the Internet, would have allowed the backers to benefit from the acquisition of the company.

For the crowd of contributors, participating in a crowdfunding campaign may be a valuable social activity, as it is associated with a community-based experience that generates community benefits for contributors (Belleflamme et al. 2014). The case of Oculus, however, like many other cases reveals that the nature of these community benefits may vary between crowdfunding vis-à-vis crowdinvesting. Backers in crowdfunding campaigns mostly derive consumption value from their experience, while crowdinvesting offers an investment experience to investors who are primarily interested in the financial prospects of the start-up. Understanding the characteristics and motivations of the crowd and how they influence funding success is important. Indeed, crowdfunding and crowdinvesting have both demonstrated potential in financing start-ups as shown by their startling rise. In 2015 alone, the global crowdfunding market raised more than USD 34 billion, thus doubling the amount of USD 16.2 billion raised in 2014.[3]

In this chapter, we first discuss the characteristics and motivations of the crowd and how they relate to success in crowdfunding. In particular, Belleflamme et al. (2014) look more closely at the relationship that the entrepreneur builds with his or her crowd by modeling the entrepreneur's choice between crowdfunding, which includes the pre-ordering scheme, and crowdinvesting. Their model stresses the role and importance of community benefits in order to "tap" the right crowd for funding success; that is, understanding the motivations of the crowd given the capital requirements. Their main finding is that entrepreneurs prefer the pre-ordering scheme if the amount of capital they need is relatively small as compared to the market size and prefer crowdinvesting otherwise.

An interesting implication of their theoretical framework is that the crowd–entrepreneur relationship is also subject to the typical asymmetric information problems of start-up financing well documented in the case of venture capital and business angel financing (see also Agrawal et al. 2014; Belleflamme et al. 2015). First, before the financing takes place, the crowd often lacks the necessary information to assess the true ability of the entrepreneur or the intrinsic quality of the start-up or product, which could lead to an adverse selection problem. In other words, portals only manage to attract low-quality entrepreneurs because high-quality entrepreneurs anticipate that they will not be identified as such by the crowd. Second, after financing takes place, the crowd may also find it difficult to induce ex post effort on the side of the entrepreneur: delays in product delivery are commonplace, and outright frauds are the most extreme cases though much less frequent (Mollick 2014). These are forms of moral hazard. Both adverse selection and moral hazard may stifle welfare-enhancing transactions between the crowd and the entrepreneur. Belleflamme et al. (2014) further show that the choice of the "right" business model (crowdfunding vs. crowdinvesting) is one important decision entrepreneurs need to make in order to overcome these potential market failures. In particular, they demonstrate that when quality uncertainty and information asymmetry are prevalent, entrepreneurs are induced to opt for crowdinvesting.

In the second part of this chapter we continue our discussion on how these two typical asymmetric information problems affect the crowd–entrepreneur relationship in the crowdinvesting context. We focus on crowdinvesting because it represents the business model for which information problems are inherently the most significant. We argue that entrepreneurs in crowdinvesting may want to supplement their crowd of contributors with other types of contributors to mitigate information asymmetry concerns. In particular, the decision to take on board a sophisticated investor (business angel or venture capitalist) or to make use of a syndicate of investors is an important strategy to reduce them. First, sophisticated investors with their expertise, knowledge and skills provide quality signals that contribute to mitigating the adverse selection problem entrepreneurs resorting to crowdinvesting face. Second, once investment has taken place, sophisticated investors are in a better position to bear the cost of monitoring entrepreneurs and to write investment contracts setting special decision-making rights (e.g. veto power on firm decisions, appointment of directors), reducing in turn moral hazard problems. Third, because these sophisticated investors co-contract with the crowd on the same terms without being compensated for their efforts, they may find it less attractive to engage in ex ante expertise and ex post monitoring. This would in turn limit the benefits for the crowd. We close the second part with a discussion on how syndication, in which a lead investor has face-to-face interaction with the entrepreneur and is compensated using carried interest, further mitigates information problems of early stage investments.

4.2 Tapping the Crowd to Get Financed[4]

Crowdfunding is an umbrella term that refers to different business models allowing entrepreneurs to raise capital: crowdfunding (including pre-sales), crowdinvesting (including profit sharing) and crowdlending. For each business model, better understanding the characteristics of the crowd of contributors—being either backers, investors or lenders—is crucial for entrepreneurs and portal managers because it determines crowdfunding successes and failures. One such important characteristic is the so-called community benefits that the crowd enjoys by participating in the crowdfunding mechanism. These extra benefits are likely to vary across business models. Because entrepreneurs perceive all business models as different, a key issue is to understand what drives entrepreneurs to choose among the different business models.

Belleflamme et al. (2014) build a stylized model to address this question. They consider an entrepreneur who intends to "tap the crowd" to meet a certain capital requirement for setting up her start-up and therefore starting production. For unmodeled reasons, the entrepreneur has not been successful in attracting sufficient external finance to cover this amount of capital. In their model, the entrepreneur can choose between two business models that dominate nowadays, namely crowdfunding and crowdinvesting. To make the comparison as clear as possible, the authors assume, without loss of generality, that (1) launching a crowdfunding campaign or a crowdinvesting campaign is equally costly for the entrepreneur, and (2) participating in one or the other business model is a priori the same for the crowd.

By "freezing" the cost and the participation dimensions, the authors want to focus on another dimension of crowdfunding that they see as crucial, namely the relationship that crowdfunding allows the entrepreneur to establish with the crowd. The key argument developed in their article is that this relationship differs across business models. That is, when choosing one or the other business model, the entrepreneur also chooses what she can learn about the crowd and what she can extract from them through the pricing of her product.

Indeed, the crowdfunding model that the authors develop is based on pre-ordering: the backers are consumers who have a strong taste for the announced product and who therefore decide to pre-order it, that is, they pay for it before it is actually produced.[5] The entrepreneur can reward the crowd in various ways, but what matters is that these rewards (called community benefits) increase the backers' willingness to pay for the product. It is assumed that this increase in willingness to pay is proportional to the backers' taste for the product, which means those consumers who like the product the most are also those who value the rewards the most. As a result, this business model allows the entrepreneur to segment her product consumers into two groups: the backers who signal themselves as high-paying consumers (and whose willingness to pay is further enhanced by the value that they attach to the rewards), and the other (regular) consumers who wait for the product to be put on the market before considering to buy it. The entrepreneur is, thus, able to price-discriminate between both consumer groups, which gives her the opportunity to raise her profits, as she is assumed to be in a monopoly position for her product.[6] However, the optimal price discrimination scheme may not be feasible if the initial capital requirement is too high. The obligation to finance the capital through pre-sales puts a constraint on the price that can be charged to those consumers who choose to pre-order the product. Therefore, the profitability of this crowdfunding model decreases with the size of the capital requirement.

The alternative business model (crowdinvesting) that the authors consider is based on profit sharing.[7] Crowdinvesting (here profit sharing) differs from crowdfunding based on two dimensions. First, the nature of contributions and compensations is different: instead of pre-ordering the product, the crowd is invited to directly provide a fixed sum of money to the entrepreneur and is promised a share of the future profits in exchange. Second, contributors also enjoy community benefits but it is assumed here that these benefits are independent of the contributor's taste for the product. This assumption makes sense as the crowd is seen here as investors, who may well decide to finance the start-up without purchasing the product. The implications of these differences are the following. On the minus side, the entrepreneur is no longer able to segment the crowd and to single out the high-paying consumers. On the plus side, all individuals value community benefits in the same way, which makes it easier for the entrepreneur to capture this extra value. Moreover, this ability to capture the value that the crowd attaches to community benefits is not impaired by the size of the capital requirement.

The comparison of the profits that the entrepreneur can achieve under the two business models yields the main result of the analysis: the entrepreneur prefers the pre-ordering model when the capital requirement is relatively small and the profit-sharing model otherwise. The intuition behind this result has been outlined earlier: pre-ordering allows the entrepreneur to practice price discrimination, which should give her a higher profit than in the profit-sharing scheme (in which she is bound to set a uniform price for her product). However, price discrimination is constrained, and hence less profitable, when the initial capital requirement grows larger than some threshold. Above this threshold, the profit-sharing model, which allows the entrepreneur to turn all individuals into investors, becomes the best option.[8]

Belleflamme et al. (2014) report consistent results when they introduce some uncertainty about the true quality of the product, which may only be known after production has taken place. In this case, both the entrepreneur and the crowd face the same (lack of) information. In another extension, the authors introduce information asymmetry between the entrepreneur and the crowd about product quality and find that information asymmetry tends to favor profit-sharing schemes. Since the uncertainty about product quality directly influences the decision (utility) of consumers to pre-order the product or not, the entrepreneur is constrained when she tries to screen backers and to induce them to pre-order. However, the inability of the crowd to ascertain the quality of the product constrains the entrepreneur less when she tries to attract investors. Indeed, under profit sharing, investors (who eventually may not consume) care about product quality only insofar as it affects the expected profitability of their investment.

These theoretical underpinnings have implications for both entrepreneurs and portal managers. First, they highlight the importance of self-revelation mechanisms in the course of the crowdfunding process. Since entrepreneurs cannot ex ante identify consumers with a high willingness to pay for their product, entrepreneurs may opt for pre-ordering as a screening device that induces high-paying consumers to reveal themselves as such.[9] For example, the singer Verity Price managed to crowdfund her first album by appealing to her fans through her own website. While her album is now released on the market at a price of ZAR (South African Rands) 116, at the time of the crowdfunding campaign her fan base pre-ordered it at ZAR 150—that is, about 30% more of what regular consumers pay today.

Second, the crowd enjoys community benefits arising from the crowdfunding experience, the nature of which varies with the business model considered.[10] Under the crowdinvesting (pre-ordering) mechanism, community benefits are linked to the consumption experience. This can be understood as the feeling of belonging to the entrepreneurial initiative, or the feeling of being part of a group of special/privilege consumers of the product. For example, backers may participate in the ideation and design of the product, as in the case of Pebble, whose creator announced the following during the Kickstarter campaign: "Without further ado, I'd like to present the Voter's Choice color ... Orange! It won with almost 2000 out of more than 10,000 qualified votes."[11] Another post by Pebble's creator further testifies the involvement of backers in the ideation of the product: "Today, we'd like to announce that your enthusiasm has helped convince us to move the entire Pebble roadmap forward and bring you a brand new feature. Bluetooth 4.0—inside every Pebble! All Pebble watches will support Bluetooth 2.1 (as before) as well as Bluetooth 4.0 (Low Energy)."[12] In addition, Mollick (2014) points out the importance of updates and comments to create and maintain a relationship between the entrepreneur and the crowd in Kickstarter. Under the crowdinvesting (profit-sharing) mechanism, community benefits are, however, related more to the investment than the consumption experience since the crowd might not eventually be consumers of the product. Indeed, investors derive value of having financed and thus contributed to the very existence of the start-up or product. An investor on FundedByMe, a Stockholm-based crowdinvesting portal, comments: "Most of all I want experience from different lines of business and to observe the operations from a close distance. It becomes interesting in a different way when you have some of your own money in it. [...The] dream is that at least one of them [projects] would turn out to be a big success."

Third, Belleflamme et al. (2014) highlight that choosing the "right" business model crucially depends on the ability of the entrepreneur to correctly estimate her capital needs. The authors predict that pre-ordering (profit sharing) is preferred when the capital needs of the entrepreneurs are low (high). This is consistent with empirical observations: From data provided by Crowdcube and Kickstarter, two market leaders in crowdinvesting and crowdfunding respectively, one easily understands that entrepreneurs resorting to crowdinvesting collect on average more capital than those relying on crowdfunding (including pre-ordering). At the time of writing, successful entrepreneurs on Crowdcube raised on average GBP 421,707 (approx. USD 554,123), whereas entrepreneurs on Kickstarter generated on average USD 8,086.[13] A similar insight applies to the target goal.

Fourth, Belleflamme et al. (2014) show that when the uncertainty and information asymmetry regarding the quality of the product are high, investors tend to favor profit sharing over pre-ordering schemes. This implies that profit sharing may be more suitable for early stage ventures, as they inherently suffer from more information asymmetries and because pre-ordering typically requires more developed projects/products at the time of the campaign—namely, the existence of a prototype or even the existence of the very product. In what follows we address these information-related concerns in crowdinvesting and discuss potential remedies; in particular, the need in some circumstances to tap other types of investors beside the crowd.

4.3 Tapping Other Types of Investors

4.3.1 Crowdfunding and the Information Problems of Start-Up Financing

The inherently uncertain nature of crowdfunding campaigns and the lack of information surrounding start-ups make it particularly difficult for the entrepreneurs to gain the crowd's trust in order to be successful in raising their funds. However, information problems are less pronounced in the cases of crowdfunding and crowdlending than in the case of crowdinvesting for several reasons. First, crowdfunding proponents believe in the "wisdom of the crowd" and its ability to efficiently make collective investment decisions. Research on reward-based crowdfunding has indeed found support for the "wise" crowd argument, for example, theater projects on Kickstarter selected by the crowd perform as well as projects selected by experts (Mollick and Nanda 2015). Second, crowdfunding portals worldwide advertise the capital campaigns raise as a strong signal of quality. Mollick (2014) argues that projects which have already attracted funding from backers more easily accumulate further funding success through a so-called Matthew Effect ("success breeds success"; Merton 1957). Similar dynamics seem to be dominating crowdlending portals (e.g. Prosper), in which well-funded borrowers attract more lenders, who in turn infer the creditworthiness of borrowers by observing peer-lending decisions ("observational learning"; Zhang and Liu 2012). Also, by taking into account observable soft information, lenders in this market substantially outperform unobservable credit scores in terms of predicting default (Iyer et al. 2016). Third, in crowdfunding and crowdlending, the relationship between the entrepreneur and the crowd is more transactional by definition: backers in crowdfunding receive their products and/or rewards shortly after the fund-raising, while borrowers in crowdlending hold a fixed claim and thus receive interest and their money back.[14]

In contrast, in crowdinvesting, contributors (i.e. investors) make an investment decision that makes them a residual claimant in typically early stage companies, a large proportion of which fails.[15] The investors have to rely on the entrepreneur to share part of her subsequent revenues or profits (in the case of revenue or profit sharing) and only see some of their money back when there is a dividend paid or an exit event such as the sale or public offering of the venture (in the case of equity).[16] Information problems are thus inherently more pressing in crowdinvesting. One can distinguish two main information problems. The first is that of hidden information or adverse selection, which occurs before the financing takes place (ex ante).[17] To mitigate this problem, some crowdinvesting portals perform an elaborate screening, in the process of which each venture undergoes due diligence, to assess whether it meets the necessary quality standards. For example, from a sample comprising about 70% of Canadian portals over the years 2013–2016, Cumming and Zhang (2016) find a positive association between due diligence and funding success. The authors conclude that active due diligence (i.e. background checks, site visits, credit checks, cross checks, monitoring accounts and third-party proof) represents an important value for portals in limiting the number of lower-quality projects.[18] The second information problem is that of hidden action or moral hazard, which occurs after investment has taken place (ex post). After the capital raising the entrepreneur can decide to invest the money in a way that does not benefit the backers or the entrepreneur might not keep her promises. Some portals reduce moral hazard by playing a monitoring role after the investment or by facilitating information disclosure of firms to investors after investment. For example, in the case of Seedrs, a crowdinvesting portal in the United Kingdom, the portal acts as the nominee shareholder on behalf of investors and offers some degree of investor protection under the subscription agreement they have with each company that crowdfunds on their portal. Symbid, a Dutch crowdinvesting portal, offers a monitoring function on which company information is provided on a regular basis to investors who invested in that company.

Last, many leading crowdinvesting portals rely on third parties to mitigate either the ex ante or the ex post information problem. In particular, they introduce a mix of different types of investors (both naive and sophisticated investors) or have a syndicate of investors among whom a lead investor engages in due diligence and monitoring on behalf of the other investors (and gets compensated for that). The following sections aim at discussing the role and importance of sophisticated investors and syndicates in the crowdinvesting context, respectively.

4.3.2 The Role of Sophisticated Investors

As technology and online networks continue to develop, sophisticated investors such as business angels and venture capitalists are starting to turn to crowdinvesting portals to gain access to relatively new steady deal flow and even invest alongside the crowd. Crowdinvesting portals are compelling to both business angels and venture capitalists, as they leverage technology to offer a wider range of investment opportunities and to facilitate more efficient information transfer, as compared to traditional means for sourcing deal flow.[19] The structure and standardized format of crowdinvesting campaigns allow for much quicker due diligence process and provide the necessary information to ease the investment decision process. Crowdinvesting portals are also a competitive marketplace that requires entrepreneurs to publicly demonstrate their potential and the strength of their team.

Although these traditional investors find interest in crowdinvesting, the reverse is also true: traditional investors play a key role in the online solicitation of funds for early stage ventures by yielding entrepreneurs both ex ante and ex post benefits. First, the important role of these more sophisticated investors comes into play when the question is raised as to whether the crowd alone is able to deal with the high levels of uncertainty and information asymmetry. Being more informed and experienced, sophisticated investors have the ability to lower the risk of funding, in that the projects they invest in are likely to be perceived by the crowd of naive contributors as higher-quality and, thus, less risky investments. Empirical research has already addressed the role of traditional investors in crowdfunding campaigns' outcomes. Block et al. (2017) document that the strategic release of updates about receiving funding from business angels or venture capitalists attracts additional investors, and also has a positive effect on the amount of funding accumulated during crowdinvesting campaigns launched on the German portals Seedmatch and Companisto. Ralcheva and Roosenboom (2016) show that companies are more successful in raising their target amount on the UK-based portal Crowdcube when they are backed by a business angel. These more sophisticated investors have done the needed screening and due diligence before deciding to invest in a given company, which is an action small armchair (crowd)investors can easily free ride on. Other studies consider information cascades and confirm that investors indeed follow more informed and sophisticated fellow investors with public profiles when deciding in which campaigns to invest (see Hornuf and Schwienbacher 2017, for evidence from German portals; Vismara 2016, for evidence from Crowdcube).

Second, crowdinvesting can lead to moral hazard, meaning that the actions of the entrepreneur may change to the detriment of the crowd after the investment has taken place. Traditionally, business angels and venture capitalists deal with moral hazard problems via investment contracts. These investment contracts give them special decision-making rights, such as the right to appoint one or more directors on the board and the right to veto company decisions (e.g. the issuance of additional equity, large investments and the sale of the company or its assets). Moreover, business angels and venture capitalists often sit on the board of directors to monitor what the entrepreneur does with the money they invested. In contrast, none of the (naive) investors engaging in crowdinvesting feel individually compelled to start monitoring the entrepreneur or write an investment contract. This is because they would have to bear all the costs involved in doing so but would only benefit to the extent of their fractional ownership in the firm, leaving the vast majority of the benefits from their efforts to be shared among the other non-monitoring investors, who would simply free ride on their efforts. By attracting a balanced mix of both naive and sophisticated investors, entrepreneurs might be able to at least partially address these crowd's concerns, as sophisticated investors are very likely to engage in monitoring activities. Business angels and venture capitalists alike have strong incentives to invest time and resources in systematically reviewing the progress of their portfolio companies, as they not only put their wealth at stake but also face serious reputational consequences in case their investees fail. At the same time, they are more experienced and have high expertise in monitoring, from which the portion of naive investors can reap significant benefits. What is more, once traditional investors have invested in a company, they pull their resources (industry knowledge, networks and services) to help their investee companies succeed (Gorman and Sahlman 1989). At the time of writing, there are only a few studies that look into the ex post performance of crowdinvesting campaigns and the role of sophisticated investors. One early study is that of Signori and Vismara (2016) who examine the expected return on investments of 212 successful equity raisings on Crowdcube and find that in one out of ten cases investors lose their money soon after the offering. However, the authors report that none of the companies backed by a business angel or venture capitals have subsequently failed. This suggests that the monitoring and value-adding role of traditional investors positively impacts subsequent performance. In a study of the realized return on investments on German crowdinvesting portals, Hornuf and Schmitt (2016) find that investors' returns have been meager (even negative according to their calculations from the entire German crowdinvesting market between 2011 and 2015) when compared to the earnings of venture capital funds and the average profits of a well-diversified crowdlending portfolio. Questioning the viability of the crowdinvesting market in Germany, Hornuf and Schmitt (2016) observe, however, that many German portals have now established pooling contracts encouraging the coexistence of the crowd and venture capital funds to overcome these performance issues.

4.3.3 The Role of Syndication

There are many crowdinvesting portals that have been successful in attracting a crowd of different types of investors (e.g. AngelList, Crowdcube, Crowdfunder, MyMicroInvest, SyndicateRoom; see Table 4.1 for a list of (selected) examples of existing types of portals with a description of the type of investments they offer). While there is evidence that business angels and venture capitalists actively engage in crowdinvesting, on portals such as Crowdcube (UK-based) and MyMicroInvest (Belgium-based), they usually co-invest with the crowd on the same terms, which means that they do not get compensated for bringing in their knowledge and expertise. This could, in turn, reduce their incentives to get sufficiently involved in ex post mentoring and monitoring, and hence limit the benefits for the other investors. However, some portals have thought of a unique portal design feature, which enables them to address this issue by formalizing the relationship between the entrepreneurs and the different types of investors. For example, SyndicateRoom (UK-based) facilitates a syndicate-like crowdinvesting, which necessitates the involvement of an experienced business angel in every round of investment. On such type of portals, individuals, business angel groups and/or venture capital funds can form syndicates and invite other investors to participate in their deals. AngelList, a US-based

Table 4.1 List and description of selected crowdinvesting portals

Portal	Description
AngelList	US-based website for start-ups that facilitates syndicate investments by accredited investors, among other things. Syndicates are brought to the portal and led by experienced angel investors who have vetted the target investment and personally invest in the deal they offer, thus demonstrating their confidence in the investment's potential. AngelList has over 200 syndicate leads who are actively bringing deals to the portal. Source: https://angel.co/
Crowdcube	UK-based crowdinvesting portal that offers individuals (everyday investors as well as professional investors) the opportunity to invest in start-up, early stage and growth businesses through equity and debt investment options. Source: https://crowdcube.com/
Crowdfunder	US-based crowdinvesting portal that connects entrepreneurs to investors online. It manages the Crowdfunder VC Index Fund, which invests into start-ups backed by top VCs at their same terms. Selected Fund investments are then shared with their online investor network. Source: https://www.crowdfunder.com/
MyMicroInvest	Belgium-based crowdinvesting portal that offers investment opportunities after validating the submitted portal projects, for which legal information and due diligence have been completed. In the majority of cases, one or several professional investors participate in the financing. It issues Participative Notes upon investment which mirror a loan or a participation in the capital of the underlying company in economic terms and give the owner the right to the same return (interest in case of loans or capital gains in the case of shares). Source: https://www.mymicroinvest.com/
Seedrs	UK-based crowdinvesting portal that facilitates equity investments by friends, family, customers, angels and other independent investors for early stage businesses. Investors receive protection through a unified nominee structure. Source: https://www.seedrs.com/
SyndicateRoom	UK-based crowdinvesting portal that promotes an investor-led crowdfunding model by necessitating the participation of an experienced business angel in every round of investment. These lead investors play an active role in evaluating the strengths of the deals they back and invest their own money. Individual investors are offered to invest alongside these angel investors on the same economic terms. Source: https://www.syndicateroom.com/

investor matchmaking website, offers investment syndicates in which start-ups raise money from accredited investors investing alongside prominent angel investors. Even Crowdcube, a portal focused on building a large base of small investors, is currently introducing different roles (e.g. a lead role) for investors.

Crowdinvesting syndicates are particularly useful for reducing both the ex ante and ex post information problems we discussed earlier. Here a (professional) lead investor posts a deal on the portal seeking the crowd to co-invest in the company together with her. The lead investor has face-to-face interaction with the entrepreneur and is compensated using carried interest (i.e. a share of the profits of the investment in excess of the amount that the lead investor contributes) by the crowd of investors for value-adding and monitoring services (such is the case of AngelList). This "carry" plays a key role in that it provides strong motivation for the lead investors to put in the hard work of correctly evaluating the entrepreneurial venture and helping it raise the funds it needs.

In the world of early stage equity financing, syndicates have been traditionally used by venture capital firms to make investments together with other venture capital firms, thus sharing a joint pay-off. There are many benefits associated with venture capital syndication. For example, syndication can be used as a mechanism to resolve information asymmetries and combine knowledge and expertise to make better investment decisions (Lerner 1994). In addition, by forming syndicates venture capital firms are able to pull together more capital, but also share the high risk inherent in early stage investments. Business angels use similar tools to overcome the information problem and benefit from an improved deal flow. They organize themselves in angel groups or business angel networks in order to collectively evaluate and invest in entrepreneurial ventures. These groups and networks offer several advantages: they make larger investments possible, while at the same time reducing the burden for individual angels; they provide more visibility, which results in receiving superior deal flow; and they usually include the most sophisticated and active investors, which allows for superior decision-making (Kerr et al. 2014). In other words, syndication encourages information flows and provides opportunities for investors to source high-quality deal flow, to benefit from additional due diligence and diversify their portfolios.

This syndicate system may prove to be especially effective in crowdinvesting in that it encourages information transfer from the more knowledgeable and sophisticated investors to the more naive-type investors composing the crowd. More importantly, crowdinvesting syndicates confer strong incentives for lead investors to conduct thorough due diligence and active monitoring.[20] Agrawal et al. (2016) coin syndication the "killer app" of crowdinvesting because they can potentially augment the role of professional investors, thus allowing for more efficient capital allocation and enhancing aggregate economic activity.

4.4 Conclusion

In this chapter, we have examined some key features of the crowd and how they relate to success in crowdfunding and crowdinvesting. In both business models, the crowd of backers/investors enjoys some extra utility (the so-called community benefits) over more traditional investors/customers. The nature of these community benefits varies across business models: community benefits are linked to the consumption experience under crowdfunding and to the investment experience under crowdinvesting. Belleflamme et al. (2014) unveil that this difference in the nature of community benefits is key in determining the entrepreneurial choice of business model. They show, consistent with empirical observations, that when the initial capital requirement is relatively small, entrepreneurs favor crowdfunding and resort to crowdinvesting otherwise.

Their theoretical framework has several entrepreneurial implications. One implication, well illustrated by the case of Oculus, is the importance for the entrepreneur to select the right business model given what she can learn about/from the crowd and what she can extract from the crowd through the pricing mechanism. Another key implication is that the crowd–entrepreneur relationship is not foreign to the typical asymmetric information problems of start-up financing and that when information asymmetries are more pressing, entrepreneurs tend to opt for crowdinvesting, rather than crowdfunding or even crowdlending, in which the crowd–entrepreneur relationship is by nature more transactional. Crowdinvesting may thus necessitate complementing entrepreneurs' relationship with the crowd by implementing various mechanisms mitigating more acute information problems. In particular, we have highlighted that the backing of sophisticated investors and the formation of a syndicate of investors do reduce information asymmetries regarding pre- and post-campaign outcomes.

Notes

1. See, for example, "Facebook to Buy Virtual Reality Firm Oculus for USD 2 Billion" by Reed Albergotti and Ian Sherr, Wall Street Journal, March 25, 2014, "Facebook Plays Platform Catch-Up with USD 2 Billion Oculus Deal" by Hannah Kuchler and Tim Bradshaw, Financial Times, March 26, 2014, or "Facebook Buys VR Startup Oculus for USD 2 Billion" by Cade Metz, Wired, March 25, 2014.
2. "When Crowdfunding Goes Corporate: Kickstarter Backers Vent over Facebook's Oculus Buy" by Victor Luckerson, Time, March 26, 2014.
3. These numbers of the crowdfunding market are sourced from the Massolution Crowdfunding Industry Report (2015), available at: http://reports.crowdsourcing.org/index.php?route=product/product&product_id=54 (last consulted on July 12, 2016).
4. This section partly draws from Belleflamme and Lambert (2014).
5. Cumming et al. (2015) consider different types of crowdfunding models (i.e. Keep-It-All vs. All-Or-Nothing) and show that they allow to allocate the risk differently between the crowd and the entrepreneur. Without loss of generality, the discussion in Belleflamme et al. (2014) does not account for this variation of crowdfunding models.
6. We have here a form of behavior-based price discrimination as consumers self-select into one group and are then charged a specific price corresponding to their choice; see Fudenberg and Miguel Villas-Boas (2006) for a general analysis of behavior-based price discrimination and Belleflamme and Peitz (2015) for a textbook treatment.
7. See also Sahm et al. (2014), who slightly correct the analysis on profit sharing and, thereby, simplify it.
8. Ellman and Hurkens (2015) also examine a crowdfunding model that allows the crowd to pre-order the product and in which entrepreneurs can commit to produce only if aggregate funding exceeds a defined threshold. Yet, in their model, pre-ordering does not confer any additional commu-

nity benefit. Their objective is to determine the optimal crowdfunding mechanism in the presence of two conflicting forces: a high threshold allows the entrepreneur to set higher prices for high-type buyers, while a low threshold raises the probability of production. Kumar et al. (2016) also model threshold choice, but they consider a continuum of consumers.

9. See Chemla and Tinn (2016) whose model emphasizes the importance of learning about demand as an essential reason why entrepreneurs engage in the pre-ordering mechanism.
10. Community benefits do not have to be confused with the rewards that are often offered by entrepreneurs to the participating crowd. Rewards simply represent, in both business models, a materialization of these community benefits.
11. See https://www.kickstarter.com/projects/597507018/pebble-e-paper-watch-for-iphone-and-android/posts/273665 (last consulted on July 11, 2016).
12. This quote is also stressed by Agrawal et al. (2014). See https://blog.getpebble.com/2012/05/08/and-one-more-thing/ (last consulted on July 11, 2016).
13. See www.crowdcube.com and www.kickstarter.com/help/stats (last consulted on July 11, 2016).
14. In most cases the products/rewards promised by the entrepreneur are delivered (see Mollick 2014) in part because a failed delivery history would also establish a negative reputation of the entrepreneur which decreases funding success when returning to raise money on Kickstarter (Li and Martin 2016).
15. According to the Small Business Administration (SBA), only about 50% of businesses survive five years or longer. See https://www.sba.gov/sites/default/files/advocacy/SB-FAQ-2016_WEB.pdf (last consulted on November 28, 2016).
16. Such an exit event might only occur several years after the original investment, if at all. Hornuf and Schmitt (2016) report that until the end of 2015 only seven start-ups that equity crowdfunded in Germany offered exit opportunities to their investors.
17. The problem of adverse selection, introduced by Akerlof (1970), can be illustrated with a simple example. Assume the venture is of either a low-quality (worth USD 100) or a high-quality type (worth USD 200). Investors know that there is an equal chance that they are dealing with a low-quality or high-quality venture but cannot distinguish between the two. In that case, backers would rationally price the venture at the average value of (50%*USD 100+50%* USD 200=) USD 150. This implies

an undervaluation of USD 50 for the high-quality venture and an overvaluation of USD 50 for the low-quality venture. As a result, low-quality ventures would quickly start to flood the market for early stage finance, which in the extreme case could lead to a market breakdown where no venture successfully gets financed.

18. Portals are of course not the only actors capable of mitigating such information asymmetries. We refer to Ahlers et al. (2015), Ralcheva and Roosenboom (2016) and Vismara (2016), among many others, whose work focuses on entrepreneurs and stresses the role of certification and quality signals.
19. Traditionally, both business angels and venture capitalists would use their personal connections and networks, and attend local start-up events or dedicated start-up conferences as means to access new potential investment opportunities. The typical way to source vital information would be through various documents and/or face-to-face communication.
20. Hildebrand et al. (2016) consider incentive effects for group leaders on the crowdlending portal Prosper. Their results suggest that similarly to crowdinvesting, group leaders on Prosper much more carefully screen and choose the listings to be funded when they have sufficient "skin in the game."

References

Agrawal, Ajay, Christian Catalini, and Avi Goldfarb. 2014. Some Simple Economics of Crowdfunding. *Innovation Policy and the Economy* 14: 63–97.

———. 2016. Are Syndicates the Killer App of Equity Crowdfunding? *California Management Review* 58: 111–124.

Ahlers, Gerrit, Douglas Cumming, Christina Günther, and Denis Schweizer. 2015. Signaling in Equity Crowdfunding. *Entrepreneurship Theory and Practice* 39: 955–980.

Akerlof, George. 1970. The Market for Lemons: Quality Uncertainty and the Market Mechanism. *Quarterly Journal of Economics* 84: 488–500.

Belleflamme, Paul, and Thomas Lambert. 2014. Crowdfunding: Some Empirical Findings and Microeconomic Underpinnings. *Revue Bancaire et Financière* 4: 288–296.

Belleflamme, Paul, Thomas Lambert, and Armin Schwienbacher. 2014. Crowdfunding: Tapping the Right Crowd. *Journal of Business Venturing* 29: 585–609.

Belleflamme, Paul, Nessrine Omrani, and Martin Peitz. 2015. The Economics of Crowdfunding Platforms. *Information Economics and Policy* 33: 11–28.
Belleflamme, Paul, and Martin Peitz. 2015. *Industrial Organization: Markets and Strategies*. Cambridge: Cambridge University Press.
Block, Jörn, Lars Hornuf, and Alexandra Moritz. 2017. Which Updates During an Equity Crowdfunding Campaign Increase Crowd Participation? *Small Business Economics*. https://link.springer.com/article/10.1007/s11187-017-9876-4. Accessed 20 Feb 2017.
Chemla, Gilles, and Katrin Tinn. 2016. Learning Through Crowdfunding. *Social Science Research Network*. https://papers.ssrn.com/abstract=2804541. Accessed 20 Feb 2017.
Cumming, Douglas, Gaël Leboeuf, and Armin Schwienbacher. 2015. Crowdfunding Models: Keep-It-All Versus All-Or-Nothing. *Social Science Research Network*. https://papers.ssrn.com/abstract=2447567. Accessed 28 Feb 2017.
Cumming, Douglas, and Yelin Zhang. 2016. Are Crowdfunding Platforms Active and Effective Intermediaries? *Social Science Research Network*. https://papers.ssrn.com/abstract=2882026. Accessed 20 Feb 2017.
Ellman, Matthew, and Sjaak Hurkens. 2015. Optimal Crowdfunding Design. *Social Science Research Network*. https://papers.ssrn.com/abstract=2507457. Accessed 20 Feb 2017.
Fudenberg, Drew, and J. Miguel Villas-Boas. 2006. Behavior-based Price Discrimination and Customer Recognition. In *Handbook on Economics and Information Systems*, ed. T.J. Hendershott, 377–436. Amsterdam: Elsevier.
Gorman, Michael, and William A. Sahlman. 1989. What Do Venture Capitalists Do? *Journal of Business Venturing* 4: 231–248.
Hildebrand, Thomas, Manju Puri, and Jörg Rocholl. 2016. Adverse Incentives in Crowdfunding. *Management Science* 63: 587–608.
Hornuf, Lars, and Matthias Schmitt. 2016. Success and Failure in Equity Crowdfunding. *CESifo DICE Report* 14: 16–22.
Hornuf, Lars, and Armin Schwienbacher. 2017. Market Mechanisms and Funding Dynamics in Equity Crowdfunding. *Journal of Corporate Finance*. http://www.sciencedirect.com/science/article/pii/S0929119916302450. Accessed 20 Feb 2017.
Iyer, Rajkamal, Asim Ijaz Khwaja, Erzo F.P. Luttmer, and Kelly Shue. 2016. Screening Peers Softly: Inferring the Quality of Small Borrowers. *Management Science* 62: 1554–1577.
Kerr, William R., Josh Lerner, and Antoinette Schoar. 2014. The Consequences of Entrepreneurial Finance: Evidence from Angel Financings. *The Review of Financial Studies* 27: 20–55.

Kumar, Praveen, Nisan Langberg, and David Zvilichovsky. 2016. (Crowd) Funding Innovation: Financing, Constraints, Price Discrimination and Welfare. *Social Science Research Network*. https://papers.ssrn.com/abstract=2600923. Accessed 20 Feb 2017.

Lerner, Joshua. 1994. The Syndication of Venture Capital Investments. *Financial Management* 23: 16–27.

Li, Emma, and J. Spencer Martin. 2016. Capital Formation and Financial Intermediation: The Role of Entrepreneur Reputation Formation. *Journal of Corporate Finance*. http://www.sciencedirect.com/science/article/pii/S0929119916300487. Accessed 20 Feb 2017.

Merton, Robert K. 1957. Priorities in Scientific Discovery: A Chapter in the Sociology of Science. *American Sociological Review* 22: 635–659.

Mollick, Ethan. 2014. The Dynamics of Crowdfunding: An Exploratory Study. *Journal of Business Venturing* 29: 1–16.

Mollick, Ethan, and Ramana Nanda. 2015. Wisdom or Madness? Comparing Crowds with Expert Evaluation in Funding the Arts. *Management Science* 62: 1533–1553.

Ralcheva, Aleksandrina, and Peter Roosenboom. 2016. On the Road to Success in Equity Crowdfunding. *Social Science Research Network*. https://papers.ssrn.com/abstract=2727742. Accessed 20 Feb 2017.

Sahm, Marco, Paul Belleflamme, Thomas Lambert, and Armin Schwienbacher. 2014. Corrigendum to "Crowdfunding: Tapping the Right Crowd". *Journal of Business Venturing* 29: 610–611.

Signori, Andrea, and Silvio Vismara. 2016. Returns on Investments in Equity Crowdfunding. *Social Science Research Network*. https://papers.ssrn.com/abstract=2765488. Accessed 20 Feb 2017.

Vismara, Silvio. 2016. Information Cascades among Investors in Equity Crowdfunding. *Entrepreneurship Theory and Practice*. http://onlinelibrary.wiley.com/doi/10.1111/etap.12261/full. Accessed 20 Feb 2017.

Zhang, Juanjuan, and Peng Liu. 2012. Rational Herding in Microloan Markets. *Management Science* 58: 892–912.

Thomas Lambert is an Assistant Professor of Finance at Rotterdam School of Management, Erasmus University. His research interests are in banking, corporate finance, entrepreneurial finance and political economy. His work has been presented at major conferences around the world and has been published in leading academic journals, including the *Economic Journal* and *Management Science*. Lambert holds a Ph.D. degree in Finance jointly from the Université catholique de Louvain and Université Lille 2, for which he has received several awards, including the Banque de France Foundation Prize for the Best Thesis in Monetary and Financial Economics.

Aleksandrina Ralcheva is a Ph.D. candidate at the Rotterdam School of Management, Erasmus University. Her interests and research efforts are targeted towards the financing of young and innovative ventures. She is particularly passionate about financial technology (FinTech), i.e. crowdfunding, blockchain, and peer-to-peer transactions in general. She carries the technological curiosity to explore creative solutions to complex issues surrounding big data, machine learning and the Internet of Things.

Peter Roosenboom is a Professor of Entrepreneurial Finance and Private Equity at the Rotterdam School of Management, Erasmus University. His work has been published in leading finance and accounting journals such as the *Review of Financial Studies*, *Journal of Financial and Quantitative Analysis*, *Review of Finance* and *Contemporary Accounting Research*. Roosenboom is an associate editor for the *Journal of Banking & Finance* and the *Multinational Finance Journal*. He is a regular advisor to the Dutch government on private equity and the financing of small- and medium-sized enterprises (SMEs).

5

Fraudulent Behavior by Entrepreneurs and Borrowers

Christa Hainz

5.1 Introduction

The crowdfunding market is a child of the digital revolution and, although still in its infancy, it is growing rapidly. Prosper.com, one of the first crowdfunding platforms to engage in peer-to-peer lending, was founded in 2006. Just like new products new markets have to demonstrate that they satisfy needs that would otherwise be unmet. The need addressed by crowdfunding platforms is to bring supply and demand of capital together.[1] As funding decisions involve significant risks, the platforms need to build up the reputation that transactions take place in a fair and trustworthy manner. Otherwise investors are not willing to invest.

To build up this reputation it is important to limit fraudulent behavior. From other financial markets we know that fraud has severely negative repercussions on the market. There is evidence from the United States that households in states that are also home to firms involved in corporate fraud cases reduce their stock market participation (Giannetti and Wang 2016). In Germany the so-called Neuer Markt (a stock market

C. Hainz (✉)
Ifo Institute for Economic Research, Munich, Germany

D. Cumming, L. Hornuf (eds.), *The Economics of Crowdfunding*,
https://doi.org/10.1007/978-3-319-66119-3_5

for small- and medium-size innovative growth firms) was dissolved in 2003 only a few years after its launch in 1997. One of the main reasons was that some major corporate scandals, such as misstatement of turnover and insider trade, eroded its reputation (Burghof and Hunger 2004). A similar effect could occur in the crowdfunding market in case of fraud. As the market is still very young, the negative effects of fraud cases might be very strong and potentially unfold a destructive power. Fraud by platforms will exert similar negative externalities.

In this chapter we investigate fraud by borrowers and entrepreneurs. Fraud has many different faces. We use the definition provided by Cummings et al. (2016, 4) for reward-based crowdfunding and formulate it for crowdfunding in general. The investor must verify that the following five different elements are present in order to prove fraud on the part of a firm: (1) the firm must have made a false statement related to a material fact, (2) the firm must have known that the statement was untrue, (3) it must have been the firm's intention to deceive the investor, (4) the investor must have reasonably relied on the statements of the firm, and (5) the investor must have been injured, which is most likely the case if funds are lost.[2]

We will begin this chapter by taking an economic perspective on fraudulent behavior. We use the sketch of a model with asymmetric information to highlight the role of uncertainty and discuss mechanisms to reduce the underlying incentives problem. We then review the existing evidence on potentially fraudulent behavior in the three different crowdfunding markets and highlight their limitations. We subsequently discuss those factors that influence the detection of fraud and conclude by offering some policy implications.

5.2 Asymmetric Information and Fraud

The behavior of agents and the relationship between agents and their principals is studied in contract theory. The idea underlying the models in contract theory is that the agents, or in the case of financial services the firms represented by their managers, have better information than their principals, the financiers; and that the former use the information asymmetry for their own benefit. The contract theoretical models deal with fraudulent behavior without calling it fraud. As the definition of fraud has shown, the challenge is to demonstrate that an agent's behavior is fraudulent and that the agent took his actions by intent. Contracts can specify variables that can be observed and verified. However, the agent's behavior cannot be stipulated in a contract because it cannot be observed and verified. At the point in time at which the contract is written there is uncertainty about the outcome of a project. In the context of finance this means that the capital that is invested in a project does not generate a return with certainty, but that there is a distribution of returns. The ultimate return is, in contrast to the agent's behavior, observable and verifiable and therefore can be the subject matter of a contract. We will discuss two problems of fraud depending on the point in time when it takes place; the agent can deceive the principal before or after the contract is concluded.

5.2.1 Adverse Selection

At the point in time before the principal and the agent enter into a contractual relationship the principal cannot observe the agent's type, that is whether the agent has a high- or low-risk production technology. The agent's type will influence the distribution of the returns and ultimately returns are observable.

An example of adverse selection from crowdfunding is Kobe beef jerky. In a Kickstarter campaign Magnus Fun Inc. offered Kobe beef jerky shortly after the import of Kobe beef to the United States was allowed, but still heavily regulated. The original goal was to raise USD 2,374. In fact more than 3,000 backers offered over USD 120,000. A team of filmmakers detected inconsistencies in the figures of Magnus Fun Inc. and the campaign stopped briefly before it would have been completed and the money of the principals could have been lost.[3]

5.2.2 Moral Hazard

The second problem of asymmetric information arises after the contract is concluded because the agent cannot commit to a certain behavior, such as investing the money as promised or exerting effort in managing the project. This problem can be referred to as moral hazard.[4] By exerting effort the agent increases the probability that the project generates a high return, enabling the agent to make payments to its principal. Similarly the agent can divert the funds instead of investing them appropriately, meaning that the project stands a relatively low chance of proving successful.

There are two fraud cases from crowdfunding that can serve as examples for moral hazard. Jen Hintz raised USD 26,000 on Kickstarter for FibroFibers, an indie yarn-dyeing business. In reality she did not spend the money on her business, but instead used it to finance her move from North Carolina to Massachusetts. Another example comes from GoFundMe. A mother raised money for paying the cancer treatments for her daughter. The daughter, however, was healthy and the money was spent otherwise (Fredman 2015).

We want to use the following simple model to illustrate the moral hazard model for the crowdlending market. Therefore the contracting parties are called borrower and lender. We study credit contracts in which borrowers first receive credit and then decide on where to invest the money. If the borrower invests the money in the proposed project the probability of success, that is of being able to repay the loan, is p_H. If he does not invest the money as proposed, but uses it for his own purposes, he will get a private benefit b with certainty, but the project will never succeed. The borrower has a return of X in the case of success and zero in the case of failure; returns are assumed to be verifiable. Furthermore, we assume that investment I is efficient from a social welfare perspective only if the borrower decides to invest the money instead of taking the private benefit, that is $p_H X - I > b$. However, the choice of the borrower is not observable and causes a moral hazard problem. We assume that the borrower possesses assets totaling the amount of A that can be liquidated by the lender in the case of failure. Thus, the borrower's liability is limited to A ($<I$). The payoffs are depicted in Fig. 5.1. It is worth noting that in the case of investing as proposed, the payoff might be *0* whereas it is certainly *0* in the case of fraud. Thus, for the investor it is impossible to distinguish between fraudulent and non-fraudulent behavior in this case because the agent's investment decision is not observable. But the lender gets an imperfect signal as to the borrower's behavior. Therefore, the contract

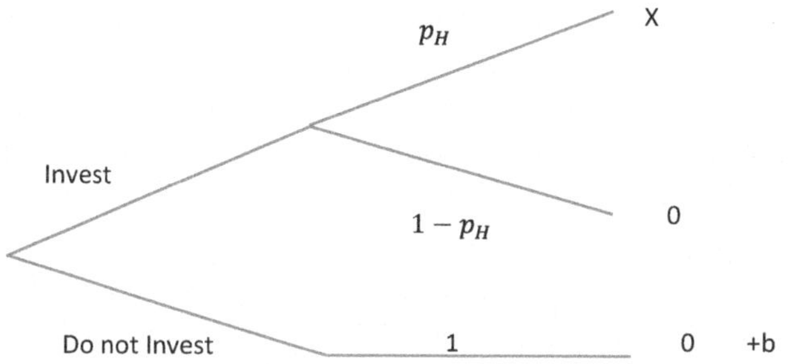

Fig. 5.1 Moral hazard model for the crowdlending market: payoff structure

terms are the means of solving the moral hazard problem; they must be set such that they give the borrower an incentive to behave non-fraudulently.

The principals offer a contract $\{R; A\}$ to the borrower, in which R is the repayment in the successful state and A is the liability in case of default. Although crowdfunding contracts do not specify collateral, borrowers are liable with all their assets in case of default and A measures the borrower's liability.[5] In order to solve the moral hazard problem, the credit contract must satisfy an incentive compatibility constraint (1), which states that the net payoff for the borrower must be higher when investing in the project than when taking the money and spending it on for its own private benefit. When investing the money the borrower will be successful with probability p_H, generating a return of X and repaying R to the lender. If the project fails, the borrower will lose all of his assets totaling the amount of A. When the borrower spends the money for its own benefit, he gains a private benefit of b, but will certainly lose its assets A.

$$p_H(A+X-R)+(1-p_H)(A-A) \geq A-A+b \tag{1}$$

$$p_H(X-R+A) \geq b \tag{2}$$

This equation helps us to understand the problems that may arise because a project is credit financed. As we assumed that $p_H X - I > b$, nobody would undertake a fraudulent project with its own means. However, if it is possible to find a lender that provides a loan, the borrower does not have to bear all the costs of his (non-)investment and therefore may have an incentive to take the money from the lender and spend it on its own purposes, getting a private benefit of b. Equation (2) states the condition a credit contract has to fulfill so that the borrower will opt for the investment. Comparative statistics provide interesting insights. The higher the private benefits from diverting the funds, the higher the incentive to opt for diverting the funds. On the other hand, the more profitable the investment project, that is the higher the probability of success p_H and the return in case of success X, the lower the incentive to divert the funds. Most importantly, the terms of the credit contract influence the borrower's incentives. The higher the repayment R and the lower the liability A, the more attractive it is for the borrower to divert the funds. The lower the liability of the borrower, the more difficult it will be to write an incentive-compatible contract. Here it is important to bear in mind that the lower the difference between $(R–A)$, the higher the incentive not to divert the funds and invest them as proposed.

Ultimately there are two ways to address problems of asymmetric information. The first way is to reduce the information asymmetry. The second way is to write a contract that gives the borrower an incentive not to exploit its information advantage. The simple model above has shown that in the case of moral hazard the difference between the repayment in the case of success and failure, that is $(R–A)$, should be low.

In the banking context, reducing information asymmetry after the contract is signed is reached by monitoring the borrower. To this end the borrower has to document the development of his business regularly by showing balance sheet and other data to the loan officer. However, monitoring imposes a fixed cost on the bank, making it unattractive for small loan sizes. For microcredit new contractual forms have emerged as a result. The first microfinance bank, the Grameen bank in Bangladesh, initially only granted microloans to groups of borrowers with joint liability. The idea was to exploit the knowledge that individual borrowers have about their peers. Thus borrowers would exert pressure on their peers to repay the loan because otherwise the well-performing borrowers would have to repay for their defaulting peers.

The microfinance loans have another important feature to improve incentives. Borrowers can build up a credit history. A good credit history gives them access to future loans and the size of those loans increases over time. This means that default leads to a loss of reputation. In our simple model above this could be captured as a higher liability whereby borrowers do not lose physical assets, but their reputation. The same mechanisms exist when a borrower and a bank have a longer-term relationship and when information-sharing devices exist in a credit market.

We have just discussed the mechanisms that could solve the moral hazard problem. Similar mechanisms exist for adverse selection. For crowdfunding to be successful it must develop ways to solve the problems created by asymmetric information, as otherwise it will attract fraudulent projects that are not financed by financial intermediaries that have mechanisms in place that solve these problems. An adverse selection problem therefore exists between different lenders, that is, between platforms and more generally between the more traditional financial market and the crowdfunding platforms. In the end there are several adverse selection problems, one between the lender and the borrower and another one between different lenders.

5.3 Empirical Evidence on Fraud

No systematic evidence on cases of fraud in crowdfunding has been collected to date. We will provide some evidence on (what we will call) performance problems in the three different areas of crowdfunding, such as non-deliveries and defaults.

5.3.1 Reward-Based Crowdfunding

Reward-based crowdfunding differs in several aspects from crowdlending and crowdinvesting. Firstly, it does not necessarily give a monetary payoff to the backers, but does provide them some other reward, such as the product or a giveaway which, for example, may be a documentary of how a product is made or a project t-shirt. Perhaps as a result it is often not perceived as an investment by the backers. Legal scholars argue that the backers' motivation to provide money is not to finance the development of the product, but rather to buy rewards or goods. This argument is illustrated by the Pebble Smartwatch project in which most backers (96 percent of the 68,929) pledged at least USD 99 which was the threshold above which one obtained the product. If backers wanted to see the Pebble Smartwatch to be developed, the fraction of contributions below the threshold should have been (much) higher. From a legal point of view the parties enter a contract for the design and manufacture of a specific good. But the important difference to other contracts for purchasing products on- or off-line is that the goods in reward-based crowdfunding have not been produced at the point in time the contract is concluded (Moores 2015).[6] This means that there is more uncertainty involved when purchasing a good via reward-based crowdfunding, which might often not be fully acknowledged by the parties of the contract, and particularly by the buyer.

Mollick (2014) studies data on performance problems on Kickstarter. He uses data on Kickstarter projects from its start in 2009 until July 2012. During that period over 23,000 projects were successfully funded on the platform (which equals a 48.1 percent share of all proposals submitted). To see how the projects perform over time the author analyzes the final outcome of the 471 projects in the categories of Design and Technology, which had specified delivery dates before July 2012. Among these 471 projects 381 had outcomes that were clearly identifiable. Within this group there were 14 projects that failed (or 3.6 percent) either issuing a refund (3 projects) or stopping to respond to backers (11). However, among the better-performing projects delivery on time is not the rule, as only 24.9 percent of the projects were not delayed. Another 33 percent did not deliver as promised until the end of the sample period. The projects with a delay (126 projects or 33 percent) delivered on average 2.4 months later.[7]

These figures provide some evidence on the performance problems in reward-based crowdfunding. However, the reasons underlying these problems can be manifold and range from intentionally deceiving investors to slipping into such deception, or even a mixture of both.[8] Fraud is only one possible explanation. If a project grants a refund, technical problems are more likely to explain non-delivery than fraud. If an individual stops responding, it could well be that "he ran away with the money." This happens in 2.9 percent of the cases in the sample. It is important to bear in mind that these projects operate under greater uncertainty than traditional sales, as products have not been produced at the point in time when they are sold. As a result, Mollick (2014) finds that delays are more likely if products are promised as compared to giveaways. The other factors increasing the risk of a delay are the size of the project and the degree of overfunding. These findings may provide some indication that performance problems increase with the complexity of the project as the latter results in uncertain outcomes.

Alternatively, one could look at fraud directly. The challenge here is that fraud—in contrast to delivery—is not readily observable. Cumming et al. (2016) search for fraud cases for projects on the two most popular platforms (Kickstarter and Indiegogo) in nine countries during the period 2010–2015. They not only collect data from the websites of the two platforms but complement it by searching for fraud cases themselves. They find only 207 fraud cases (which corresponds to a rate of 0.01 percent).

The figures on fraud cases (0.01 percent) and non-deliveries (about 3 percent when deducting the refunds from the non-deliveries) could act as lower and upper bounds for fraudulent behavior in reward-based crowdfunding. As fraud is not readily observable, the fraud cases that this figure is based on are only the tip of the iceberg (we will discuss the detection of fraud cases below). By contrast, non-deliveries will exaggerate fraudulent behavior because in an uncertain world non-fraudulent projects also fail.

5.3.2 Crowdlending

There are no figures on fraud in crowdfunding available to date. However, default rates are observable and are used for research. Just as for non-deliveries there are many different reasons that lead to a default, and one of them is fraud.

To determine the performance of a loan it is optimal to study loans that have matured. Therefore the evidence on loan performance is mostly on loans that were granted relatively early in the life of the platforms and have matured already. Iyer et al. (2015) provide a very rich analysis of peer-to-peer lending on prosper.com (henceforth Prosper). They use data for the period February 12, 2007 until October 16, 2008. All loans are unsecured personal loans, with a duration of three years and a fixed interest rate. During this period 194,033 funding proposals were listed, of which 17,212 were eventually funded (representing 8.9 percent).

The following Table 5.1 from Iyer et al. (2015) provides data on default for the loans that received funding (funded listings). Default occurs when the loan is three or more months late at the end of the three-year loan term. For the entire loan portfolio the default rate is 30.6 percent. Not surprisingly, the default rate depends strongly on the credit category of the borrower. Credit categories are assigned by the platform based on the borrower's credit score from Experience ScoreX PLUS; they are observable for the lenders. The (Experian ScoreX Plus) credit score uses numerous hard financial variables in its default prediction model. In the lowest credit category (HR) over half of the borrowers (51.6 percent) default on Prosper. But even in credit category AA with the best borrowers the default rate is 14.7 percent.

Table 5.1 Default rates and expected repayments on Prosper

	Funded listings	
	Mean	SD
Loan outcomes		
Annual lender interest rate	0.166	0.068
Default dummy	0.306	
Credit category HR	0.516	
Credit category E	0.424	
Credit category D	0.356	
Credit category C	0.318	
Credit category B	0.305	
Credit category A	0.234	
Credit category AA	0.147	
Fraction of loan repaid	0.797	0.334
Credit category HR	0.625	0.406
Credit category E	0.708	0.377
Credit category D	0.762	0.352
Credit category C	0.793	0.334
Credit category B	0.798	0.329
Credit category A	0.852	0.292
Credit category AA	0.910	0.235

Source: Iyer et al. (2015, 1559)

When considering these figures one has to make several qualifications. The loans were granted in the United States just before and during the great recession. This means that borrowers faced a significant macroeconomic shock with a doubling of the unemployment rate. The following figure shows developments in the rate for repayments that are overdue for over 30 days among the three major peer-to-peer lending platforms in the United States over time. This rate is measured on a daily basis and therefore is much lower than default rates in Iyer et al. (2015). Moreover, this rate is calculated taking the delinquencies relative to the loans outstanding at a platform.[9] However, the graph shows some interesting dynamics over time. A short while after the start of the platforms, which was when the financial crisis hit the real economy, the default rates increased considerably. But in 2010 they fell again and have not changed dramatically since. It is also interesting to note that although delinquency rates vary strongly between the different platforms, the differences are much lower now than in the first few years. Not only the macroeconomic conditions, but also changes in the way borrowers and lenders interact on the platform in terms of which kind of information borrowers are required to reveal, for instance, could explain this development.

To put the figures from Iyer et al. (2015) into perspective, one might compare them to the delinquency rates reported by commercial banks to the Federal Reserve Board (see Fig. 5.2). Here again the rates are computed as the ratio of delinquent loans to total loans. The highest delinquency rates of around 10.5 percent were observed among residential real estate loans in 2010. The delinquency rate among credit card loans peaked as early as 2009 at 6.8 percent. By comparison, the current delinquency rates (first quarter 2016) are 4.8 percent for residential real estate and 2.2 percent for credit card loans (Federal Reserve Board 2016). Of course, these figures depend on the whole population of borrowers and how it is composed of borrowers of different creditworthiness. Borrowers in the high-risk loan categories of Prosper are most likely to find it very difficult, or even impossible, to obtain loans in the formal banking sector. Indeed, borrowers at Prosper have lower average credit scores than the general population (610 versus 680, with higher numbers indicating higher creditworthiness). The detailed data from Prosper makes it possible to compare default rates for individual loan categories. Here the

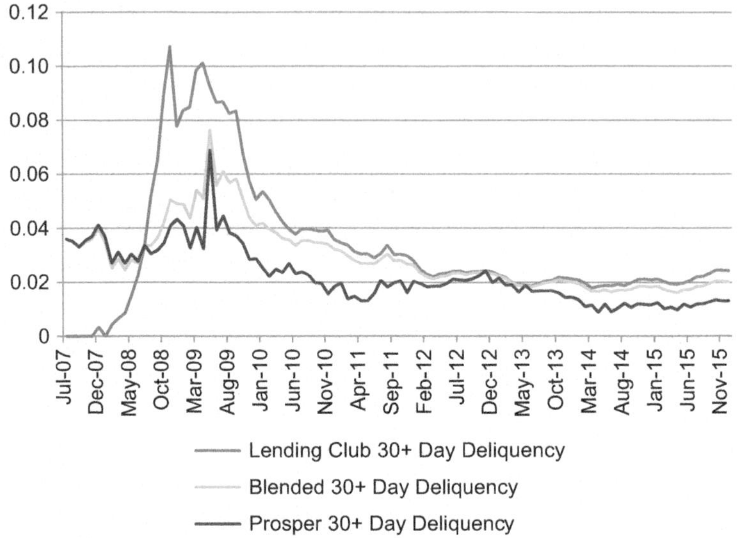

Fig. 5.2 Marketplace lending 30+day delinquency

default rate of 14.7 percent of the best borrowers is higher than the average figure in the market. Thus borrowers at Prosper were less likely to repay than their credit rating may have suggested. But we do not know whether the default happened by intent, or whether the borrowers slipped into difficulties repaying the loan.

When interpreting this finding we have to acknowledge that the potential lenders only observe the loan category (as reported in the table), but not the actual credit score. However, the lending rate the borrowers are willing to accept may be another important measure from which one can infer the lenders' risk evaluation of the loan. It is worth noting that borrowers on Prosper had to announce the interest rate they are willing to accept until 2009 when interest rates were determined in a (Dutch style) auction. Iyer et al. (2015) compare different measures for risk and find that the predictive power of this announced interest rate outperforms that of the credit score: the interest rate is 45 percent more accurate in predicting default than the credit score. This result provides evidence that the lenders in peer-to-peer lending make informed choices. They not only use the hard financial information contained in the credit category (which is based on the credit score), but they also have soft information about the borrower that helps them to predict how the loan will perform. The results also indicate that soft information is particularly helpful for evaluating the future performance of the borrowers in the lower credit categories. The most important piece of soft information that influences the lenders' evaluation is the maximum interest rate a borrower posts that s/he is willing to pay.[10]

Knowing the risk they are taking, lenders should be compensated for the risk they are bearing. To calculate the expected repayment one needs to know what the lenders would receive in case of default. If a borrower does not repay for four months or more, his/her loan is sold to a collection agency. The proceeds from selling the loan are distributed among the lenders. As shown in the Table 5.1 in the "fraction of loan repaid" column, which is calculated from the probability of repayment and the recovery value Prosper gets from selling defaulting loans to a collecting agency, the lenders in expected terms get 79.7 percent of the principal. Thus, in expected terms, the defaults are too high and the recovery rates too low to be compensated by an interest rate of 16.6 percent. The puzzling result of this analysis is that while the lenders seem to be quite good at rating the risks of loans in relative terms, they do not get enough compensation in absolute terms.

5.3.3 Crowdinvesting

Compared to the other two forms of crowdfunding, crowdinvesting is relatively new. Unlike for the two other forms, we do not have any evidence from the United States as Title III of the JOBS Act, which sets the rules for crowdinvesting, did not take effect until May 2016. But there is some evidence about the performance of firms financed by crowdinvesting from the United Kingdom and Germany. Again, there are no studies on fraudulent behavior in this market.

In the United Kingdom, the world's first and largest platform for crowdinvesting, Crowdcube, was launched in 2011. By the end of 2015 318 equity offerings had been successfully funded. Signori and Vismara

(2016) study 212 initial offerings, the other offerings were left out because they were too small or were follow-up campaigns. Out of these firms 22 have failed (10.4 percent). Such a failure rate may not seem too surprising among start-up firms. An investment in the crowdinvesting market would pay off if the losses could be offset by high returns on successful firms. The figures available seem to suggest that this is indeed the case. For the 64 firms (30.2 percent) that are involved in an equity deal after raising equity by Crowdcube, the average return on the deal is 63.5 percent.

Hornuf and Schmitt (2016) provide similar figures for Germany, but unlike Signori and Vismara (2016), they calculate actual returns. For nearly the same period of time, September 2011 until December 2015, 303 campaigns were started on German equity crowdfunding platforms. 210 of these campaigns successfully obtained funding, 54 did not reach their funding goal and publicly available information is missing for 39 campaigns due to the intransparency of the platform. Among the firms financed, 85 percent are still operating three years after their incorporation. This is a higher rate than for the general population of start-ups in Germany for which the survival rate is 70 percent. This may be due to the fact that crowdinvesting platforms screen firms and select which firms are allowed on the platform. Through this process the majority of "applicants" is denied access to the platform (Hornuf and Schwienbacher 2018).

5.4 Fraud and Detection

Data on fraud is scarce because it is not readily observable. The number of fraud cases observed depends on the prevalence of fraudulent behavior and on the probability of fraud being detected; and there is even an interaction between the two processes (Wang 2013).

The model outlined in Sect. 5.2 shows the parameters that influence whether an agent chooses a fraudulent project. Basically, the higher the private benefit of diverting the funds are relative to the net return of a project, the more likely fraud is to occur. This formulation does not take behavioral aspects into account like preferences for truthfulness or self-concept maintenance (Gibson et al. 2013; Hornuf and Haas 2014).[11] Although the behavioral aspects might change the trade-offs for part of the population, and thereby the number of fraud cases, the comparative statistics of the model still provide important insights. The model has shown that the net payoff received by the agent in cases with success relative to failure influences the choice. Thus, it depends on the contract, in the case of crowdlending on the loan contract, what the incentives are. Ultimately the contract should be such that the agent's payoff in case of success is high relative to the case of failure. In the contracts offered by banks or microfinance organizations, this is achieved through the collateralization of physical assets, through social collateral, group contracts or reputation effects.

Thus, the challenge for crowdfunding platforms is (1) to reduce information asymmetries themselves and (2) to offer contracts that give incentive for non-fraudulent behavior. To reduce asymmetric information, either the platform itself or the principal (the backer, the lender or the investor depending on the type of crowdfunding) needs to collect information about the agent. There seem to be very different attitudes towards the involvement of the platforms depending on the type of crowdfunding in question. In crowdinvesting platforms screen firms ex ante and reject a large share of the proposed offers (Hornuf and Schwienbacher 2018). For potential investors too, the widespread availability of information made possible by the digital revolution provides new possibilities for screening and monitoring projects (for more details see, Morse (2015) and Vismara (2017), in Chap. 3 of this book). Agents, for instance, can describe their projects on the platform and even show videos of their products.[12] Ultimately, there is a lot of soft information in their appearance: text features, for instance, can help to predict default (Gao and Lin 2015). However, as research shows which features are more often used by failing or fraudulent projects, the dishonest agents can adjust their behavior (Morse 2015).

The design of the contracts plays a crucial role for the agent's incentives. This is demonstrated for crowdlending on Prosper. Hildebrand et al. (2017) study the incentives of group leaders in lending. On Prosper everybody can become a group leader or member. The group leader has the right to allow new members into the group and to deny access. Moreover, the group leader can request additional information from members, as well as reviewing the members' new listings. The group leader used to be able to decide whether to offer its service for free or to demand a reward. These rewards were eliminated by Prosper at some point in time. The authors use this change in the platform's policy and show in a difference-in-difference-analysis that the rewards had adverse effects on group leader incentives, leading to higher default rates (and lower interest rates). This example demonstrates how important the policies of platforms are for the outcomes of the contracts that are concluded.

We have acknowledged that evidence on fraud cases is scarce. This should be due to the fact that fraud has not been detected to date. The wave of corporate scandals in the United States since the turn of the millennium inspired researchers to investigate corporate fraud. Dyck et al. (2013) estimate that the probability that a firm in the United States commits fraud is 14.5 percent. In their estimation they use the fact that after the demise of the auditing company Arthur Anderson, firms had to change their auditor. In these firms three times more fraud cases were detected. Based on these figures, the authors conclude that three out of four fraud cases remain undetected; and they use this figure to estimate the total fraud from observed fraud.

The relationship between detected and undetected fraud cases depends on whether there are incentives for reporting fraud. Therefore it is instrumental to know who reports fraud cases. Dyck et al. (2010) study a sample of 216 corporate fraud cases taking place between 1996 and 2004 in the United States. They find that the SEC and auditors account for 17 percent of the detected cases, debt and equity holders for 3 percent, short sellers for 11 percent, equity holders' agents (analysts and auditors) for 24 percent, employees for 17 percent, non-financial-market regulators for 13 percent and the media for 13 percent. The crowd is missing in the enumeration, but might be relevant as the following example suggests: "[…] Mythic: The Story of Gods and Men was a 2012 Kickstarter campaign for a videogame. Research by potential backers revealed that the creators plagiarized nearly all of the components of the campaign. With this information revealed to the public, the project creator withdrew the campaign before reaching the funding goal and backers did not lose any money" (Moores 2015, 406).

Generally, the incentive to report fraud will depend on the cost of gathering the information relevant for detecting fraud and the rewards that could result from a legal obligation, from a residual claim or from reputation. On the one hand, one would argue that the widespread availability of information, in particular for firms that operate mainly online, which is often the case for firms seeking crowdfunding, implies that the (monetary) costs of gathering information are low. On the other hand, the return on exerting this effort for the individual investors is also low if they have invested a small amount, which is often the case. Thus, there is a coordination problem between the large number of investors. Unless there are other mechanisms, like reputation, which increase the benefit of a single investor, incentives for fraud detection should be low among investors. As crowdfunding firms differ in many respects like size, age and sector from the larger corporations, some of the groups listed above that may possibly detect fraud like non-financial-market regulators or equity holders' agents might simply drop out as potential fraud detectors.

5.5 Conclusions and Policy Implications

Although fraud certainly exists in crowdfunding, evidence is scarce. This chapter discusses the incentive to engage in fraud and identifies that the terms of the underlying contract influence the incentives. The reduction of information asymmetries can also help to limit fraud. The fact that we observe hardly any fraud cases may be due to low incentives to detect fraud. Although the costs of gathering information leading to the detection of fraud in crowdfunding might be lower than in the corporate world in general, the benefits could be lower as well. If only a small amount of money is at risk, the low costs in absolute terms might be high in relative terms.

As the crowdfunding markets are young, they need to establish a reputation for being a "fair market place." Therefore, market-based mechanisms that try to avoid fraud are essential. One important measure is suggested by the financial analysts' roundtable: "Crowdfunding platforms must develop and adopt disclosure standards that make identifying and tracking issuers easy. Such standards may include unique identifiers for both individuals and companies that seek financing, and they should require issuers to provide full legal names and brief biographies of all principals" (Conrad et al. 2016). This may help to reduce asymmetric information between different platforms and between other financial service providers more generally; and thereby makes collecting information cheaper. It also allows the agent to build up a reputation as a trustworthy contracting party that acts as social collateral. Another important aspect is that platforms need to carefully design the rules that determine how contracts are formed and the incentives they provide for different groups of participants. Finally, a potential drawback of transparency must be mentioned: "The problem with uncovering success cues is of course once they are disclosed, their predictive power disappears" (Morse 2015, 469).

Acknowledgment I would like to thank Manuel Wiegand for helpful discussions and comments. Of course, all remaining errors are my own.

Notes

1. Note that crowdfunding platforms usually do not offer services traditional financial intermediaries like banks offer (e.g. screening or monitoring in the case of crowdlending).
2. Cumming et al. (2015) provide an overview on the literature on financial market misconduct in general.
3. See http://money.cnn.com/2013/06/17/technology/kickstarter-scam-kobe-jerky/ and http://www.digitaltrends.com/cool-tech/biggest-kickstarter-and-indiegogo-scams/.
4. We do not study the third problem of asymmetric information, costly state verification. It arises after the returns of the project to be financed are realized. The entrepreneur could claim that the project was not profitable although it was and he diverted the project's return of this own purposes.
5. In countries with a well-functioning legal system the claims can be enforced. The crowdlending platform Prosper, for example, sells its outstanding debt to a collection agency (see Sect. 5.3.2).
6. Note that there might be a tension between timely delivery and the quality of the product (Moores 2015).

7. The literature does not always acknowledge this difference. For example, Moores (2015, 402) gives the following reference to Mollick (2014): "Recent figures suggest that less than five percent of crowdfunding projects result in **fraud**" (highlight by CH).
8. The mini drone Zano raised EUR 3 million on Kickstarter in the United Kingdom. When they stopped responding Kickstarter asked a journalist to investigate the case. He found that the firm was surprised by its large funding success and the huge demand. At the same time the firm did not describe the state of development properly initially (Nezik 2016).
9. Note that therefore we cannot directly compare the default rates.
10. Prosper changed the design and now determines the interest rates itself.
11. Other behavioral economic effects are not modeled either. Schwartz (2015, 566) argues that "Crowdfund investors with negative returns will not simply have *lost* their money, but rather they will have *spent* it (at least in part) on nonpecuniary benefits, including entertainment, political expression, and community building." While investors may derive utility from these benefits, they may also suffer from being deceived.
12. This gives rise to another type of fraudulent behavior, namely stealing of ideas, as the example of a smartphone case selfie-stick shows that was posted on Kickstarter and copied by a Chinese manufacturer (Horwitz 2016).

References

Burghof, Hans-Peter, and Adrian Hunger. 2004. The Neuer Markt—An (Overly) Risky Asset of Germany's Financial System. In *The Rise and Fall of Europe's New Stock Markets (Advances in Financial Economics Vol. 10)*, ed. Giancarlo Giudici and Peter Roosenboom, 295–327. Bingley: Emerald Group Publishing Limited.

Conrad, Jennifer, Jonathan Karpoff, Craig Lewis, and Jay R. Ritter. 2016. Statement of the Financial Economists Roundtable: Crowdfunding. *Financial Analysts Journal* 72: 14–16.

Cumming, Douglas, Robert Dannhauser, and Sofia Johan. 2015. Financial Market Misconduct and Agency Conflicts: A Synthesis and Future Directions. *Journal of Corporate Finance* 34: 150–168.

Cumming, Douglas, Lars Hornuf, Moein Karami, and Denis Schweizer. 2016. *Disentangling Crowdfunding from Fraudfunding.* Max Planck Institute for

Innovation and Competition Research Paper, No. 16-09. https://ssrn.com/abstract=2828919. Accessed 28 Feb 2017.

Dyck, Alexander, Adair Morse, and Luigi Zingales. 2010. Who Blows the Whistle on Corporate Fraud? *Journal of Finance* 65: 2213–2253.

Dyck, Alexander, Adair Morse and Luigi Zingales. 2013. *How Pervasive is Corporate Fraud?* Rotman School of Management Working Paper No. 2222608. doi: https://doi.org/10.2139/ssrn.2222608

Federal Reserve Board. 2016. *Charge-Off and Delinquency Rates on Loans and Leases at Commercial Banks.* https://www.federalreserve.gov/releases/chargeoff/delallsa.htm. LAst modified 18 May 2016.

Fredman, Catherine. 2015. *Fund Me or Fraud Me? Crowdfunding Scams are on the Rise.* Consumer Reports, October 5. http://www.consumerreports.org/cro/money/crowdfunding-scam. Accessed 22 Mar 2017.

Gao, Qiang, and Mingfeng Lin. 2015. *Lemon or Cherry? The Value of Texts in Debt Crowdfunding.* Working Paper. doi: https://doi.org/10.2139/ssrn.2446114

Giannetti, Mariassunta, and Tracy Yue Wang. 2016. Corporate Scandals and Household Stock Market Participation. *Journal of Finance* 71: 2591–2636.

Gibson, Rajna, Carmen Tanner, and Alexander F. Wagner. 2013. Preferences for Truthfulness: Heterogeneity Among and Within Individuals. *American Economic Review* 103: 532–548.

Hildebrand, Thomas, Manju Puri, and Jörg Rocholl. 2017. Adverse Incentives in Crowdfunding. *Management Science* 63: 587–608.

Hornuf, Lars, and Georg Haas. 2014. Regulating Fraud in Financial Markets: Can Behavioral Designs Prevent Future Criminal Offences? *Journal of Risk Management in Financial Institutions* 7: 192–201.

Hornuf, Lars, and Matthias Schmitt. 2016. Success and Failure in Equity Crowdfunding. *CESifo DICE Report* 14: 16–22.

Hornuf, Lars, and Armin Schwienbacher. 2018. Internet-Based Entrepreneurial Finance: Lessons Form Germany. *California Management Review.* Forthcoming.

Horwitz, Josh. 2016. *Your Brilliant Kickstarter Idea Could be on Sale in China Before you've Even Finished Funding It.* http://qz.com/771727/chinas-factories-in-shenzhen-can-copy-products-at-breakneck-speed-and-its-time-for-the-rest-of-the-world-to-get-over-it/. Accessed 22 Mar 2017.

Iyer, Rajkamal, Asim Ijaz Khwaja, Erzo F.P. Luttmer, and Kelly Shue. 2015. Screening Peers Softly: Inferring the Quality of Small Borrowers. *Management Science* 62: 1554–1577.

Mollick, Ethan R. 2014. *Delivery Rates on Kickstarter*. Social Science Research Network. https://ssrn.com/abstract=2699251. Accessed 28 Feb 2017.

Moores, Christopher. 2015. Kickstart My Lawsuit: Fraud and Justice in Rewards-Based Crowdfunding. *UC Davies Law Review* 49: 383–424.

Morse, Adair. 2015. Peer-to-Peer Crowdfunding: Information and the Potential for Disruption in Consumer Lending. *Annual Review of Financial Economics* 7: 463–482.

Nezik, Ann-Kathrin. 2016. Sauercrowd. *Spiegel* 34: 64–66.

Schwartz, Andrew. 2015. The Nonfinancial Returns of Crowdfunding. *Review of Banking and Financial Law* 34: 565–580.

Signori, Andrea, and Silvio Vismara. 2016. *Returns on Investments in Equity Crowdfunding*. Social Science Research Network. http://ssrn.com/abstract=2765488. Accessed 28 Feb 2017.

Vismara, Silvio. 2017. Signaling to Overcome Market Inefficiencies. In *The Economics of Crowdfunding Startups, Portals and Investor Behavior*, ed. Douglas Cumming and Lars Hornuf. London: Palgrave Macmillan.

Wang, Tracy. 2013. Corporate Securities Fraud: Insights from a New Empirical Framework. *Journal of Law, Economics and Organization* 29: 535–568.

Christa Hainz is Senior Researcher and Deputy Head of the Ifo Center for International Institutional Comparisons and Migration Research. She was assistant professor at the University of Munich and guest professor at the University of Augsburg and visited the New York University and SITE at the Stockholm School of Economics. Her research focuses on banking, corporate finance and institutions. Her work has been published in the *Economic Journal*, the *Journal of Public Economics* and the *Journal of Comparative Economics*. She recently wrote an expert report for the Federal Ministry of Finance on the Small Investor Protection Act.

Part II

Market Structure

6

Fintech and the Financing of SMEs and Entrepreneurs: From Crowdfunding to Marketplace Lending

Mark Fenwick, Joseph A. McCahery, and Erik P.M. Vermeulen

6.1 Introduction

Bank lending to small and medium sized enterprises (SMEs) has changed dramatically since the time of the financial crisis of 2008. That shouldn't be too surprising. Banks' lending capacity shrank between 2008 and 2013 due to higher risk aversion in a time when economic growth had slowed. The higher sensitivity to external market shocks led to changes in the supply of short- and long-term financing to SME borrowers. In the Netherlands, for example, we observed a 6–8% year-on-year decline in

M. Fenwick (✉)
Kyusha University – Graduate School of Law, Fukuoka, Japan

J.A. McCahery
Faculty of Law and Tilburg Law and Economics Center, Tilburg University, Tilburg, The Netherlands

E.P.M. Vermeulen
Tilburg Law and Economics Center, Tilburg University, Tilburg, The Netherlands

D. Cumming, L. Hornuf (eds.), *The Economics of Crowdfunding*,
https://doi.org/10.1007/978-3-319-66119-3_6

bank loans to SMEs and the highest loan rejection rate in Europe (OECD 2013). SMEs continue to face numerous obstacles in borrowing funds because they are small, less diversified, and have weaker financial structures. Moreover, ample evidence suggests that smaller companies face greater perceived and actual constraints than larger firms. Collectively, they have been considered unfavorable borrowers due to their difficulty in providing high-quality collateral or their relative opaqueness with respect to their creditworthiness (Boot et al. 1991; Ayadi and Gadi 2013).

In recent years, policymakers and researchers have increasingly begun to explore the impact of the recent financial crisis on the rationing of credit. The effect, in the case of SMEs, was on the reduction income reflected in their balance sheet and overall collateral levels. Not only did small businesses look less creditworthy, but they also faced greater perceived and actual constraints than larger firms and that this would play a critical role in the narrowing of available finance options (European Central Bank 2015). Also, data on small business credit scores, such as PAYDEX, indicate that lending to small business is lower than before the financial crisis (Mills and McCarthy 2014). While bank loans remain of vital importance for small businesses, changes in lending standards have placed significant demands on banks focused in the SME, prompting a significant decline in small business credit. The literature suggests that regardless of the change in credit conditions in 2014, lending standards remained comparatively tight and interest rates high for SMEs in countries hard hit by the financial crisis (OECD 2016).

There are a number of specific, efficient strategies that have been developed and demonstrated to alleviate credit rationing. In general, these strategies involve three types of mechanisms. First it is clear that the presence of information asymmetries and principal/agent problems may induce sellers of financial service to offer products that, due to monitoring problems, leave potential borrowers without access to credit. Past studies show that banks' local network ties and relationships have reduced the uncertainties and mitigated some of the risks opportunism associated with bank lending to SMEs. Moreover, this literature has emphasized how enabling environmental initiatives may have actually reduced information asymmetries by establishing effective monitoring techniques. Second, the use of collateral gives the SME with a serious credit problem an incentive to repay the loan. Research suggests that if collateral is not available, a credit guarantee system offsets the reduced reliability of non-audited financial statements and may improve access to credit as well as improve loan terms (Beck et al. 2010). So, if collateral is not available, a credit guarantee system for SMEs that offsets the reduced reliability of non-audited financial statements may improve access to credit as well as improve the loan terms. Thus, governments tend to invest in a loan guarantee program because they address the market imperfections that cause credit restrictions to SMEs and spur innovation in the SME sector. The presence of the guarantee can result in a lower rate paid for the loan.

However, as banks retreat from SME financing, strong online lending has made it easier for low-income businesses and small young firms to secure credit without government support (OECD 2015). This growth of alternative online lending has supplied new competition to traditional banks and venture capitalists, and is beginning to disrupt the tradition of business of lending in a number of ways—not only by bringing competition to the corporate market, creating efficiencies and competition that reduces online risk, but also making SMEs more profitable (Ahmed et al. 2017). Another important consequence of the new models of finance is the reduction of systemic risk and more diversified lending options. Established industry players confronting the reality of alternative online platforms are improving the profitability of small business lending (Deutsche Bank 2017).

More specifically, the booming demand for fintech—broadly defined as the use of new technology and innovation to compete in the marketplace of financial institutions and intermediaries—is the result of fast funding and online applications, which has lowered costs for their clients. This, in turn, has helped these lenders in the United States, for example, to become an important provider of capital to low-income businesses and small young firms while helping to bridge the funding gap in the SME credit market (GAC 2015).

Fintech has disrupted or is disrupting the financial service sector in at least three ways. First, online platforms, which differ from traditional funding channels, allowing financial service providers to offer a wide range of new services that remove intermediaries and administrative layers to make transactions more effective and less prone to error. In this way, financial services are decentralized and made flatter. Most obviously, there is the growth of mobile banking that allows customers to perform a wide range of transactions online. Second, networked access to financial services facilitates quicker access to all manner of transactions from checking financial status, making payments, and withdrawing and transferring funds. Third, behind-the-scenes activities of financial institutions are similarly transformed. In part, this involves the use of Big Data to deliver a more efficient service, but it also allows firms to use technology to manage legal risk more effectively. Finally, in the absence of industry-wide standardization (i.e., no capital requirements) it is clear that peer-to-peer ('P2P') platforms will enjoy lower operating and capital expenses compared to traditional banks.

To many observers, one of the most disturbing aspects of the 2008 financial crisis was the subsequent introduction of vast swaths of new banking regulation. The rapid introduction of regtech—which involves using new technologies to meet regulatory and compliance requirements—suggests that using big data analytics allows firms to accelerate the cumbersome and costly process of implanting new regulation. There are a number of areas of compliance and reporting where technology can have significant benefits, such as risk data aggregation, modeling and real-time transactions monitoring. Machine learning, artificial intelligence, and biometrics have been particularly promising in tackling compliance challenges.

Fintech has also facilitated the emergence of start-ups that offer an alternative source of financial services. Fintech lenders, including equity crowdfunding, invoice and supply chain financing, and marketplace lending, are beginning to challenge traditional business models in a number of ways—not only by bringing competition to the corporate market, creating efficiencies and competition that reduces online risk, but also making SMEs more profitable (WEF 2015). In particular, app-based companies are emerging everywhere. They challenge and disrupt incumbents, such as traditional banks, by supporting a wide range of financial services, namely marketplace lending platforms; equity crowdfunding platforms; insurance services; algorithm-driven robo-advisors offering smarter, more personalized financial advice; and blockchain-based crypto-currency and payment systems. This trend is borne out by the

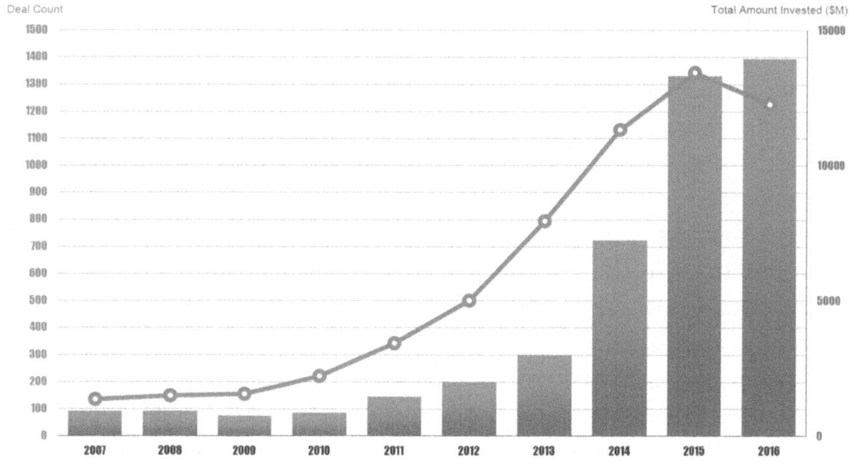

Fig. 6.1 Global venture capital investments in fintech start-ups

investment data. Since around 2010, more and more investment is being made into fintech. And even though deal activity has slowed over the last year, there is little evidence that indicates that fintech is likely to permanently stall or collapse (see Fig. 6.1).

Millennials—defined as the demographic cohort that reached maturity around 2000—are thought to be one of the primary drivers of fintech innovation. To begin, millennials are prompting changes in the need of firms to focus on the consumer. Three aspects of the contemporary consumer expectations that seem pertinent in this context include state-of-the-art consumer experience, speed, and convenience (PWC 2016). The delivery of innovative fintech solutions will require a degree of cooperation between multiple partners, including millennials, as stakeholders and investors, in maintaining a focus on the core task of innovating.

In this chapter, we examine how fintech lenders target the SME segment, connecting companies and investors that want to lend or provide some form of equity capital or debt to start-ups. To gain a better understanding of the online alternatives to bank financing, we provide an overview of the different platforms and external financing providers such as crowdfunding, peer-to-peer and marketplace lenders. We also discuss the factors responsible for the expansion of these well-developed credit systems to SMEs and the ecosystem that supported the creation of a sector-wide secondary market. The question that arises, however, is whether fintech's low-cost expansion of credit to SMEs and individuals, based on a more efficient credit-assessment model, weaker underwriting standards, and packaged loans to institutional investors, could persist in the long run, and eventually become more profitable than traditional banks. A significant body of literature has already sought to explain these developments. On the one hand, new market mechanisms can facilitate the introduction of explicit barriers to entry and new systems that become oligopolies and other forms of intellectual property protection where the governance and enforcement issues are quite difficult to enforce. On the other hand, through such well-designed mechanisms, such as platform ecosystem, the business benefit would be large leading to low-cost trading systems that are open-access, transparent, and facilitate economic growth. Recent studies show that that current of regulatory approach to fintech and its financial practices are blocked by significant political economy and coordination costs and are to promote much structural change (Philippon 2016). In this chapter, we investigate the regulatory response to fintech start-ups, distinguishing between two broad categories of response—reactive and proactive.

The plan of this chapter proceeds as follows. Section 6.2 provides a comprehensive overview of the crowdfunding platforms, analyzing the advantages and disadvantages of the different portals and whether equity crowdfunding platforms will provide a competitive new funding channel for young companies and SMEs. Section 6.3 examines the features of the peer-to-peer and marketplace lending process, including the lenders, lending, and credit process. Section 6.4 will then discuss the results of our empirical analysis of the regulatory determinants that have influenced the formation of fintech start-ups in 12 countries. Section 6.5 concludes.

6.2 Crowdfunding

Crowdfunding is a method for raising finance in which start-ups can sell directly or indirectly shares or equity in a company to a group of investors through the Internet. Historically, crowdfunding has evolved from a way to finance creative projects, such as books, films, and games, into a new type of entrepreneurial finance which has the potential to dramatically change the venture capital ecosystem. Crowdfunding makes it possible for early-stage start-up companies to raise 'venture capital' from a large group of individuals, sidestepping the traditional fundraising process that includes lengthy due diligence periods and tough negotiations over the pre-money valuation and contractual terms. The 'crowd' investors, who invest relatively small amounts through Internet-based platforms (crowdfunding websites) and/or through social networks—such as Facebook, Twitter, and LinkedIn—need less contractual protection (the small investment amounts do not justify close involvement in the growth process of the start-up companies).

As noted above, accessibility and speed are the key drivers behind the emergence and development of crowdfunding platforms. Another factor likely to influence the rise of crowdfunding platforms is that they can generate information about risks that can be interpreted as effective signals of project quality and thus effect the probability of funding success (Ahlers et al. 2015). Thus, in addition to providing access to information about credit scoring of potential borrowers, the platforms allow investors through real-time notifications of lender bids on projects to diversify their portfolio of investments (Morse 2015).

In their quest to answer these questions, many academics have examined crowdfunding from an economics perspective. Within economics, there have been several approaches to the study of crowdfunding, including the 'wisdom of the crowds' perspective. Management researchers have also begun to look at why investors are likely to enter a crowdfunding platform. Underlying this view, investors on equity crowdfunding platforms tend to be a dispersed group who invest small denominations in a start-up, and have little incentive to do due diligence research before the investment and thereafter the investment will monitor managerial effort. Platforms can attract investors by offering their own due diligence and process a project before it is offered to the public or is likely to turn to co-investment with a business angle or VC firm.

While these mechanisms have been influential and helpful, there exists a wide array of mechanisms, each of which could be more or less significant in shaping the dynamics of the business relationship. For example, the Australian platform ASSOB requires every start-up to engage in a business relationship with a professional business advisor, who guides the company through the process and monitors the company after the offering. Note that the British platform, Crowdcube, discloses the largest investment in a project. Underlying this approach is the view that if the largest investment is highly proportional to the total amount, this signals to the market that there is a higher chance of monitoring and due diligence.

We can roughly distinguish among four categories of crowdfunding platforms: (1) donation-based crowdfunding; (2) reward-based crowdfunding; (3) lending-based crowdfunding; and (4) equity-based crowdfunding. If investors follow the donation-based crowdfunding model, they generally contribute to a charitable, creative, or social project without the expectation of being compensated. The donation model stands in contrast to the reward-based model where the 'crowd' that decides to donate receives a reward, such as a finished product, perks, or recognition in the credits of a movie, in return. The popularity of the latter approach is confirmed by the results that it is the second largest sector within European online alternative market (E&Y 2015, see Fig. 6.2).

Given the apparent benefits, start-up companies and entrepreneurs typically use lending-based crowdfunding and equity-based crowdfunding to attract investments from the general public. Lending-based and equity-based crowdfunding are jointly called 'investment crowdfunding'. If the companies grow and prosper, the investors usually receive a financial return. For example, in the lending-based model, they will receive their investment back plus interest (the rate of which is dependent on the risk level). Investors that contribute cash through equity-based crowdfunding platforms indirectly or directly become beneficial owners or shareholders of the start-up company.

Equity-based crowdfunding increasingly attracts attention from start-up companies, investors, and the media. This is not surprising since recent research on equity crowdfunding platforms suggests that they, in the presence of information asymmetries, are likely to mitigate distance-related costs, such as monitoring investments, in early-stage financing (Agrawal et al. 2015). That said, it is only to be expected that the number

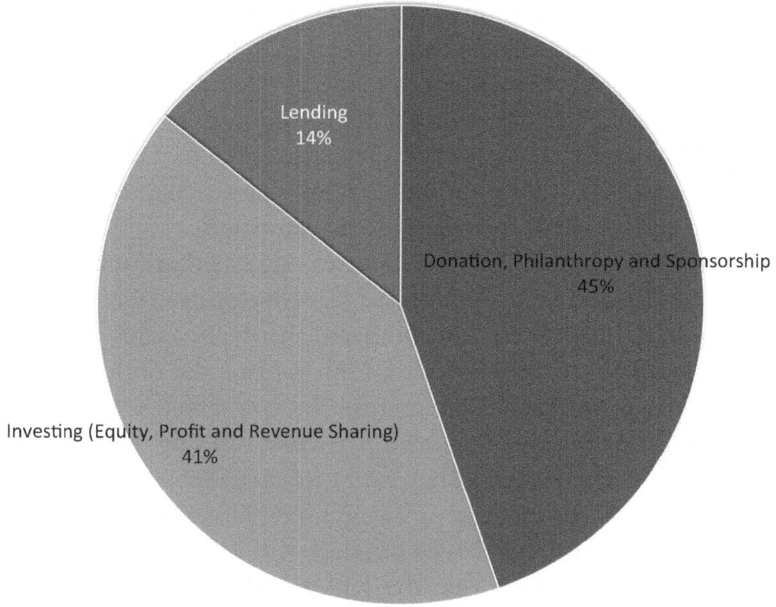

Fig. 6.2 Crowdfunding platforms in Europe in 2015

of equity-based crowdfunding platforms will increase further in the near future as we increasingly observe several regulatory initiatives that are intended to give a boost to equity crowdfunding (by increasingly allowing non-professional investors to participate in deals).

So far, we have been focusing on the growth of equity-based platforms. An important source of participation is the within-group effects of funders and fundraisers on crowdfunding platforms. Faced with cross-group and within-group external effects, crowdfunding platforms need strategies to effectively mitigate coordination failures while minimizing the risks posed by asymmetric information as the number of potential fundraisers on the platform increases (Belleflamme et al. 2016). Scholars have sought to show that within the group of funders, it is likely that the external effects will be positive. Applied to the design of crowdfunding platforms, these studies show that the external effects are positive if a project has to reach their funding goal, reducing the risk that undercapitalized projects may be realized. For example, the 'All-Or-Nothing'

(AON) or fixed-funding model, which has been adopted by most platforms, allows the fundraiser to collect any funds received if they reached the specific goal by the end of the campaign period. In practice, a second model has emerged. The 'Keep-It-All' (KIA) model permits fundraisers to keep any of the money raised even if they raised only part of the threshold level. In the latter context, fundraisers are charged higher fees on the money that was raised in the unsuccessful campaign.

Current research on non-price strategies suggests that fundraisers may prefer the flexibility of the KIA model. To check this claim empirically, Cumming et al. (2015) recently compared the AON versus KIA models based on the Indiegogo platform that offers firms the option to choose between the two models. In comparing the two different models, they analyze the company types that use a particular funding model as well as their disclosures and success. They find evidence that is consistent with the view that AON fundraising campaigns have larger fundraising targets for their projects and tend also to be successful in realizing their capital goals. Moreover, they show that the KIA model is likely to be used by firms that can scale their business. Thus, the results in Cumming et al.'s study indicate that flexible platforms are likely to be attractive to a number of firms, creating sustainable user growth, for example, of Indiegogo's fund.

Another factor likely to influence the dynamics of investor behavior is whether investors have a public profile. In fact, an informational advantage may occur when investors have chosen a public profile. This information in turn may lead to more bids as well as interest from other investors. Prior research points to numerous examples of investors with expertise, particularly venture capitalists and business angels are likely to disclose this information and their investment decisions, particularly in first-come-first-served environments. Vismara (2016) found, using a sample of 111 equity offerings posted in 2014 on Crowdcube, information cascades among individual investors are crucial for the success of crowdfunding campaigns. For example, successful campaigns have a higher fraction of public investors, particularly in the first five days of the launch. Looking at the numbers, most investors prefer not to make their profile public. However, Vismara further showed, using a group of 200 public profile investors in Crowdcube, that the public profile investor numbered more than 4.8 investments in the platform whereas the average made 2.7 investments. He then mapped the public profile investors to their level of entrepreneurial and project-specific expertise and found that 88% of the public profile investors had entrepreneurial and start-up skills and 44% had experience in the funded project's industry. In combination with augmented data from Crunchbase, the results support the view that public profile investors are more likely to be sophisticated than other blind investors.

The importance of signaling to potential small investors in a start-up is also likely to have implications for the success of proposed campaigns. In the context of hidden information, start-up firms tend to employ a range of signals to induce investors to devote resources to the project. Some evidence from a recent study, Ahlers et al. (2015), reveals that the signals that investors are more likely to rely on, as a proxy for project quality, include the number of board members, and board experience, measured in terms if a board member has an MBA. Yet external certification (patents and government grants) has no impact on the probability of attracting investors.

Despite its popularity and growth, equity crowdfunding poses several challenges. First, it requires some experience in making a pitch to smaller investors (Lewis 2013). Moreover, there are usually no one-to-one conversations with interested investors. All the relevant information should be made available upfront, which in turn could easily lead to confidentiality and transparency issues. Second, unlike business angels and venture capitalists, crowdfunding investors typically do not intensively monitor and support the business in the post-investment period. Current research suggests that, in order for the start-up to succeed, risk investors must be willing to provide the entrepreneur with 'value-added' services. These services include identifying and evaluating business opportunities, including management, entry, or growth strategies; negotiating further investments; tracking the portfolio firm and coaching the firm participants; providing technical and management assistance; and attracting additional capital. When assessing the potential of crowdfunding, the absence of real value-added services could become significant and may have the potential to retard growth.

The third challenge is that crowdfunding may lack connectivity to follow-on investors, key stakeholders, and other advisors. High-potential growth companies, particularly in highly capital-intensive sectors (such as biotechnology and medical), must be able to attract follow-on funding from later-stage investors. The connectedness between early-stage investors and the venture capital community provides companies with improved access to external financing. Clearly, crowdfunding investors that typically follow a 'spray and pray' strategy (spreading small investments among as many firms as possible) when it comes to making investment decisions have fewer resources and/or incentives to assist portfolio companies in securing the next stage of finance. A related problem is that this strategy may be exacerbated by the fact the companies that pitch for crowdfunding investors are more likely to end up with a multitude of investors. As such, these circumstances not only enhance the free-rider problem among investors but also add an additional 'negotiation challenge' to potential follow-on investor, as it is easier to negotiate the funding with only a few investors (Kolodny 2013).

If one adds to these challenges the legislative and regulatory issues that surround crowdfunding, the jury is still out on whether this source of capital will have a significant impact on the new venture capital industry in the near future. The crowdfunding provisions of Title III of the JOBS Act that took effect on May 16, 2016, are not promising. The fact that these provisions require start-up companies to have public accounting firms audit their financials will arguably have a deterrent effect on the use of equity crowdfunding in the United States. High-profile venture capitalists have already announced that they will most likely pass on 'crowdfunded' start-up companies (Mittal 2016).

We have seen that Regulation Crowdfunding (Reg CF) has provided some early evidence on the type of issuers that are using the new securities exemption created by the JOBS Act of 2012 and the quantified utilization during the period of May 2016 to December 2016.

Saha and Parsont (2017) documented how during the first 100 days since implementation that a majority (72%) of companies were organized within five years and are technology firms. Moreover, as of October 10, 2016, 14 out of 33 companies succeeded in reaching their funding goals and the average capital raised was about USD 400,000 (and the median was approximately USD 266,000). Finally, the relationship between the level of prior capital raising and successful Reg CF issues seems to be significant. An analysis shows that 42 (49%) companies succeeded in earlier capital raising efforts, with a majority of the successful examples raised funds from accredited investors. The results suggest that while 49% of the firms have been successful in earlier funding rounds, Reg CF is perhaps more suitable for the follow-on financing needs of firms.

Along similar lines, Abrams (2017) found that 141 companies had, as of November 12, 2016, started securities issues across 19 portals with 5 companies already having completed an issue under Reg CF, and collectively these companies have raised over USD 13.6 million in funds. The typical successful equity issue has raised USD 90,000 from 120 investors with a minimum offering amount of USD 100,000 with 37 days to collect the rest. Start-up firms represent the majority of firms pursuing issues, with the median issuer age of 10 months. From this perspective, the median issuer has three employees, assets of USD 26,000, and seeks to raise USD 70,000. The evidence shows that 26 of the 50 closed issues were successful in meeting the minimum offering amount by their deadline. While investors appear to be sophisticated, they commonly invest in issues that make more information available to the SEC, have more assets, less long-term debt, and higher Stratifund ratings. In addition, sophisticated investors tend to appear within one month of the issue and are located on average 900 miles from the firms seeking funds. In sum, the growing number of platforms and successful issues in a range of industries in the United States suggests that the market could play a key role in the fundraising activities of SMEs and young firms.

6.3 Peer-to-Peer or Marketplace Lending Model

Despite the attention given to crowdfunding over the last decade, we have seen the rapid development of peer-to-peer lending ('P2P'). More a hybrid of crowdfunding and marketplace lending, P2P is best understood as a form of debt-based crowdfunding.

When it comes to debt, the P2P transactional marketplaces take three forms. They may be organized as either: (1) balance sheet lenders that fund loans off their own balance sheet; (2) marketplace lending which is non-bank based Internet lending; and (3) peer-to-peer lending focused on retail investors and borrowers. If lenders follow the balance sheet lending model, they are considered to be more diversified financial institutions that, in contrast to the marketplace or P2P model, retain some loans on their own balance sheet and are also less dependent financially on directly selling loans. The marketplace lending model, which stands in contrast to the fintech balance sheet lending model, serves to connect borrowers to investors, which receives a higher rate of return than being offered by traditional banks.

Furthermore, the P2P model, unlike a traditional bank, matches borrowers who are seeking a loan with investors, who obtain revenue from a portion of the interest that borrowers pay on the loan. Platforms operate by assisting in the collection, scoring and distributing the credit qualifications of potential borrowers, reporting real-time bids on projects, and supplying online servicing and monitoring of the loan (Morse 2015). Using this information, lenders are able to review the applications. Generally speaking, investors may choose to invest algorithmically, directly, or through a group. Unlike traditional banks, the P2P loan process involves the direct matching of lenders and borrowers via online auctions in which bid/ask is matched until a loan is fully funded, or is matched by fixed rate and category. For the most part, platforms have adopted the AON rule, which requires projects to meet their funding goal in order to be funded. Other bidding rules provide that lenders cannot underbid each other, but loan applicants can raise the offered interest rate during the bidding period.

There are a number of factors that explain the success of P2P lending platforms and their potential to be disruptive. On the one hand, platform-based data tools can be used to lower transaction costs in matching financing requests and investment opportunities, leading to smaller loan amounts and the splitting of large loans (Feng et al. 2015). On the other hand, P2P enables modern investors to have direct access to an asset class that was limited previously to large institutional investors, which may allow them to diversify their portfolios and create enhanced risk-adjusted returns through the savings achieved by a lower-cost operating model.

As a result, the P2P model has experienced significant growth rates in the United States and United Kingdom. Evidence indicates that P2P lending in the United States reached USD 12 billion at the end of 2014 (Morgan Stanley Research 2015), with similar loan levels for the United Kingdom. Moreover, the P2P market is expected to be worth between USD 150 and USD 490 billion globally between 2016 and 2020, from USD 26.16 billion in 2015. In the United Kingdom, the volume of P2P consumer lending rose to EUR 366 million in 2015 whereas business lending rose to EUR 212 million for the same period (Cambridge/KPMG 2016). Unsurprisingly, commercial banks have not been shy about jumping into this sector once they witnessed the earlier success of the fintech business model. In fact, large commercial banks pursuing this strategy have purchased new fintech start-ups and created competitive platforms designed not only to improve the efficiency of their traditional financial products but to look for other market opportunities (Parker et al. 2016).

Despite its popularity and growth the P2P lending poses several challenges. First, there are likely to be some agency costs involved with this new channel of funding. We can expect, based on prior research, that borrowing history has a significant impact on the success rate of loans (Iyer et al. 2015). Second, if lenders believe that there are adverse selection problems, this is likely to lead to high interest rates and low rates of success (Yum et al. 2012). Third, a major concern for lending platforms is whether any loan is in arrears and could potentially default. A primary concern is that investors maintain a close watch on developments in marketplace lending, such as ensuring that the modeling of the assumed default rate is accurate, or that there is clear identification of the servicing cost (for the outsourced loans) for platforms. Finally, another factor likely to influence the efficiency of the online P2P markets is the high risk from borrowers that are unable to finance their projects to completion, leading to loans that are illiquid and cannot be withdrawn ahead of maturity.

6.4 Regulatory Determinants of Fintech Start-Ups

This section considers the regulatory factors that are influencing fintech start-ups. Several researchers have written about the influence of country-level factors on fintech. A primary factor that prior researchers have examined is the relationship between country-level legal and cultural traits and their impact on platform formation (Dushnitsky et al. 2016). Second, as highlighted by Cumming and Schwienbacher (2016), the extent of venture capital deals in the fintech sector can be seen as a function of the differential enforcement level of financial rules among start-ups and large financial institutions. In addition to legal and cultural factors, researchers have also considered the primary economic and technical factors influencing the number of fintech start-ups, including the presence of a well-developed capital market, ready availability of the latest technology, and people more likely to possess telephone subscriptions (Haddad and Hornuf 2016). The magnitude of the labor market is associated with the increase of new fintech start-up formations. While the degree of soundness of banks has a negative effect on the formation of start-ups, the variable VC financing has a significant effect on the number of new fintech start-ups that provide payment services.

To be sure, prior work suggests that fintech innovations will take place with or without changes in regulation. Thus, one possibility is that policymakers might wish to create incentives so that fintech will lower the cost of services to end-users and encourage entry in highly concentrated markets so that regulators could ensure a level playing field. As noted above, another possibility is that the recent fintech innovations are stifled due to the strength of industry groups and labor that might want to curb incentives to fintech firms and support existing subsidies and barriers to entry. We thus attempt to shed light on whether lawmakers respond to the ongoing development of fintech firms or attempt to support the extant financial system and their own style of regulation.

In this section, we provide some preliminary evidence of 12 country-level regulators' responses to fintech. In general, if we look around the world today we can distinguish between two broad categories of government response—reactive and proactive—each of which has a number of sub-categories.

Reactive. The first group includes countries in which nothing is being done. There is No Regulatory Talk or Action. The second group consists of countries in which there is partial or Fragmented Regulation of fintech. Certain institutions, such as the Consumer Financial Protection Bureau (CFPB) in the United States, may offer certain safe harbor provisions for certain type of fintech companies. Yet there appears little willingness to genuinely embrace the technology and its regulatory implications, nor is there any comprehensive plan as to how fintech can or should be regulated.

Proactive. In such countries, there is a significant amount of regulatory attention paid to fintech. Such attention can take the form of consultation papers, White Papers, or conferences. But action is limited and there is a risk that prioritizing fintech can slide into an empty lip service aimed at projecting an image of regulatory action when, in reality, action is limited.

A second group of countries engage in what might be characterized as regulatory guidance. Regulators provide advice to fintech start-ups and incumbents in order to help navigate them through the regulatory system. This does not necessarily entail changes in regulatory structure, but it does promote a collaborative dialogue between regulators, traditional service providers, and fintech companies.

A final group of countries have embraced the possibilities of fintech by creating a so-called regulatory sandbox. We characterize this approach as Regulatory Experimentation. Regulators create a regulatory sandbox in which they facilitate and encourage a space to experiment. This allows the testing of new technology-driven services, under the supervision of regulators. This ensures that meaningful data can be gathered for the evaluation of risk in a safe environment. Such data can then facilitate evidence-based regulatory reform.

A key point about this last approach is that it is collaborative and dialogical, in the sense that regulators, incumbents, and new service providers are engaged in an ongoing dialogue about the most effective means to gather relevant information and to identify the most appropriate regulatory model.

6.4.1 Empirical Study of Regulatory Effects on Fintech Start-Ups

In order to better understand the effects, risks, and opportunities associated with these regulatory choices, we focus on the regulatory responses to fintech in 17 jurisdictions (see Fig. 6.3). In particular, we looked at first-time venture capital investments in fintech companies. The intention was to see whether there was a meaningful connection between levels of investment and regulatory choice.

Five jurisdictions were cut due to a lack of reliable data. For instance, we were unable to find a sufficient number of companies receiving investment; or there were doubts about the veracity of the data and it was difficult to independently verify; or there was conflicting information. The 12 remaining jurisdictions were examined. When we look at the results of year-on-year percentage growth of first-time venture capital backed companies, we get the following in Fig. 6.4.

In many cases, this data confirms anecdotal evidence of a slow-down of interest in fintech in 2015. From 2015 to 2016, the total fintech funding declined approximately 50 percent, down to USD 25 billion from USD 47 billion in 2015 (KPMG 2017a). But interestingly, in 6 of the 12 jurisdictions there was an increase in investment activity in 2016. The question this data raises is whether there are any signals as to a correlation between regulatory initiative and increased activity in the fintech sector.

In contrast, in those countries with a more proactive response—particularly involving Regulatory Guidance or Regulatory Experimentation—there is evidence that this proactive approach makes the jurisdiction more attractive as a potential location for starting fintech operations (Fig. 6.5).

This suggests that the regulatory environment does affect the degree of investment and—perhaps as importantly—affects the willingness of companies to start operations in one jurisdiction, rather than another. Regulation matters, but we have to realize that there are other components that make up an attractive ecosystem for fintech. Consider Israel. A market known for its venture capital industry, a strong R&D focus, and large multinationals that are open to fintech. These ingredients play a

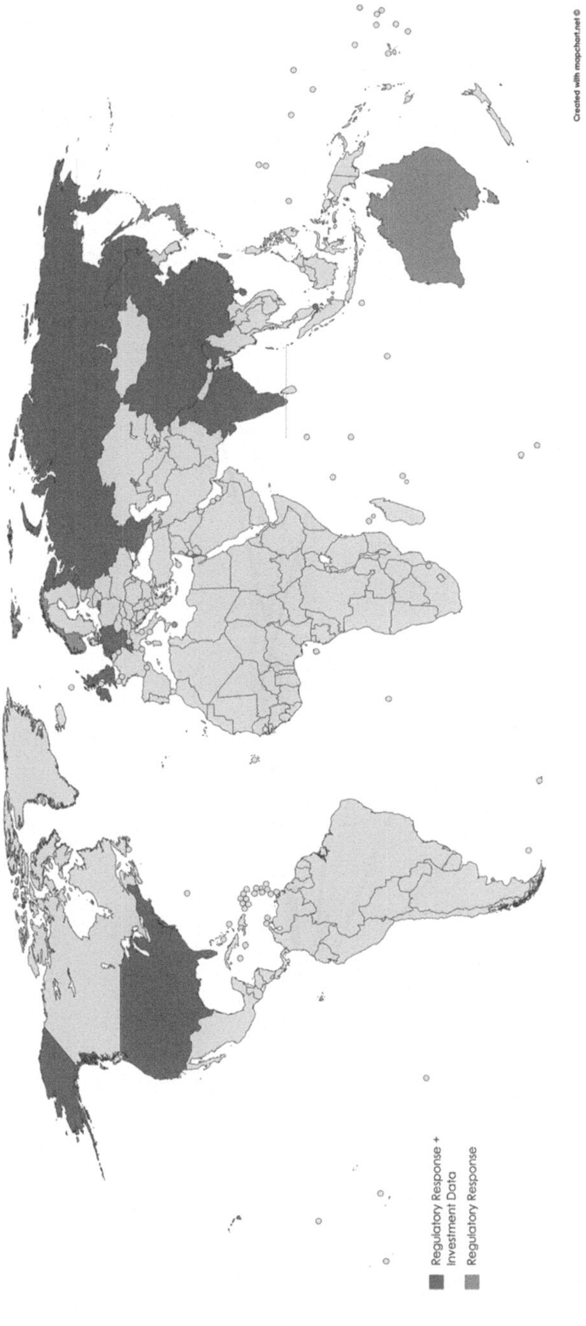

Fig. 6.3 Overview of countries in our study

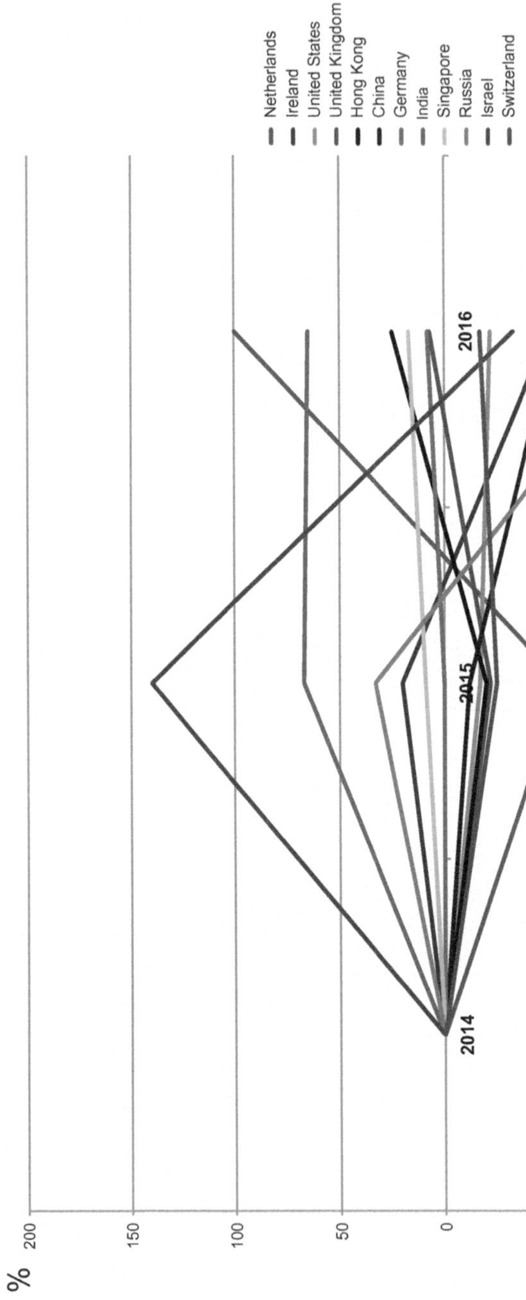

Fig. 6.4 Year-on-year percent growth of first-time venture capital backed fintech companies (country)

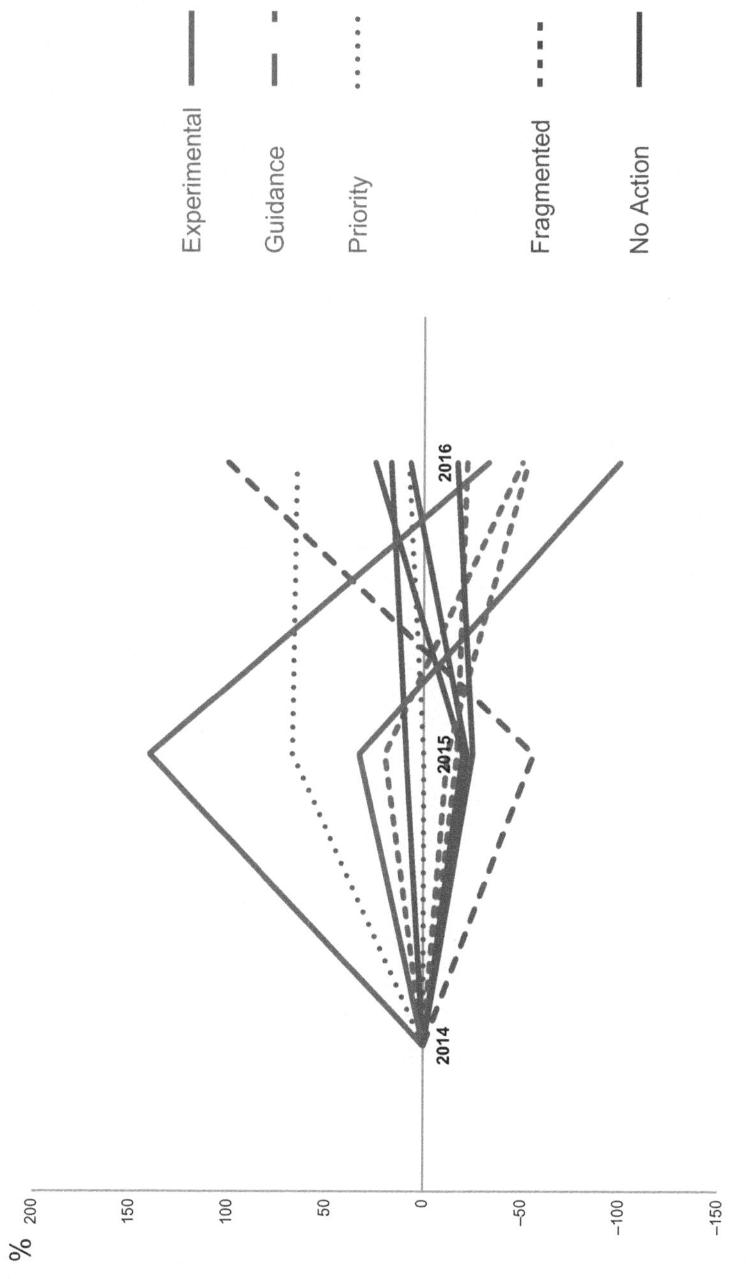

Fig. 6.5 Percentage growth of first-time venture capital backed fintech companies (regulatory approach)

crucial role in making Israel an attractive site for investing. But the evidence does suggest that collaborative regulation that facilitates experimentation is key. For now, policy experimentation seems to be the way to go for regulators. It is, therefore, crucial that we track the effectiveness of regulatory sandboxes in 2017. After all, they are relatively new and we need to build a better understanding of their effectiveness in order to improve their design. To be sure, such knowledge will show whether other countries can follow this more proactive and experimental model and whether it might work also in other industries that have a tradition of being heavily regulated.

6.5 Conclusion

This chapter considered how alternative sources of business lending can help to fill the financing gap for SMEs and young firms. By canvassing the empirical literature on alternative finance, we evaluated the benefits and costs of the respective alternative lending models.

We initially examined crowdfunding, which is a new funding source that complements traditional forms of finance. In particular, we reviewed the efficiency benefits of the respective non-price strategies and considered whether the differences are likely to attract more investors. AON fundraising campaigns have larger fundraising targets for their projects and tend also to be successful in realizing their capital goals. In contrast, the KIA model is used by firms that can scale their business. In sum, flexible platforms are attractive to a number of firms, creating sustainable user growth. We also discussed whether an investor has a public profile and whether it influences the dynamics of investor behavior. An informational advantage is likely to occur when investors have chosen a public profile. This will likely lead to more bids as well as interest from other investors.

We then considered the P2P model, which matches borrowers who are seeking a loan with investors. In short, platforms operate by assisting in the collection, scoring, and distribution of the credit qualifications of potential borrowers, reporting the real-time bids on projects and providing the online servicing and monitoring of the loan. Using this information, lenders are able to review the loan applications. Generally speaking, investors may choose to invest algorithmically, directly, or through a group. Unlike traditional banks, the P2P loan process involves the direct matching of lenders and borrowers via online auctions in which bid/ask is matched until a loan is fully funded, or is matched by fixed rate and category. For the most part, platforms have adopted the AON rule, which requires projects to meet their funding goal in order to be funded. In terms of the factors which explain the success of P2P lending platforms, platform-based data tools can be used to lower transaction costs in matching financing requests.

At the same time, P2P offers investors access to an alternative asset class that has been limited solely to large institutional investors, which also enables SMEs to obtain short-term credit at attractive rates and enables investors to achieve higher benchmarked returns.

Finally, this chapter focused on the regulatory responses to fintech in 17 jurisdictions. We examined the first-time venture capital investments in fintech companies to determine whether there is a meaningful connection between levels of investment and regulatory choice. The findings here have implications for how regulation is likely to play an important role in the development of the fintech market.

References

Abrams, E. 2017. *Securities Crowdfunding: More than Family, Friends and Fools?* Social Science Research Network. https://papers.ssrn.com/abstract=2902217. Accessed 20 Feb 2017.

Agrawal, Ajay, Christian Catalini, and Avi Goldfarb. 2015. Crowdfunding, Georgraphy, Social Networks, and the Timing of Decision. *Journal of Economics and Management Strategy* 24: 253–274.

Ahlers, Gerrit K., Douglas Cumming, Christina Günther, and Denis Schweizer. 2015. Signalling in Equity Crowdfunding. *Entrepreneurship Theory and Practice* 39: 955–980.

Ayadi, R., and S. Gadi. 2013. *Access by MSMEs to Finance in the Southern and Eastern Mediterranean: What Role for Credit Guarantee Schemes?* European Commission, MEDPRO Technical Report No. 35/2013.

Beck, Thorsten, Leora F. Klapper, and Juan Carlos Mendoza. 2010. The Typology of Partial Credit Guarantee Funds Around the World. *Journal of Financial Stability* 6: 10–25.

Belleflamme, Paul, Nessrine Omrani, and Martin Peitz. 2016. Understanding the Strategies of Crowdfunding Platforms. *CESifo DICE Report* 2: 6–10.

Boot, Arnoud W.A., Anjan V. Thakor, and Gregory F. Udell. 1991. Secured Lending and Default Risk: Equilibrium Analysis, Policy Implications and Empirical Results. *The Economic Journal* 101: 458–472.

Cambridge Centre for Alternative Finance/KPMG. 2016. *Sustaining Momentum: The 2nd European Alternative Finance Industry Report*. September. https://assets.kpmg.com/content/dam/kpmg/xx/pdf/2016/09/sustaining-momentum.pdf. Accessed 20 Feb 2017.

Cumming, Douglas J., Gaël Lefoeuf, and Armin Schweinbacher. 2015. *Crowdfunding Models: Keep-it-All vs. All-Or-Nothing*. Social Science Research Network. https://papers.ssrn.com/abstract=2447567. Accessed 20 Feb 2017.

Cumming, Douglas J., and Armin Schwienbacher. 2016. *Fintech Venture Capital*. Social Science Research Network. http://ssrn.com/abstract=2784797. Accessed 20 Feb 2017.

Deutsche Bank. 2017. *Synthetic Securitisation: Making a Silent Comeback*. EU Monitor: Global Financial Markets, February 21. http://dbresearch.de

Dushnitsky, Gary, Massimiliano Guerini, Evila Piva, and Cristina Rossi-Lamastra. 2016. Crowdfunding in Europe: Determinants of Platform Creation Across Countries. *California Management Review* 58: 44–71.

———. 2015. *Moving Mainstream—The European Alternative Financing Benchmark Report*. February. http://www.ey.com/Publication/vwLUAssets/EY-and-university-of-cambridge/$FILE/EY-cambridge-alternative-finance-report.pdf. Accessed 20 Apr 2017.

European Central Bank. 2015. *Survey on the Access to Finance of Enterprises in the Euro Area, October 2014 to March 2015*. June. https://www.ecb.europa.eu/pub/pdf/other/SAFE_website_report_2014H2.en.pdf. Accessed 20 Apr 2017.

Feng, Yan, Xinlu Fan, and Yeujun Yoon. 2015. Lenders and Borrowers' Strategies in Online Peer-to-Peer Lending Market: An Empirical Analysis of PPDai.com. *Journal of Empirical Research* 16: 242–260.

Global Agenda Council. 2015. *The Future of FinTech: A Paradigm Shift in Small Business Finance*. October. www3.weforum.org/

Haddad, Christian, and Lars Hornuf. 2016. *The Emergence of the Global Fintech Market: Economic and Technological Determinants*. CESifo Working Paper No. 6131. https://papers.ssrn.com/abstract=2830124. Accessed 20 Feb 2017.

Iyer, Rajkamal, Asim Ijaz Khwaja, Erzo F.P. Luttmer, and Kelly Shue. 2015. Screening Peers Softly: Inferring the Quality of Small Borrowers. *Management Science* 62: 1554–1577.

Kolodny, Lora. 2013. AngelList and Beyond: What VCs Really Think of Crowdfunding. *Wall Street Journal*. October 8. http://blogs.wsj.com/venture-capital/2013/10/08/angellist-and-beyond-what-vcs-really-think-of-crowd-funding/. Accessed 20 Apr 2017.

KPMG. 2017a. *The Pulse of FinTech Q4 2016: Global Analysis of Investment in FinTech*. February 21. https://assets.kpmg.com/content/dam/kpmg/xx/pdf/2017/02/pulse-of-fintech-q4-2016.pdf. Accessed 20 Apr 2017.

———. 2017b. *US Fintech Funding Drops in 2016: KPMG Report*. February 21. https://home.kpmg.com/us/en/home/insights/2017/02/us-fintech-funding-and-deal-volume-drop-significantly-in-2016-kpmg-q4-16-pulse-of-fintech-report.html. Accessed 20 Apr 2017.

Lewis, Neil. 2013. *Business Angels vs Equity Crowdfunding: 7 Key Differences*. iBusinessAngel. http://www.ibusinessangel.com/2013/04/business-angels-vs-equity-crowdfunding/. Accessed 20 Feb 2017.

Mills, Karen, and Brayden McCarthy. 2014. *The State of Small Business Lending: Credit Access during the Recover and How Technology May Change the Game*. Harvard Business School Working Paper 15-004. https://papers.ssrn.com/sol3/abstract=2470523. Accessed 20 Feb 2017.

Mittal, Alex. 2016. *Read the Fine Print Before You Turn to Equity Crowdfunding*. Mattermark. April 25. https://mattermark.com/read-fine-print-turn-equity-crowdfunding/. Accessed 20 Feb 2017.

Morgan Stanley Research. 2015. Can P2P Lending Reinvent Banking? June 17. https://www.morganstanley.com/ideas/p2p-marketplace-lending. Accessed 20 Feb 2017.

Morse, Adair. 2015. Peer to Peer Crowdfunding: Information and the Potential for Disruption in Consumer Lending. *National Bureau of Economic Research*. http://www.nber.org/papers/w20899. Accessed 20 Feb 2017.

OECD. 2013. *SMEs and Entrepreneurs 2013: An OECD Scorecard*. April 17. http://www.oecd.org/officialdocuments/publicdisplaydocumentpdf/?cote=CFE/SME(2012)12/FINAL&docLanguage=En. Accessed 20 Feb 2017.

———. 2015. *New Approaches to SME and Entrepreneurship Financing*. https://www.oecd.org/cfe/smes/New-Approaches-SME-full-report.pdf. Accessed 20 Feb 2017.

———. 2016. *Financing SMEs and Entrepreneurs 2016: Highlights*. April. http://www.oecd.org/cfe/smes/financing-smes-and-entrepreneurs-23065265.htm. Accessed 20 Feb 2017.

Parker, Geoffrey G., Marshall W. van Alsyne, and Sangeet P. Choudary. 2016. *Platform Revolution: How Networked Markets Are Transforming the Economy—*

And How to Make Them Work For You. New York: W.W. Norton and Company.
Philippon, Thomas. 2016. The FinTech Opportunity. *National Bureau of Economic Research*. http://www.nber.org/papers/w22476. Accessed 28 Apr 2017.
———. 2016. *Blurred Lines: How Fintech is Shaping Financial Services*. March. https://www.pwc.se/sv/pdf-reports/blurred-lines-how-fintech-is-shaping-financial-services.pdf. Accessed 20 Feb 2017.
Saha, A., and J. Parsont. 2017. *Regulation Crowdfunding: A Viable Capital-Raising Method for Tech Companies?* http://clsbluesky.law.columbia.edu/2017/03/06/regulation-crowdfunding-a-viable-capital-raising-method-for-tech-companies/
Vismara, Silvio. 2016. Information Cascades Among Investors in Equity Crowdfunding. *Enterpreneurship Theory and Practice*. https://doi.org/10.1111/etap.12261.
World Economic Forum. 2015. *The Future of FinTech: A Paradigm Shift in Small Business Finance*. October. http://www3.weforum.org/docs/IP/2015/FS/GAC15_The_Future_of_FinTech_Paradigm_Shift_Small_Business_Finance_report_2015.pdf. Accessed 20 Feb 2017.
Yum, Haewon, Byungtae Lee, and Myungsin Chae. 2012. From Wisdom of the Crowds to my Own Judgment in Microfinance Through Online Peer-to-Peer Lending Platforms. *Electronic Commerce Research and Applications* 11: 469–483.

Mark Fenwick is Professor of Law at Kyushu University. His research areas are white-collar and corporate crime, terrorism, emergencies and the law, bioethics and criminal law and theoretical criminology and social theory. He received his PhD from Cambridge University.

Joseph A. McCahery is Professor of International Economic Law at Tilburg University Law School and TILEC. He has held visiting appointments at Auckland University, Columbia University, Solvay Business School and University of Pennsylvania. His research interest areas include: banking regulation and supervision, corporate finance, financial market regulation, and corporate law and governance. He has published widely in the top finance and law journals and is author and editor of more than ten books, including *Law,*

Economics and Organization of Alliances and Joint Ventures (Cambridge University Press, forthcoming); *Institutional Investor Activism: Hedge Funds and Private Equity, Economics and Regulation* (Oxford University Press, 2015); and *Corporate Governance of Non-listed Companies* (Oxford University Press, 2008). He has served as a consultant to publicly traded firms, governmental agencies, investment companies, and law firms.

Erik P.M. Vermeulen is Professor of Business and Financial Law at Tilburg University and Tilburg Law and Economics Center (TILEC) in the Netherlands. He is also Senior Counsel Corporate of Philips in the Netherlands. He serves as a Vice President at the legal department where he advises on corporate governance, corporate venturing activities, international joint ventures, and mergers and acquisitions. He teaches courses on corporate governance, venture capital, entrepreneurship, joint ventures, and company law. He frequently lectures on these and other topics at universities around the world. In addition, he has served as an expert advisor to various organizations, such as the European Commission, the Organisation for Economic Cooperation and Development (OECD), the World Bank, the International Finance Corporation, the Dutch Development Finance Institution, the United Nations Commission on International Trade Law (UNCITRAL) and several national and local governments, concerning innovation, financial and venture capital markets, corporate law, and corporate governance of listed and non-listed companies.

Part III

Backers and Investors

7

Crowdfunding as a Font of Entrepreneurship: Outcomes of Reward-Based Crowdfunding

Ethan Mollick

Despite the relatively low level of consequences for failure, I find that crowdfunding project creators deliver their promised rewards the vast majority of the time (over 90%), and seem to make great efforts to fulfill their obligations. Additionally, a large number of projects, especially those in product-oriented categories, turn into ongoing ventures. Overall, the data suggests that crowdfunding is a viable method of producing new enterprises.

7.1 Surveys and Methods

I conducted two surveys with the help of Kickstarter.[1] The first survey was of project creators. The creators of all 61,654 successful Kickstarter projects that raised over USD 1000 before May 2015 were surveyed via email. Of those projects, 10,078 completed part of the survey (16.3%)

E. Mollick (✉)
The Wharton School, University of Pennsylvania, Pennsylvania, PA, USA

D. Cumming, L. Hornuf (eds.), *The Economics of Crowdfunding*,
https://doi.org/10.1007/978-3-319-66119-3_7

and 8448 (13.7%) completed most or all of the survey. These response rates are comparable with other web-based surveys in non-traditional industries within the management literature (Kriauciunas et al. 2011). Additionally, it is likely that many of the email accounts were set up for completed projects and were no longer actively used, artificially lowering response rates, though the proportion of these emails is difficult to determine. Therefore, in order to provide a more accurate accounting of actual responses, open rates on emails were tracked (Nickerson 2007), with an open rate of 47.8%. Open rate tracking works well for web-based email addresses (Gmail, Yahoo, Hotmail), but may not work in all cases, and could result in an underestimate of read emails. Nonetheless, using open rates suggests that overall response rates were between 16% and 34% of delivered email. Response rates varied by amount raised, with larger projects responding at a higher rate. After controlling for this factor, there was no significant difference between respondents and non-respondents in the types of backers they attracted (those who had backed projects before or those who had never backed projects), or the number of projects backed or launched by the creator.

The second survey was of project backers. In total 456,751 backers were surveyed, representing 65,326 projects. All projects from 2009 through May 2015 that raised over USD 1000 were included in the sample, as well as half the projects that raised less than USD 1000 but over USD 250, and a quarter of projects raising less than USD 250. Backers were selected randomly, without replacement, to maximize the number of backers per project. A mean of 7.2 backers were surveyed per project, with 7 backers surveyed in 89% of projects and 10 backers surveyed in 7.8% of projects.

A total of 47,188 backers (10.3%) responded. In total, there is at least one response for 30,323 projects, (46.4% of all projects), with 1.56 backer responses per project on average. The mean backer in the sample contributed USD 76.43 to the project they backed.

Response rates were not entirely representative of the project backer population, as response rates were higher for projects that traditionally produce consumer products, such as games (83% of all projects), technology (72% of all projects), design (70% of all projects), and comics (72% of all projects). They were lower for categories focused more on traditionally artistic pursuits, such as those in theater (35% of all projects), dance (31%), music (36%), and film (37%). Larger projects and more recent projects also had higher response rates. Across all categories, however, response rates were acceptable, and are unlikely to bias the findings.

For analyses of economic impact, responses were adjusted by iterative proportional fitting ("raking") to create weighted observations based on the total population of projects using the "ipfweight" command in STATA (Bergmann 2011). The raking model was based on the amount pledged, the degree to which projects raised more than their goal, and project category. This standard approach reduces non-response bias and increases representation.

Several questions in the surveys used ranges as potential answers. These included questions about age, children, personal earnings, and total earnings by projects. For the analyses, I converted these answers to a single scale, taking the midpoint of each range.

7.2 Measuring Failure Rates

First, I will examine the degree to which projects fail to deliver their promised rewards to project creators. Since creators raise money before trying to fulfill their promises, it is likely that many unanticipated problems could emerge that could interfere with project completion. Since budgets are fixed by the amount raised, these problems could be unsurmountable if they include cost overruns. Additionally, there are few clear legal recourses available to backers of failed projects (though see Cumming et al. 2016 for exceptions), making the consequences of failure somewhat unclear. Thus, project failure represents a real possibility. However, we have little evidence about how often failure occurs.

One challenge is determining what a "failed" project might be. Backers might consider a project failed if it did not deliver on its promises, if it delivered something different than expected, or for any one of a number of reasons. For the purpose of this chapter, I focus specifically on the rewards promised to project backers in return for backing projects (rewards on Kickstarter include a mix of physical, digital, and intangible rewards). The delivery of rewards seems to be the major way in which project backers evaluate the success of a project. At the same time, it is important to note that rewards are but one potential outcome of a project as there are many ways by which a project could "succeed" but still fail to deliver rewards—for example, an art exhibit may have been successfully staged, but not deliver a promised t-shirt or sticker to backers. Given this caveat, the degree to which backers believe they receive the expected outcome is a reasonable measure of one kind of success or failure.

There are many potential ways to classify projects as failed, based on my data. Respondents were asked to select from one of five reward status options, see Table 7.1.

For this chapter, I consider failures to be those projects where backers answer that they "never expect to get the promised reward" (5.2% of all responses) or that they "received the reward but it was not what was promised" (2% of all responses). It is important to note, however, that there may be a number of reasons that people may never expect to get the promised reward, including reasons unrelated to failure.

This issue becomes more complicated when considering projects rather than individual backer opinions, because there might be multiple backers who answer the survey about a single project, and they might disagree about whether promised rewards were delivered. Thus, at the level of projects, rather than respondents, there is a need to decide how to classify projects as failures. The broadest definition is to say if anyone reported the project as a failure, then the project has failed. This would classify 9.95% of all projects as failures. However, given that individual complaints are not uncommon, this is likely too harsh a definition. If instead, we classify projects where at least half of backers considered the project as

Table 7.1 Respondents' selection of reward status options

Category	Response	*N*	%
Completed	I received the reward	28,503	60.40
Completed	I was not expecting a reward	6398	13.56
Waiting	I am still expecting to get the promised reward	8879	18.82
Failed	I never expect to get the promised reward	2456	5.20
Failed	I received the reward, but it was not what I was promised	951	2.02

a failure (which I will refer to as the "middle definition" of failure), the rate drops to 8.6%, and if we take the strict definition that all backers should consider the project a failure, the failure rate is 5.6%.

Failure rates are highest for smaller projects, lowest for mid-size projects, and somewhat elevated for the largest projects. Using the middle 50% failure standard, in terms of dollars, 8.2% of all dollars pledged to successfully funded projects goes to those that ultimately fail to deliver promised rewards.

We might also be concerned that a number of the projects that are currently waiting for delivery will ultimately fail. If we look at older projects from 2012 or earlier, it may provide a better sense of long-term success rates. For projects from 2012 or earlier, the failure rate is 13.9% for the broadest definition, 12.3% by the middle definition, and 8.6% by the strictest definition. Part of the reason for this failure is mechanical, longer projects may fail at a higher rate. While these historical failure rates are higher, it is also likely that overall failure rates have decreased since 2012, as creators have climbed the learning curve of how to create successful projects, and backers have become more educated on which projects to support.

Combining all of these results, the overall failure rate for Kickstarter projects at the project level is around 9%, and likely in a range between 5% and 14%. A total of 7.2% of all backers reported that the project they were surveyed about failed. At the same time, it is important to note that even these numbers might overestimate project failure, as a project may have failed to deliver its reward, but still succeeded in accomplishing the goals of the creator.

Innovation involves risk, and so some failure rate in innovative projects is to be expected. At the same time, it is important to know if there are any observable factors that can serve as a warning for backers that a particular funded project is more likely to fail than another. A logistic regression (see Table 7.9) sheds some light on these questions.

As previously mentioned, the most-funded and least-funded projects are more likely to fail, though the smallest projects are more at risk than the largest ones. Controlling for the amount pledged and the year of the project creation, however, there are also some category-based risks. Film, technology, and food projects have greater chances of failure, while music projects are much less likely to fail. Again, this may be because of differences in ambition level across categories—it may be that film or technology products are aiming for more breakthrough products or are offering more complicated rewards (a completed movie or gadget, rather than a band t-shirt), and are thus at a higher risk of failure.

Other than category differences, there were few factors apparent to backers during the campaign that predicted failure, though projects that showed signs of creator effort, by having videos or by posting updates before the fundraising deadline, were less likely to fail (Mollick 2014). These had relatively small effects, however. This is consistent with prior research that has determined that crowds do a good job assessing project quality (Mollick and Nanda 2016).

Given that one effect of crowdfunding is to increase the diversity of people who can get access to funds, there was also a notable non-finding in the analysis of failures—the characteristics of the project creator were not significantly related to failure. There was no significant difference in failure rates between women and men (though women are more likely to raise funds, see Greenberg and Mollick 2016), between highly educated and less-educated creators, between teams and individual projects, between single or partnered creators, or between creators with children and those without. Systematic differences may exist, but those that do are not clearly observable to project backers.

Overall, for backers considering funding a project, there are currently few signs about which project will fail, assuming it has reached its goal. In general, for funded projects, a failure to deliver seems relatively rare, accounting for around 9% of all projects, with a possible range of 5% to 14%. The fact that failures seem to be distributed in non-predictable ways should offer some comfort about the underlying ability of backers to weed out projects that might offer obvious signs of trouble. Project backers should expect a failure rate of around 1-in-10 projects, and to receive a refund 13% of the time when a project does fail. Since failure can happen to anyone, creators need to consider, and plan for, the ways in which they will work with backers in the event a project fails, keeping lines of communication open and explaining how the money was spent. Ultimately, there does not seem to be a systematic problem associated with failure (or fraud) on Kickstarter, and the vast majority of projects do seem to deliver. At the same time, it is important to realize that these results apply only to Kickstarter, and other crowdfunding methods (such as equity crowdfunding) and platforms that have different policies or approaches may have higher failure rates.

Though many projects on Kickstarter have gone on to be artistic or financial successes for project creators, to date there has been no clear evidence about how often projects actually deliver on their promises to backers. What evidence we have suggests that creators are generally honest, if overconfident—many projects take longer to deliver than creators estimate[2] and overall fraud rates are low.[3] However, while Kickstarter warns potential backers about the risk of non-delivery in supporting projects, the actual share of projects that fail—that is, either do not deliver a promised reward, or deliver a reward that is very far from expectations—has been unknown, and a subject of considerable speculation. This chapter provides a first attempt to systematically understand delivery rates on Kickstarter.

7.3 Measuring Economic Impact

Projects therefore tend to deliver on their goals, but this does not mean that they lead to viable long-term impacts. I next examine this issue, which is complicated by the fact that Kickstarter projects span artistic and commercial ventures, and encompass a wide range of different goals, ambition levels, and expected outcomes. The first step in understanding the long-term impact of reward-based crowdfunding is to understand the variation among projects on Kickstarter. A logical way to do this would be to use the categories Kickstarter uses to define projects. However, these often span a wide range of project types—for example, the Design category includes both product design and architecture.

For this analysis, I have regrouped the categories somewhat to add clarity and to ensure that no one category makes up less than 2.5% of the total projects. The revised categories are based on the original categories in Kickstarter, with changes to rationalize and consolidate them. Unchanged from Kickstarter are the Games, Fashion, and Comics categories. Categories with minor variations include: Food (the same as the original, minus cookbooks and some gadgets), Technology (the same as the original, without makerspaces), and Film (the same as the original, without movie theaters). The Art category now includes projects in art, photography, graphic design, crafts, architecture, civic design, and typography. The Publishing category includes cookbooks and journalism, as well as the original publishing category. Dance and Theater are combined. Product Design only includes product design projects and unclassified design projects. Finally, I created a small category, Spaces, for projects supporting movie theaters, makerspaces, and practice spaces; however, due to its small size I exclude it from most further analyses.

We can further cluster these categories into two general groups: "product-oriented" and "art-oriented." Examining all 11 of the newly defined categories by whether the goal of the creator was to create or sustain an organization, or else to launch a one-time project, the contrast between types of projects becomes clear. The five "product-oriented" categories are dominated by attempts to build organizations: three quarters or more of the projects in these categories are started by current or new formal organizations (mean = 0.84). On the other hand, the six "art-oriented" categories are generally created by one-time or informal groups, with less than half the projects involving organizations. Qualitatively, the artistic categories tend to also contain a higher proportion of purely creative projects, while the product categories are more likely to be commercial in nature (see Fig. 7.1).

Using these rough divisions, we can now begin to examine the multiple types of impacts these projects have had, both for the creators themselves and for society overall. In the charts below, I often separate projects into art-oriented and product-oriented categories. When I do, I also separately rake both categories to yield more accurate weighting.

7.3.1 Careers and Salaries

One potential impact of crowdfunding is on the careers of the individuals seeking funding. As part of the survey, I asked creators whether their Kickstarter projects helped advance their career, increase the money they earned, switch careers, and whether it created new job opportunities. The career impact appeared to be substantial—a third of creators reported that the project advanced their careers (see Table 7.2).

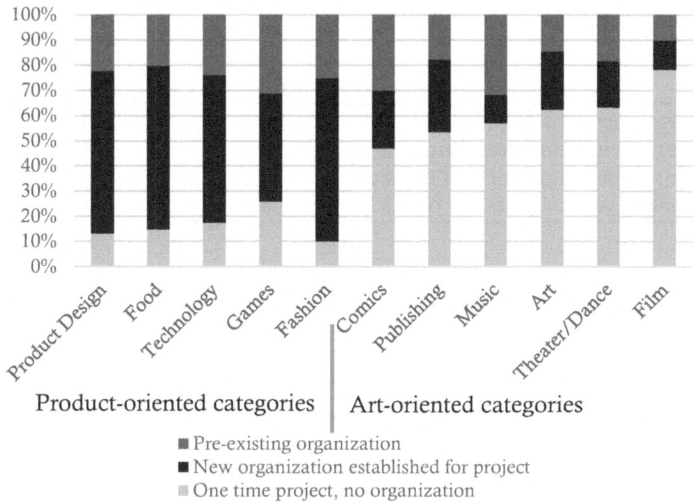

Fig. 7.1 What kind of organization created the project?

Table 7.2 Percent agreeing that "my Kickstarter campaign helped me..."

	Advance in my career (%)	Increase the money I made (%)	Switch careers (%)	Find new job opportunities (%)
Product-oriented	26	28	14	16
Art-oriented	41	18	5	21

I was also able to use salary data from the survey to examine the claims of those individuals who felt that their project helped increase the money they earned. Looking at creators who raised money before 2014, the total earnings of those who say that Kickstarter increased their earnings went up by USD 16,339 (SE = USD 1602) compared with USD 10,504 (SE = USD 689) for creators who reported that Kickstarter did not have an impact on their earnings.

Projects also became the jobs for many creators. Almost 19% of project creators said the project was their full-time job, even after the project was completed (see Table 7.3).

In addition to direct career benefits, crowdfunding seemed to lead to personal accomplishment as 60.1% of successful creators said their project "helped fulfill a dream."

Table 7.3 Creator job status on projects

	Ongoing projects (%)	Completed projects (%)
Project is my current full-time job	23.6	18.7
Project was my full-time job, but isn't now	13.0	14.9
I am working on the project on the side	57.5	49.0
I am no longer working on the project	6.0	27.3

7.3.2 Economic Impact

Moving from careers to the wider economy, there are a number of ways to measure the potential economic impact of crowdfunding. One useful measure is to look at the organizations and companies that were founded as a result of crowdfunding (see Table 7.4). Many projects did not attempt to create organizations, while others are projects from pre-existing companies, and still others are new organizations created for Kickstarter.

Using the weighted sample and extrapolating to the population, I find that, in total, through May 2015, around 4994 new formal organizations (companies or partnerships) were created for Kickstarter projects (95% confidence: 4642–5347). Of these, 3082 new for-profit companies and 1048 new not-for-profit companies are still in operation. Additionally, 11,314 (95% CI: 10,798–11,830) existing organizations raised money.

Another way of examining impact is to consider the earnings of projects outside of Kickstarter. The majority of projects created in Kickstarter campaigns generated additional sales beyond the money they raised from backers (see Table 7.5).

These results are lowered by the fact that many projects (30.8%) never generate additional revenue. Of these, it is likely that most actually do not seek additional outside revenue, as they could represent one-time events or artistic efforts. Removing those we find the mean revenues are higher (Table 7.6).

Extrapolating from the data, Kickstarter projects in total have generated non-crowdfunding revenues of around USD 3.4B (with a 95% confidence interval of USD 2.8B to USD 4.0B). Overall, projects generate an average of USD 2.46 of revenue from each dollar of pledges.

Figure 7.2 shows the ratio of dollars generated to dollars pledged for projects by category, for those projects where creators stated that a project

Table 7.4 Organization types used by Kickstarter project creators

	Product-oriented (%)	Art-oriented (%)
No organization	48	73
Ongoing pre-existing	30	15
Ongoing new for-profit	15	2
Ongoing new non-profit	1	2
Organization now shut down	2	1

Table 7.5 Average yearly revenues (outside of Kickstarter campaign money)

	Product	Artistic
No organization	USD 29,068 (5252)	USD 1918 (356)
Ongoing pre-existing	USD 89,642 (13,211)	USD 12,151 (2705)
Ongoing new for-profit	USD 106,910 (21,329)	USD 26,926 (11,487)
Ongoing new non-profit	USD 25,587 (12,771)	USD 49,454 (29,272)

Standard errors in parentheses

Table 7.6 Average yearly revenues (outside of Kickstarter campaign money) for projects that earned any income

	Product	Artistic
No organization	USD 38,271 (6882)	USD 3088 (572)
Ongoing pre-existing	USD 104,020 (15,246)	USD 17,854 (3959)
Ongoing new for-profit	USD 121,739 (24,144)	USD 35,760 (15,178)
Ongoing new non-profit	USD 34,949 (16,730)	USD 71,069 (41,928)

Standard errors in parentheses

is complete (that is, projects not still trying to deliver promised rewards to backers). The lines represent 95% confidence intervals. All ratios are positive and do not cross 0 except for the Film category.

In addition, the average project in the product-oriented category added 0.6 permanent employees (SD = 0.1) (outside of founders), and hired a maximum of 2.21 temporary employees (SD = 0.34) on average.

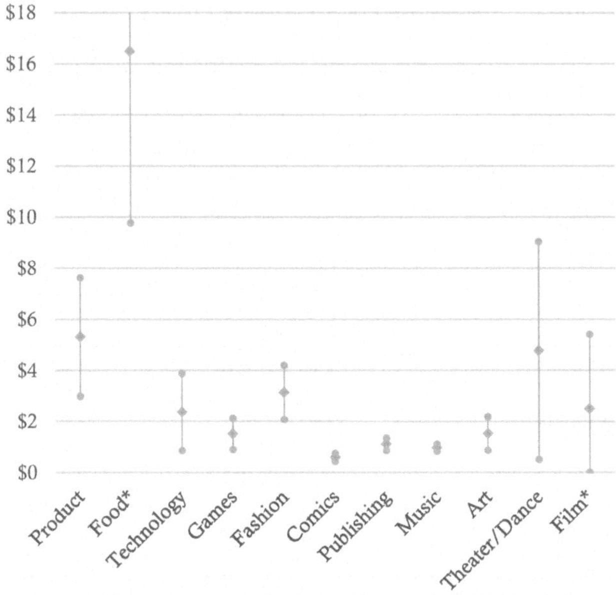

Fig. 7.2 Dollars in non-crowdfunding revenue per dollar in crowdfunding pledges for completed projects

Art-oriented projects did not add permanent employees (in fact, the number of permanent employees is slightly lower after the campaign, −0.08, SD = 0.03), but hire a maximum of 2.69 temporary employees (SD = 0.13). Thus, through May 2015, Kickstarter projects have created 5135 new ongoing jobs beside those that go to creators (though the 95% confidence interval is large, ranging from 1188 to 9082), and led to the hiring of 160,425 temporary workers (CI: 145,330 to 175,518).

Further, 11% of projects received additional funding after receiving crowdfunding. A total of 6.6% (CI 6%–7%) received funding from angel investors, VCs, or other companies. This suggests that crowdfunding can be part of the fundraising mix available to entrepreneurs (Cosh et al. 2009). Indeed, recent research suggests that crowdfunding can lead to a geographic expansion of venture capital (Sorenson et al. 2016).

While a hazard model examining the chances for failure, future funding, or exit would be ideal, it is difficult to do a longitudinal analysis with the dataset. Nonetheless, failure rates do not seem particularly high, as

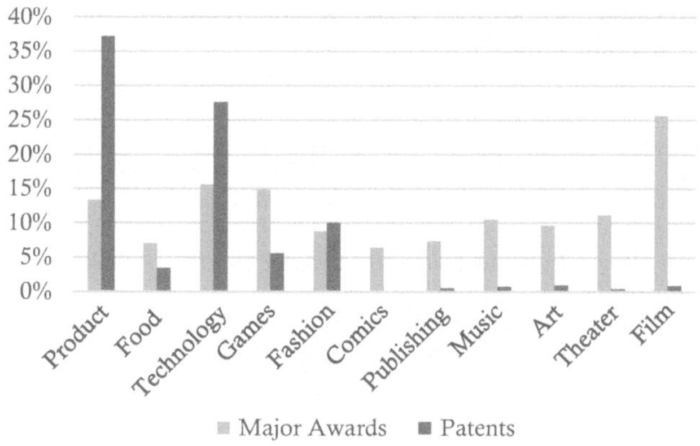

Fig. 7.3 Measures of innovation: percent of projects in category reporting winning major awards or applying for patents

compared to other estimates of organizational failure rates for new startups. Of the organizations that raised money on Kickstarter, 10.71% report ceasing operations, and another 5.02% report ceasing operations after acquisition.

7.3.3 Innovation and Creative Impact

Creators believe they are doing innovative work: 66% of them agreed or strongly agreed that their project was innovative (see Fig. 7.3). There is reason to believe that this self-assessment is largely accurate. In a separate survey of backers, backers classified 50.1% of successful projects as innovative. This innovativeness had a variety of measurable impacts. Around 4% of projects filed patents, meaning that, through May 2015, at least 2601 patents were filed by projects (CI = 2349–2854), though this could be much higher since some projects likely filed multiple patents. In addition, 13.7% of projects reported winning major awards, which would mean that 8446 projects (CI = 7975–8917) won these awards.

Additionally, all project creators were asked whether they agreed or disagreed with the statements about the creative impact of the campaign on their work in Table 7.7, with 1 being strongly disagree, 5 being strongly agree, and 3 being neutral.

Table 7.7 Responses to questions about artistic freedom (from 1, "strongly disagree," to 5, "strongly agree")

	Mean (1–5 scale)	SE
This campaign afforded you the creative independence you would not have been able to find through other funding avenues	4.00	0.011
This campaign allowed you to bring the project to life without compromising your vision	4.28	0.001
This campaign allowed you to pay collaborators you would not have been able to pay otherwise	3.61	0.014
This campaign allowed you to pursue your vision full time	2.79	0.015
This campaign helped you build a following or customer base that patronized your work after your Kickstarter campaign ended	3.53	0.013

7.3.4 Social Impact

Many projects reported a social impact to their work—either assisting a community, building something for society, or engaging in charitable work (see Table 7.8).

7.4 Conclusions

This data presents a consistent (and remarkably sunny) view of the value of reward-based crowdfunding. Projects seem to deliver the vast majority of the time, despite the frequent barriers they face and the low cost of failure. Further, successful crowdfunding projects have implications that go beyond the interactions of the backers and creators who participate in projects. Crowdfunding campaigns lead to new organizations that ultimately generate billions in non-crowdfunding revenue and have hired thousands of employees. Individual project creators often use crowdfunding campaigns to transition or advance their careers, or else to start new ventures. There also appears to be substantial new innovations and positive social good that comes from crowdfunding campaigns, though this can be difficult to quantify. While it is not possible in this

Table 7.8 Social impact of projects

	Percent responding yes (%)	SE
Did your project produce something aimed at helping a community?	53	0.0
The project helped do something important for society	27	0.0
Project helped create something important	67	0.0

Table 7.9 Factors predicting campaign's failure to deliver (Middle failure case)

	(1)	(2)
Variables	Logit coeff	Odds ratio
Log(Pledged)	−1.511***	0.221***
	(0.257)	(0.057)
Log(Pledged)^2	0.161***	1.174***
	(0.033)	(0.039)
Category: Comics	−0.272*	0.762*
	(0.139)	(0.106)
Category: Crafts	0.313*	1.368*
	(0.178)	(0.244)
Category: Dance	−0.424*	0.655*
	(0.224)	(0.147)
Category: Design	0.065	1.067
	(0.111)	(0.118)
Category: Fashion	0.077	1.080
	(0.136)	(0.147)
Category: Film & Video	0.375***	1.455***
	(0.085)	(0.124)
Category: Food	0.441***	1.555***
	(0.108)	(0.168)
Category: Games	0.166	1.181
	(0.108)	(0.127)
Category: Journalism	−0.068	0.934
	(0.281)	(0.262)
Category: Music	−0.220**	0.802**
	(0.088)	(0.071)
Category: Photography	0.004	1.004
	(0.150)	(0.150)
Category: Publishing	−0.179*	0.836*
	(0.106)	(0.088)
Category: Technology	0.466***	1.594***
	(0.117)	(0.186)

(*continued*)

Table 7.9 (continued)

	(1)	(2)
Variables	Logit coeff	Odds ratio
Category: Theater	0.028	1.028
	(0.120)	(0.123)
Provided updates during campaign	−0.015***	0.985***
	(0.005)	(0.004)
Had video	−0.191***	0.827***
	(0.063)	(0.052)
Creator commented during campaign	0.000	1.000
	(0.001)	(0.001)
Days project was live	0.003*	1.003*
	(0.002)	(0.002)
Constant	0.860	2.362
	(0.573)	(1.353)
Observations	30,323	30,323
df_m	26	26
χ^2	665.7	665.7
Pseudo r^2	0.037	0.037

Omitted category is Art. Year controls included. Standard errors in parentheses
***$p < 0.01$; **$p < 0.05$; *$p < 0.1$

study to compare the efficiency of crowdfunding to other methods of encouraging entrepreneurship or subsidizing creative work, it is clear that, overall, the money raised from campaigns leads to positive returns across a variety of measures.

An important question is whether these results apply to other forms of crowdfunding. In equity crowdfunding, early work suggests that many of the same factors apply. In particular, equity crowdfunded companies in Germany appear to have relatively low failure rates but also low exit rates (Hornuf and Schmitt 2016). This appears consistent with startups on Kickstarter, which also have low failure rates and relatively few companies achieving large scale. Similarly, signal quality seems to matter in both equity and reward crowdfunding (Ahlers et al. 2015). At the same time, the equity crowdfunding market is rapidly evolving, and the lessons from reward crowdfunding may attenuate as time goes on.

There is much to learn about crowdfunding, but these early results are encouraging. In general, reward-based crowdfunding appears to be a viable way for founders to launch sustainable organizations. Innovative projects appear common, as do projects that improve social good.

Notes

1. Kickstarter collaborated on data gathering, but these results are independent and solely my own work. I was not paid by Kickstarter, and all analyses were conducted independently of Kickstarter. Kickstarter was offered the chance to comment on, but not change, this chapter before it was made public. For the survey of project creators, the survey was conducted by me alone, and responses were not shared with Kickstarter. For the backer data, Kickstarter conducted the survey using questions jointly developed with me, but shared all relevant non-private data. All errors and omissions are mine. I would also like to acknowledge the help of Derya and Matt Lane, who assisted me with the research. Funding for the project was provided in part by the Kauffman Foundation.
2. Based on this survey, it appears that backers receive (or expect to receive) their rewards on time in the majority of cases. Backers agreed or strongly agreed with the statement that "the reward was delivered on time" for 65% of projects (i.e. the average answers from backers for a project ranged from 4 to 5 on a 5-point scale); they disagreed or strongly disagreed with the statement for 17% of projects (1–2 on the scale); and for the remainder neither agreed nor disagreed that delivery was on time (2.01–3.99 on the scale). This only includes cases where backers were expecting a reward of some kind.
3. See Mollick (2014), The Dynamics of Crowdfunding: An Exploratory Study, *Journal of Business Venturing*, 29 (1).

References

Ahlers, Gerrit K.C., Douglas Cumming, Christina Günther, and Denis Schweizer. 2015. Signaling in Equity Crowdfunding. *Entrepreneurship Theory and Practice* 39: 955–980.

Bergmann, Michael. 2011. IPFWEIGHT: Stata Module to Create Adjustment Weights for Surveys. *Statistical Software Components*. Boston College Department of Economics.

Cosh, Andy, Douglas Cumming, and Alan Hughes. 2009. Outside Enterpreneurial Capital. *The Economic Journal* 119: 1494–1533.

Cumming, Douglas J., Lars Hornuf, Moein Karami, and Denis Schweizer. 2016. Disentangling Crowdfunding from Fraudfunding. *Social Science Research Network*. https://papers.ssrn.com/abstract=2447567. Accessed 28 Feb 2017.

Greenberg, J., and E. Mollick. 2016. Activist Choice Homophily and the Crowdfunding of Female Founders. *Administrative Science Quarterly* 62 (2): 341–374.

Hornuf, Lars, and Matthias Schmitt. 2016. Success and Failure in Equity Crowdfunding. *DICE Report* 14: 16–22.

Kriauciunas, Aldas, Anne Parmigiani, and Miguel Rivera-Santos. 2011. Leaving Our Comfort Zone: Integrating Established Practices with Unique Adaptations to Conduct Survey-based Strategy Research in Nontraditional Contexts. *Strategic Management Journal* 32: 994–1010.

Mollick, E. 2014. The Dynamics of Crowdfunding: Determinants of Success and Failure. *Journal of Business Venturing* 29: 1–16. https://doi.org/10.2139/ssrn.2088298.

Mollick, E., and R. Nanda. 2016. Wisdom or Madness? Comparing Crowds with Expert Evaluation in Funding the Arts. *Management Science* 62: 1533–1553. https://doi.org/10.1287/mnsc.2015.2207.

Nickerson, David W. 2007. Does Email Boost Turnout. *Quarterly Journal of Political Science* 2: 369–379.

Sorenson, Olav, Valentina Assenova, Guan-Cheng Li, Jason Boada, and Fleming Lee. 2016. Expand Innovation Finance via Crowdfunding. *Science* 354: 1526–1528.

Ethan Mollick is the Edward B. and Shirley R. Shils Assistant Professor of Management at the Wharton School. He studies innovation and entrepreneurship and has published papers in top academic journals on topics ranging from crowdfunding to entrepreneurial strategy. He is a Schultze Distinguished Professor and Kauffman Foundation Junior Faculty Fellow.

8

Crowdfunding Creative Ideas: The Dynamics of Project Backers

Venkat Kuppuswamy and Barry L. Bayus

8.1 Introduction

An important barrier to commercializing new ideas is the availability of early stage funding (Cosh et al. 2009). Given the difficulties that new ventures face in attracting financing from angel investors, banks, and venture capital funds, some entrepreneurs are tapping into large, online communities of consumer-investors (Schwienbacher and Larralde 2012; Agrawal et al. 2015). A relatively new form of informal venture financing called "crowdfunding" allows entrepreneurs to directly appeal to the general public for financial help in getting their innovative ideas off the ground. Related to crowdsourcing (Bayus 2013), crowdfunding involves an open call (through the Internet) for the provision of financial resources either in the form of donation or in exchange for some form of reward in order to support initiatives for specific purposes (Belleflamme et al. 2014).

V. Kuppuswamy • B.L. Bayus (✉)
Kenan-Flagler Business School, University of North Carolina at Chapel Hill, Chapel Hill, NC, USA

D. Cumming, L. Hornuf (eds.), *The Economics of Crowdfunding*,
https://doi.org/10.1007/978-3-319-66119-3_8

Prominent examples include Sellaband (which offers consumer-investors an interest in the venture in the form of some sort of profit-sharing agreement; Agrawal, et al. 2015), Prosper (involving crowdlending in which it is expected that the original principal is repaid along with some fixed interest; Zhang and Liu 2012), JustGiving (in which funders voluntarily donate their money with no expectations of any tangible reward; Smith et al. 2014), and Kickstarter (where project backers receive nonfinancial rewards for their contributions; Mollick 2014). Kickstarter, which is the leading crowdfunding platform in the United States, has raised USD 2.14 billion in pledges to fund 108,000 creative ideas (Kickstarter 2016). By itself, Kickstarter has provided more funding than the National Endowment for the Arts (Boyle 2013; Mollick and Nanda 2016), and is one of the biggest publishers of graphic novels in the United States (Flood 2012).

Despite the rapidly growing interest in this online form of venture financing, research into this phenomenon is in its infancy (see the reviews by Kuppuswamy and Bayus 2017; Moritz and Block 2016). To date, the majority of empirical studies in this domain focus on identifying the project and entrepreneur characteristics associated with successful funding outcomes. For example, research shows that funding success is positively related to project quality signals such as preparedness (Mollick 2014), narrative in the project description (Herzenstein et al. 2011b; Allison et al. 2015), information disclosure (Hornuf and Schwienbacher 2017), and others' contributions (Herzenstein et al. 2011; Zhang and Liu 2012; Burtch et al. 2013; Smith et al. 2014), as well as individual quality signals like gender, race, personal characteristics (Pope and Sydnor 2011; Gorbatai and Nelson 2015; Marom et al. 2015), creditworthiness (Herzenstein et al. 2011; Zhang and Liu 2012), internal social capital accumulated from supporting other projects (Colombo et al. 2015; Zheng et al. 2014), social networks (Lin et al. 2014), and the geographic distance between entrepreneurs and their supporters (Agrawal et al. 2015). With few exceptions, the level of analysis for the vast majority of existing crowdfunding studies is the project (i.e., studies are cross-sectional in nature; see Kuppuswamy and Bayus 2017). Researchers do not generally use panel data to model the dynamics of project-funding behavior over the project-funding cycle and, more importantly, to control for unobserved project-level heterogeneity (e.g., with fixed project effects). While many studies attempt to include appropriate controls with measured variables, the reported conclusions from project-level (cross-sectional) studies should be viewed with caution due to unobserved differences in the inherent quality of projects that can potentially explain observed project-funding outcomes.

Our interest in this chapter is to complement the existing cross-sectional research by explicitly considering the dynamics of project support over time using panel data. Because most crowdfunding campaigns last for only a few weeks, understanding funding behaviors over time is important as we do not expect contributions to be uniform over the project-funding cycle. For example, as suggested by related research in online auction bidding (Ariely and Simonson 2003), the key drivers of contribution decisions may vary over the beginning, middle, and later stages of a crowdfunding campaign. Thus, the purpose of this chapter is to add to our empirical understanding of crowdfunding by focusing on the number of project backers added to a project each day over its funding cycle. We refrain from formally developing and testing specific hypotheses because our empirical study is exploratory in nature. We believe this approach is appropriate for a nascent and evolving topic like online crowdfunding as very little prior work on backer dynamics exists with which to guide our research. Instead, we expect that our empirical findings will be useful for future theory-building.

8.2 Empirical Setting and Available Data

In this section, we briefly discuss the empirical setting of our study. Based in the United States, Kickstarter is one of the world's largest crowdfunding platforms. According to their website, "Kickstarter is focused on creative projects. We're a great way for artists, filmmakers, musicians, designers, writers, illustrators, explorers, curators, performers, and others to bring their projects, events, and dreams to life." Projects are grouped into broad categories: Art, Comics, Dance, Design, Fashion, Film and Video, Food, Games, Music, Photography, Publishing, Technology, and Theater. The website defines a project as "something finite with a clear beginning and end. Someone can be held accountable to the framework of a project—a project was either completed or it wasn't—and there are definable expectations that everyone can agree to." Kickstarter does not accept projects created to solicit donations to causes, charity projects, or general business expenses.

In order to participate, individuals must join the Kickstarter community (at no cost) by selecting an anonymous username. Like most online communities, information on demographics and personal characteristics are not collected (the Kickstarter community is a large, undefined "crowd"). Community members can propose projects for funding, back a project by financially contributing (with a credit card via Amazon), and/or comment on projects. Kickstarter projects can only be proposed by US residents (for tax purposes); project contributors have no geographic restrictions.

To use Kickstarter, an entrepreneur (called "creator" in Kickstarter) creates a webpage for the project on the platform explaining the purpose of the project and the specific deliverables that they aim to produce with the contributed funds. Along with an end date for the project-funding cycle, the creator also indicates the funding goal of the project, that is, the amount of money they require to execute the project as specified. Creators can communicate with their supporters by posting public updates that everyone can see.

When a potential funder (called "backer" in Kickstarter) visits an active project's webpage, they are presented with all the project information initially posted by the creator. Moreover, potential backers are shown the current funding status of the project (i.e., the funds raised thus far), the ultimate funding goal, and the number of days remaining until the project-funding cycle expires. A potential funder can also see a listing of the other backers who have contributed to the project, as well as the timing of these contributions.[1] To help potential backers discover projects they want to support, Kickstarter has a number of search options. In particular, projects can be sorted based on the first week after their initial launch ("Recently Launched"), the last week before the project funding closes ("Ending Soon"), or popularity (based on the number of backers recently added to a project).

There are two important features of Kickstarter that distinguish it from many other smaller crowdfunding platforms, as well as more traditional forms of entrepreneurial finance. The first is the "all-or-nothing" aspect of fundraising on the platform. A project must be fully funded before its funding cycle concludes or no money pledged by any backer is transferred to the project creator. An overambitious funding goal may thus result in the fundraising effort falling short and, consequently, raising no funds whatsoever. At the same time, once a project has reached its funding goal, it can continue to receive contributions until its deadline. As a result, funded projects can exceed their original funding goal.

The second important feature of the Kickstarter model is the fact that individuals contributing to a project do not receive equity in the project in return for their funds. Specifically, backers do not receive any financial incentives, returns, or repayment in exchange for their contributions. Instead, project creators typically offer more modest "rewards" to contributors which vary by the level of contribution. According to the Kickstarter website, the four most common reward types are (a) copies of the thing (e.g., the actual product, an assembled version of a DIY kit); (b) creative collaborations of various kinds (e.g., a backer might appear as a hero in the comic, or he or she may be painted into the mural); (c) creative experiences (e.g., a visit to the film set, a phone call from the author, dinner with the cast, a concert in the backer's backyard); and (d) creative mementos (e.g., photos sent from filming location, or explicit thanks in the closing credits of the movie).

Data for our study come from publicly available information on the Kickstarter website. We extracted information on all backed projects posted on the platform from its inception in May 2009 through February 2012. We focused on projects with at least one backer since we were interested in the dynamics of backer behavior (projects with zero backers would not contribute any information to our analyses). To allow a time buffer for community activity around a project to stabilize, projects completed after 2011 were dropped from the analysis. In addition, projects started in 2009 were not used in the analysis because the look and feel of the website underwent several revisions in the first few months after launch. We restricted our analyses to projects with a duration of at least 21 days to ensure an adequate length of time to examine backer behaviors during the early, middle, and late stages of the funding cycle. After cleaning the data for inaccuracies and incomplete information, daily data of two years on 14,704 projects that began on or after January 1, 2010, and concluded by December 31, 2011, are available for analysis purposes.

Descriptive statistics for these projects are reported in Table 8.1. The average project[2] has a goal of just over USD 9,900 but only receives a little more than USD 2,100 in pledged contributions.[3] Projects tend to last for around six weeks; a relatively large proportion of backers support a project in the first or last weeks of its funding cycle. Almost 80 percent of the projects include a video. The average project offers more than seven reward categories as incentives for their donors and receives about USD 70 per backer. Creators generally post a couple of project updates. Over 90 percent of creators only propose a single Kickstarter project.

There is a considerable amount of variance in the funding outcomes for Kickstarter projects. Figure 8.1 shows the distribution of project success: projects that reach their funding goal do so by a small margin (almost half of all the successful projects are within 10 percent of their original funding goal), while projects that miss their targets do so by a large margin (almost half of all the unsuccessful projects achieved less than 10 percent of their goal).

Table 8.1 also reports descriptive statistics by funding level achieved. While unsuccessful projects have a funding goal more than four times as large as successful projects (USD 14,686 compared to USD 3,486), these projects receive less than half of the amount contributed to successful projects (USD 1,214 compared to USD 3,496). Successful projects tend to be shorter in duration. All projects receive a relatively large proportion of their backers in the first week, and successful projects also get a lot of support in the last week of their funding cycle. Not surprisingly, successfully funded projects have significantly more backers than unsuccessful projects, and add more backers each day. Successful projects tend to communicate more to the community and their backers by posting updates.

8.3 Empirical Analyses

In this section, we attempt to shed some empirical light on the dynamics of backer behaviors in reward-based crowdfunding. To do this, we exploit the panel structure of the Kickstarter data to explore the relationship

Table 8.1 Summary statistics for *Kickstarter* projects 2010–2011 (*N* = 14,704)

		Funding level achieved		
Variable	(1) Total sample mean (*N* = 14,704)	(2) <100% of goal (*N* = 8681)	(3) 100% of goal (*N* = 897)	(4) >100% of goal (*N* = 5126)
Goal (USD)	9,907.24	14,686.4	3,485.68	2,937.36
Total amount pledged (USD)	2,160.22	1,214.07	3,496.46	3,528.72
Percent of goal funded	62.39	15.44	100.23	135.27
Percent of goal achieved in first week	21.32	6.09	30.33	45.53
Percent of goal remaining in last week	51.8	87.01	26.81	−3.45
Duration (days)	43.47	46.72	40.1	38.53
Number of backers	28.63	17.27	30.34	47.55
Number of backers in first week	9.31	6.57	7.93	14.19
Number of backers in last week	6.21	2.39	9.1	12.19
Number of backers added per day	0.64	0.36	0.74	1.2
Average contribution per backer (USD)	70.57	59.52	129.35	78.99
Number of reward categories	7.59	7.62	7.04	7.64
Maximum reward claimed (USD)	339.94	255.68	471.53	456.26
Percent of rewards claimed	79.63	79.44	74.39	80.87
Has video (1 = yes)	0.78	0.78	0.77	0.8
Number of days on top 50 most popular list	0.32	0.12	0.19	0.67
Number of updates	1.95	1.56	1.91	2.63
Number of updates in first week	0.49	0.49	0.38	0.56
Number of updates in middle period	1.15	0.93	1.08	1.54
Number of updates in last week	0.42	0.24	0.63	0.7
Number of active projects (×1000)	1.86	1.86	1.82	1.87

(continued)

Table 8.1 (continued)

		Funding level achieved		
Variable	(1) Total sample mean (*N* = 14,704)	(2) <100% of goal (*N* = 8681)	(3) 100% of goal (*N* = 897)	(4) >100% of goal (*N* = 5126)
Maximum number of backers on competing projects	0.28	0.28	0.27	0.28
Proposed by a serial creator (1 = yes)	0.07	0.06	0.1	0.08
Creator previously backed a project (1 = yes)	0.21	0.18	0.22	0.27

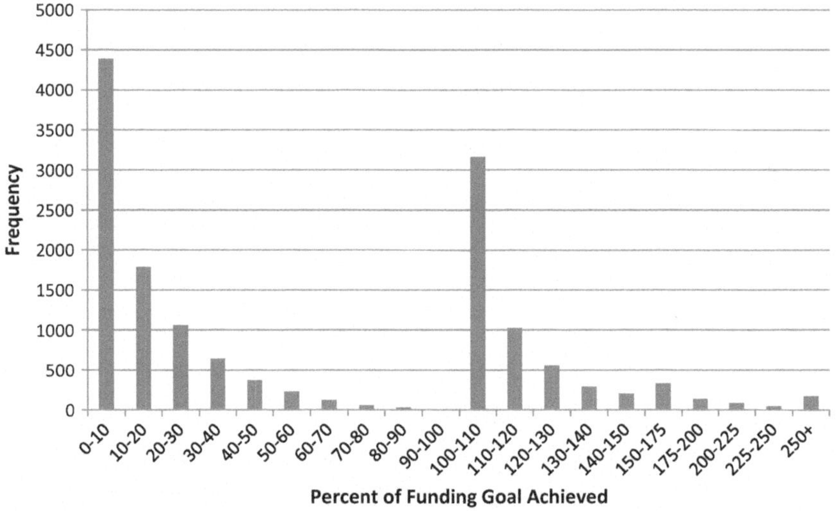

Fig. 8.1 Distribution of project-funding outcomes

between the daily support a project receives and various explanatory and control variables. The key dependent variable in our analyses is *BackersAdded*, a count variable which is the number of backers project *i* receives on day *t*. Because the dependent measure is a non-negative integer, our empirical strategy is to estimate appropriate panel count models (using a Poisson Quasi-Maximum Likelihood estimator). To account for any unobserved project heterogeneity (e.g., projects may differ in unobserved "quality"), we estimate fixed-effects models. Essentially, fixed-effects models incorporate project-specific intercept terms. Based on a Hausman-type test (see Allison 2005), fixed-effects models are preferred over random-effects models for the Kickstarter data. Importantly, a fixed-effects model removes any unobserved time-invariant heterogeneity across projects and allows these unobserved differences to be correlated with the independent variables (and thus is less likely to be biased). Although time-invariant characteristics are controlled, estimation of the fixed-effects models is accomplished using a conditional maximum likelihood estimator where all time-invariant project effects are conditioned out of the model using an individual's total count (Cameron and Trivedi 2009). Cluster-robust standard errors for the estimated coefficients are used for statistical tests due to dependence among the errors over time within a project.

8.3.1 The Dynamics of Project Support

We begin by empirically exploring the dynamics of project support over its funding cycle. The average number of backers added to a project over its relative funding cycle is depicted in Fig. 8.2. Consistent with the descriptive statistics in Table 8.1, projects tend to get a lot of backer support in the first and last weeks of their funding cycle. A high level of initial project support in the first few days is followed by generally decreasing support over most of the first week. A pronounced lull in project activity occurs during the middle period of the funding cycle. As the project approaches its conclusion, there is an increase in contributions. To better understand the dynamics of project-funding behaviors, we next turn to an econometric analysis of these data.

We define binary variables to capture the first seven days (*Day T*, where $T = 1, \ldots, 7$) and last seven days (*L LastDay*, where $L = 1, \ldots, 7$) in the project-funding cycle. Here the reference category is the middle period. In addition, several time-varying variables that account for possible effects due to other project or situational factors are included in our analyses. As suggested by Fig. 8.2, several projects in our sample exceed their original

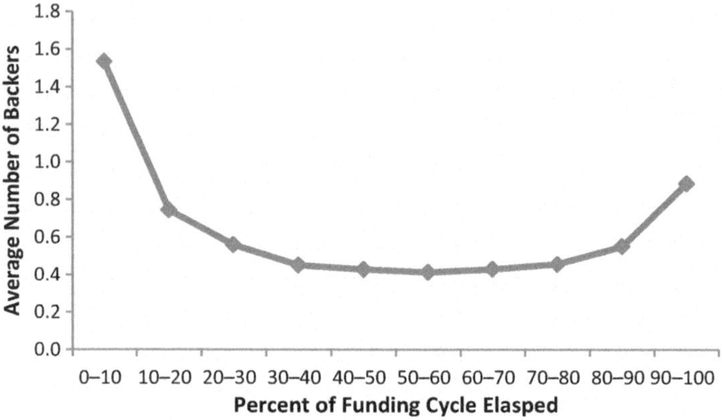

Fig. 8.2 Average number of backers added to a project on any day

funding goal. To account for any differences in backer behaviors for these projects, we include *PostFunded*, defined to be one for each day a project has already been funded and zero otherwise. We control for competition among projects for backer support by including *ActiveProjects* (the number of Kickstarter projects across all categories[4] that are accepting pledges on day *t* in thousands) in our estimations. We also include *MaxCompetingBackers* (the maximum number of cumulative backers across all competing projects accepting pledges on day *t*) to control for any possible negative effects due to other projects that are receiving a lot of backer support. Finally, we control for the possibility that pledges concentrate on certain days by including separate dummy variables for day of week and account for any other unobserved time-varying effects by including month-year dummy variables. This framework with the dummy variables for time in the project-funding cycle, along with control variables, is the basic econometric model used in most of our analyses.

The results of estimating a conditional fixed-effects Poisson model that corrects for overdispersion and allows for cluster-robust standard errors (Wooldridge 1999; Cameron and Trivedi 2009) are given in Table 8.2. While we do not report the estimation details for day of week and month-year to conserve space, we can make a few observations. First, projects are more likely to receive contributions on weekdays compared to weekends, with activity increasing from Sunday to a peak on Wednesday; thereafter,

Table 8.2 Panel estimation results for the dynamics of backer support (cluster-robust standard errors; t-statistics in parentheses)

	Model 1	Model 2	Model 3	Model 4	Model 5
Variable	(All)	(Funded)	(Unfunded)	(Goal ≤ USD 3,500)	(Goal > USD 3,500)
Day in the project-funding cycle					
Day 1	1.30 (0.02)***	1.13 (0.02)***	1.58 (0.02)***	1.27 (0.02)***	1.32 (0.02)***
Day 2	1.11 (0.02)***	1.00 (0.02)***	1.31 (0.02)***	1.06 (0.02)***	1.14 (0.02)***
Day 3	0.81 (0.01)***	0.68 (0.02)***	1.03 (0.02)***	0.75 (0.02)***	0.85 (0.02)***
Day 4	0.61 (0.02)***	0.49 (0.02)***	0.83 (0.02)***	0.56 (0.02)***	0.64 (0.02)***
Day 5	0.47 (0.02)***	0.36 (0.02)***	0.66 (0.03)***	0.43 (0.02)***	0.50 (0.02)***
Day 6	0.37 (0.02)***	0.28 (0.02)***	0.56 (0.03)***	0.32 (0.02)***	0.42 (0.02)***
Day 7	0.28 (0.02)***	0.19 (0.02)***	0.44 (0.02)***	0.24 (0.02)***	0.31 (0.03)***
7th LastDay	0.34 (0.02)***	0.45 (0.02)***	0.04 (0.04)	0.38 (0.03)***	0.31 (0.03)***
6th LastDay	0.42 (0.02)***	0.55 (0.02)***	0.11 (0.03)**	0.47 (0.02)***	0.39 (0.03)***
5th LastDay	0.53 (0.02)***	0.69 (0.02)***	0.15 (0.04)***	0.59 (0.03)**	0.48 (0.03)***
4th LastDay	0.69 (0.02)***	0.87 (0.02)***	0.31 (0.04)***	0.76 (0.03)***	0.63 (0.03)***
3rd LastDay	0.94 (0.02)***	1.16 (0.02)***	0.51 (0.04)***	1.02 (0.02)***	0.88 (0.03)***
2nd LastDay	1.23 (0.02)***	1.53 (0.02)***	0.73 (0.03)***	1.31 (0.02)***	1.16 (0.03)***
LastDay	1.02 (0.03)***	1.45 (0.03)***	0.46 (0.04)***	1.22 (0.03)***	0.87 (0.04)***
Explanatory variables					
PostFunded	−0.94 (0.02)***	−1.41 (0.03)***	NA	−1.20 (0.03)***	−0.63 (0.04)***
Control variables					
Active projects	−0.20 (0.07)**	0.36 (0.08)***	−0.56 (0.10)***	0.18 (0.09)*	−0.40 (0.09)***
MaxCompetingBackers	−0.05 (0.04)	−0.04 (0.05)	−0.06 (0.07)	−0.10 (0.05)	−0.03 (0.06)
Fixed-effects					
Day of week	Yes	Yes	Yes	Yes	Yes
Month-year	Yes	Yes	Yes	Yes	Yes

(continued)

Table 8.2 (continued)

Variable	Model 1 (All)	Model 2 (Funded)	Model 3 (Unfunded)	Model 4 (Goal ≤ USD 3,500)	Model 5 (Goal > USD 3,500)
Project	Yes	Yes	Yes	Yes	Yes
N (observations)	653,820	239,520	414,300	311,150	342,670
N (projects)	14,704	6,023	8,681	7,499	7,205
Chi-square	22,021.77***	12,647.52***	12,595.90***	12,856.73***	10,590.52***

*Significant at 0.05 level; **significant at 0.01 level; ***significant at 0.001 level

activity decreases to its lowest point on Saturday. Month-year fixed effects indicate that projects are less likely to add backers as we move from the beginning of the sample period (January 2010) to the end (December 2011).

The coefficient estimates for *MaxCompetingBackers* are insignificant in Table 8.2. These results do not strongly support the idea of a "Blockbuster Effect" in which a project with a large number of backers steals potential backers from other projects (Kickstarter 2013). Across all the models in Table 8.2, the coefficient estimate for *PostFunded* is negative and significant. This indicates that backer support drops off considerably once a project surpasses its goal. From Model 1, we find the effect of *ActiveProjects* on backer support is negative and significant. This is consistent with the idea of "Kickstarter Fatigue" as proposed by some industry followers in which potential backers are becoming weary due to an increasing number of projects asking for their financial contributions (Goninon 2013; Maxwell 2013; Nelson 2013). This particularly seems to be the case for projects with high goals (Model 4). Further, the results in Models 2 and 3 indicate that a large number of competing projects is associated with more backer support for projects that are eventually funded and less for unsuccessful projects. Together, these results suggest that there are limits to the financial support of backers.

Strongly confirming a U-shaped pattern of backer support, the coefficient estimates for the *Day* and *LastDay* binary variables are jointly significant and positive in all the models. Moreover, these variables significantly decrease in magnitude over the first week and significantly increase in magnitude over the last week.[5] The positive coefficient estimates indicate that backers are more likely to pledge in the first and last week as compared to the middle period in the project's funding cycle. Deadline effects in which a lot of action occurs as the end of an experience is approached has been widely observed in many contexts (Webb and Weick 1979; Ariely and Simonson 2003). Consistent with the idea of a deadline effect, almost two-thirds of the projects in our sample achieved their target goal in the last week of their funding cycle. More persuasively, the significant and increasing coefficient estimates for the *LastDay* variables strongly suggest a deadline effect.

Models 2 and 3 demonstrate that both successfully and unsuccessfully funded projects also exhibit a U-shaped pattern of backer support, as do projects with different goal targets (Models 4 and 5). It is interesting that successfully funded projects exhibit the same dip in activity during the middle period of the funding cycle as projects that do not meet their goal. Thus, even successful projects find it very difficult to maintain their initial momentum in continuing to get pledges over the entire funding cycle. In our extended working paper (Kuppuswamy and Bayus 2015), we confirm that this U-shaped pattern of project support is pervasive across different project types (Art, Product Design, Film and Video, Games, Music, Technology). These results extend common thinking that only successfully funded projects exhibit a U-shaped pattern in project support over its funding cycle (de Witt 2012; Steinberg 2012)—in fact, this U-shaped pattern is systematic and persistent across Kickstarter projects.[6]

8.3.2 Inside the Dynamics of Project Support

In this section, we consider several factors that have been related to project-funding success by other researchers. We extend these prior studies by empirically exploring the dynamics associated with these factors. Specifically, we consider four questions: (1) Is the U-shaped pattern of project support due to collective attention effects, that is, do backers simply support projects that are easily found and most visible from using the available platform project-sorting options (Qui 2013)? (2) What is the role of family and friends over the project-funding cycle (Agrawal et al. 2015)? (3) What are the dynamic effects of social influence in supporting a project (Herzenstein et al. 2011; Zhang and Liu 2012; Agrawal et al. 2015; Hornuf and Schwienbacher 2017; Vismara 2015)? (4) What is the role of project updates over the project-funding cycle (Mollick 2014; Block et al. 2017)?

8.3.2.1 Collective Attention Effects

One interesting perspective that might account for the U-shaped pattern of backer support comes from research on the effects of consumers' limited attention in the digital economy where information is abundant

(Falkinger 2008; Wu and Huberman 2007; Hodas and Lerman 2013). The problem of collective attention is at the center of online communities and the spread of ideas—"a wealth of information creates a poverty of attention" (Simon 1971: 40). This collective attention framework is extended by Hodas and Lerman (2013), who find little evidence that the novelty of news stories decays over time (i.e., older stories are just as appealing as newer stories). Instead, they argue that people pay more attention to recent stories because they are easy to find and more visible. This idea is consistent with Nelson (2013), who suggests that the majority of pledges to a crowdfunding campaign come at the beginning and end of a project because projects are most visible then. In an online environment, there are often several website features and sorting options that lower search costs, making projects more visible (Bakos 1997).

In the case of Kickstarter, projects can be sorted based on whether they were "Recently Launched" (the first week after a project's initial launch) or will be "Ending Soon" (the last week before a project's funding closes). Thus, the collective attention argument is that the significant coefficient estimates for the first and last weeks' daily variables in Table 8.2 are due to the use of these sorting options in Kickstarter—potential backers simply support projects that are most visible from using these sorting options. If this were true, however, we would also expect that the positive effects of the first and last weeks will be accentuated when there are more potential backers who can use these options to view the projects. To examine this idea, we incorporate information on daily traffic to Kickstarter over time in our basic econometric model (from Quantcast.com, *KickstarterTraffic* is the number of unique visitors to the Kickstarter website on day *t* in hundred thousands). If visibility is a plausible explanation for the U-shaped pattern of project support, the marginal effects of time in the funding cycle should be increasing as traffic to the website increases. Based on the analyses reported in our extended working paper (Kuppuswamy and Bayus 2015), we find an insignificant trend in project support as Kickstarter traffic increases. Thus, the greater project support observed in the first and last weeks does not seem to be due to higher project visibility associated with the "Recently Launched" and "Ending Soon" sorting options available with Kickstarter.

8.3.2.2 The Role of Family, Friends, and Followers

Even though there are relatively few empirical studies, it is generally acknowledged that financial support from family and friends is an important source of early stage funding for new ventures (Cumming and Johan 2009; Agrawal et al. 2015). Agrawal et al. (2015) empirically show the importance of friends and family investors in the SellaBand crowdfunding community. This is consistent with the general belief among crowdfunding pundits who argue that successful projects create a critical mass of early funding from the people in their close social circles (de Witt 2012; Steinberg 2012).

To explore this idea, we examine the timing of Kickstarter pledges from direct family relatives. Given the anonymous nature of members in the Kickstarter community, we rely on a manual coding of usernames to construct an indicator variable for whether a project was supported by a backer who has the same last name as the project creator. Based on an analysis reported in our extended working paper (Kuppuswamy and Bayus 2015), we find that family members are most likely to support a Kickstarter project in the first week after launch, as well as just before it ends. Further, we find evidence that Kickstarter project creators attract most of their funding by mobilizing their own social network of friends (who are directly known by the project creator) and followers (who indirectly know the project creator from social media connections).

8.3.2.3 The Effects of Social Influence

As noted by several researchers in lending and donation-based settings (Herzenstein et al. 2011; Zhang and Liu 2012; Burtch et al. 2013; Agrawal et al. 2015), an important factor that can influence the behavior of backers in crowdfunding communities is information on others' prior funding decisions. In particular, the level of financial support for each project as well as its timing is publicly visible on most platforms. Figure 8.1 highlights an interesting phenomenon in Kickstarter that involves social influence within the community. Commonly known as the "Kickstarter Effect," as a project nears its goal there can be a flurry of activity that pushes it over its target (Galinsky 2010; Nelson 2013). Matt Haughey, a backer of more than 150 Kickstarter projects, sums it up this way (Steinberg 2012: 149):

> *[O]nce you pass 50 percent of your funding, at any point, you have a 95 percent chance of reaching your goal. ... Only a handful of projects have finished unsuccessfully having reached 85 percent or more of their funding. The people who are at like 60, 70 percent with a week to go, it's gonna be OK!*

Clearly, there is solid empirical support for this notion from the strong U-shaped pattern of project support over the project-funding cycle. While much of the research studying the reasons for goal pursuit has emphasized individuals and their personal goals, this work can be used to understand the motivations for individuals to contribute to the shared goals of a group (Fishbach et al. 2011). When group identification is relatively weak (as in crowdfunding communities with anonymous members), research finds that individuals decide to pursue a shared group goal if they believe the goal is worthwhile (Fishbach et al. 2011). Here, others' prior contributions can positively influence the assessment of goal value. In the case of crowdfunding, whether or not a project is deemed worthy of support depends on how much of the goal has already been pledged. Backers want the project to succeed, and projects closer to their target goal are more likely to reach their funding objective.

Given that a project is considered to be worthwhile, the Kickstarter Effect further suggests an acceleration in funding activity as a project nears its goal. Such an increase in motivation and effort to reach a goal as it is approached has been found in humans and other animals (Liberman and Forster 2008; Toure-Tillery and Fishbach 2011). Rats run faster through a maze as they get closer to food (Hull 1932), people increase their purchases as they approach rewards from loyalty cards (Kivetz et al. 2006), and groups of donors contribute more to charitable campaigns close to reaching their goals (Fishbach et al. 2011; Cryder et al. 2013). More formally, the "goal-gradient" hypothesis is that motivation to reach a goal increases monotonically with proximity to the desired end state (Hull 1932). One key reason for goal-gradient behavior is that the perceived impact of later-stage decisions tends to increase over the course of goal pursuit (Toure-Tillery and Fishbach 2011). For example, the marginal impact of a USD 100 contribution to a project that is halfway toward its goal of USD 1,000 is much less than the marginal impact of the same contribution if this project has already achieved 90 percent of its goal. As discussed by Cryder et al. (2013), perceived impact is an important rationale for prosocial acts like crowdfunding. Even in situations when there are no financial rewards, backers still perceive that later-stage funding decisions close to the goal have more impact and thus they are even more likely to make a donation when the target is in sight.

Based on analyses reported in Kuppuswamy and Bayus (2017), we find strong evidence for the goal-gradient pattern of increasing project support as the target goal is approached. Thus, there does seem to be empirical evidence for positive effects of social influence linked to how much has already been pledged to the project goal.

8.3.2.4 The Role of Project Updates

To reach their crowdfunding goals, industry pundits insist that project creators need to develop and execute an effective campaign that communicates with the media, bloggers, and potential contributors (Steinberg 2012; Dushnitsky and Marom 2013). While comprehensive and detailed information on any marketing efforts external to the Kickstarter community is not available, project creators can communicate with potential backers via project updates. In fact, many experts highly recommend updates as a way to generate visibility and excitement around crowdfunding projects (Budman 2012). Based on an analysis of updates reported in our extended working paper (Kuppuswamy and Bayus 2015), we find that higher levels of project support are positively related to updates.

We also find that updates tend to occur during the early and late stages of a project and that it is difficult to maintain the initial excitement that comes right after project launch. This especially seems to be the case for successfully funded projects—as reported in Table 8.1, successful projects have significantly more updates than unsuccessful projects, and add significantly more backers each day (and during the first and last weeks). In addition, creators tend to use updates more aggressively as their project nears its goal.

8.4 Discussion and Implications

Given the difficulties that new ventures face in attracting financing from traditional sources, many entrepreneurs are directly appealing to the general public for help through large, online communities of consumer-investors. These crowdfunding campaigns typically involve relatively small contributions of many individuals over a fixed time limit (generally a few weeks). The aim of this chapter is relatively modest; we seek to add to our empirical understanding of backer dynamics over the project-funding cycle. The empirical setting for our study is Kickstarter, one of the oldest and largest reward-based crowdfunding communities on the Web. Publicly available information of two years on successfully and unsuccessfully funded projects is used to obtain the following empirical findings.

- Backer support over the project-funding cycle is not uniform. Potential backers are more likely to pledge in the first and last weeks as compared to the middle period of the funding cycle.
- A U-shaped pattern of project support is persistent across crowdfunding projects—including both successfully and unsuccessfully funded projects, those with large and small goals, and projects in different categories like Art, Design, Film and Video, Games, Music, Technology.
- There is a strong deadline effect in which project support tends to increase in the last week of the project-funding cycle.
- Potential backers are less likely to contribute once a project reaches its goal.
- For the full sample of projects, there is evidence supporting the idea of Kickstarter Fatigue in which the number of other active projects on the platform is negatively related to backer support.
- For the full sample of projects, there is no evidence for a Blockbuster Effect in which a project with a lot of backers draws potential contributors away from other projects.

- Most backer contributions do not come in during the first and last weeks because projects are more visible then due to sorting options available on the platform.
- Support from family members tends to occur in the first week and just before the project ends.
- Most of the contributors at any point in the funding cycle are one-time backers that likely come from the creator's own social circle.
- As the end goal is approached, project support monotonically increases. Thus, there is strong and consistent evidence for the Kickstarter Effect in which projects nearing their goal often see a flurry of activity that pushes it over its target.
- Potential backers are influenced by how much of the goal has already been pledged.
- Project support is positively related to updates, and updates are more likely to be posted during the first week and last three days as compared to the middle period of the funding cycle.
- Project creators tend to post updates as their project nears its goal.

These empirical findings significantly extend our understanding of backer dynamics over the project-funding cycle. While all of our findings only apply to the Kickstarter reward-based crowdfunding community, we can make some comparisons with other crowdfunding settings. Our analyses confirm the general results of Agrawal et al. (2015) in a crowdinvesting community regarding the importance of friends and family investors, particularly in the early stages of the funding campaign. At the same time, the vast majority of Kickstarter contributors are one-time backers who only pledge to a single project (most of these backers join the community and pledge on the same day). In contrast, serial backers with prior experience are the primary investors in other forms of crowdfunding (Agrawal et al. 2015). This distribution of backer experience suggests that the project creator's own social network of family, friends, and followers is even more important in reward-based crowdfunding than in crowdinvesting, crowdlending, or donation-based crowdfunding. Further research with appropriate data is needed to map out the details of project backers and their social connections with the project creators.

The effects of social influence from others' prior funding decisions are of great interest in crowdfunding, particularly since the level of financial support and its timing is publicly visible on most platforms. The effects of social influence are found to be positive in crowdinvesting and crowdlending communities (Herzenstein et al. 2011; Zhang and Liu 2012; Agrawal et al. 2015) and negative in a donation-based setting (Burtch et al. 2013). In this chapter, we find strong evidence for positive effects of social influence in reward-based crowdfunding. Because consumer-investors in crowdinvesting and crowdlending expect a financial return on their contributions, the literature on rational herding and information cascades argues that positive herding based on the number of prior contributors signals that a project is of high quality (Devenow and Welch 1996). In this case, herding behavior is a "rational" way for individuals to reduce their own risk in the face of uncertainty about a proposed new idea. For reward-based crowdfunding, we find positive herding based on how much of the project goal has already been pledged by others. We believe that the positive effects of social influence in reward-based crowdfunding involve rational herding that comes from payoff externalities in which a project closer to its goal is more likely to succeed and, thus, a backer expects that their contribution will have more impact if they also support this same project (Devenow and Welch 1996). Cryder et al. (2013) present some empirical results from field and lab experiments that are consistent with this idea. Further research is needed to confirm the individual-level details of perceived impact of contributions near the end of goal completion and whether payoff externalities do indeed explain the observed goal-gradient behavior.

While there are some hints for other crowdfunding platforms that project contributions follow a U-shaped pattern (Ceyhan et al. 2011) and additional contributions are less likely once a project reaches its goal (Herzenstein et al. 2011), further research is needed to firmly establish whether these backer behaviors generalize across settings and projects. For example, Hornuf and Schwienbacher (2017) find that the contribution pattern in crowdinvesting is L-shaped and very little is known about the dynamics associated with different reward-based crowdfunding models (does the entrepreneur keep all of the funds contributed no matter whether the target goal was reached versus the entrepreneur not receiving any of the contributed funds if their target goal is missed; Cumming et al. 2015).[7] Outside of our results not supporting collective attention effects in Kickstarter, little is known about the search costs of potential investors and project visibility due to the sorting options available on other crowdfunding platforms. And, other than our findings regarding the importance of project updates in Kickstarter, not much is known about the possible effects of communications between project creators and their potential contributors in other crowdfunding settings (for an exception, see Block et al. 2017). Additional research can help establish whether any further empirical regularities exist across the various types of crowdfunding communities.

8.4.1 Implications for Entrepreneurs

With very few notable exceptions, the vast majority of creative ideas on Kickstarter involve relatively modest amounts of money (from Table 8.1, the average project has a goal of USD 9900 and successful projects on average receive around USD 3,500). Typically, crowdfunding involves small contributions from many people (from Table 8.1, the average contribution is USD 70 and more than 25 backers support the average project). As emphasized in the "how to crowdfund" books (e.g., de Witt 2012; Steinberg 2012), setting appropriate funding goals is paramount to having a successful project. Many project failures set unreasonable funding targets given the scope of their creative idea (from Table 8.1, the average goal for unsuccessful projects is almost five times the goal for successful projects). In general, projects with large goals are less likely to be funded (Mollick 2014). Our results emphasize the importance of setting appropriate project goals—potential backers make their pledging decision based on how much of the project goal has already been funded by others. In light of these results, entrepreneurs may be tempted to artificially set low goals so as to ensure that their project will achieve its target, at the same time hoping that their project will exceed its low goal. Such a strategy, however, may backfire as potential backers are also much less likely to contribute to a project once it reaches its goal. If the project creator actually requires more funding than their goal to make their creative idea a reality, they may end up with insufficient funds. While the importance of setting goals is usually noted in the various types of crowdfunding communities, further research is needed to test whether goal-gradient behavior generalizes across platforms.

Very few Kickstarter projects achieve at least 50 percent of their goal and are not eventually funded (Fig. 8.1). This suggests that the Kickstarter community is generally sympathetic to an entrepreneur's plea for help: Kickstarter reports an overall success rate of almost 45 percent. At the same time, our econometric results highlight the difficult challenge facing project creators. Inherent to the Kickstarter crowdfunding model is a strong U-shaped pattern of project support over its funding cycle—the initial excitement around a new project is quickly followed by a sharp drop in support and a prominent lull in activity until the last week of the funding cycle. As a result, some entrepreneurs want to allow as much time as possible to raise funds by setting their funding cycle as long as possible. Due to goal-gradient behavior and deadline effects, however, it is difficult if not impossible to overcome this period of low activity between the first and last weeks of the funding cycle. In fact, research finds that project duration is negatively related to funding success (Mollick 2014). Kickstarter also lowered the maximum project duration from 90 to 60 days because they observed that most pledges come in the first and last weeks of the funding cycle, with the length of the middle period not really mattering to eventual project success (Strickler 2011). Even though contributions during the middle period of the funding cycle are generally lower than in the first and last weeks, these pledges are still important for a project to experience the Kickstarter Effect (e.g., see Table 8.1). Further research on the "optimal" project duration might explore these trade-offs.

Because most project supporters in Kickstarter are one-time backers, entrepreneurs must rely on their own social circle of family, friends, and followers. Indeed, project creators need to be proactive by communicating with their social network. We find that project support is positively related to updates at any point in the funding cycle, even though project creators currently tend to only post updates in the first and last weeks of the funding cycle. Clearly, our analysis of project updates is very basic. Data limitations prevent us from considering the potential role of other social and online media in generating buzz around a crowdfunding project. Several guidebooks stress the importance of crafting an online marketing campaign and its importance in generating excitement and project support throughout the funding cycle (de Witt 2012; Steinberg 2012). At this point, however, only anecdotal case studies of success stories and their marketing efforts exist, indicating that further research would be helpful in carefully sorting out the various possible effects and whether the lull in activity between the first and last weeks can be overcome.

8.4.2 Implications for Policy Makers

With the passing of the JOBS Act by the US Congress in 2012, policy makers are persuaded by the potential of crowdfunding to help fund small businesses and entrepreneurs with creative ideas (Stemler 2013). At the same time, however, many pundits have sounded alarms at the potential for fraud associated with unregulated investing behavior, especially by consumer-investors (the "crowd"). Of particular concern is that project creators with unreasonable ideas will still find funding from naive investors due to "irrational" herding behavior (i.e., consumers will simply mimic each other without any regard to project quality). In contrast to this perspective, we find no evidence for irrational herding in the Kickstarter community. Instead, we argue that goal-gradient behavior is an example of rational herding that comes from payoff externalities, that is, others' previous funding decisions signal that a project is likely to succeed and thus a contribution to the same project will have greater impact. Further research is needed to determine if our findings generalize to other financial-based crowdfunding communities.

Another possible fear is that project creators propose projects, receive the funding from consumer-investors, and then never complete the project or deliver the promised rewards. Interestingly, Mollick (2014) concludes that most Kickstarter project creators make serious efforts to fulfill their obligations, but the majority deliver the promised rewards later than expected. Although explicitly disclaimed by Kickstarter, many consumer-investors believe that the website is essentially an online retail storefront in which project creators presell products.

To explore the idea of new product pre-orders and the possible effects of product rewards on backer behavior, we consider a separate model for only Design, Games, and Technology projects—categories that typically offer tangible new products as rewards for contributions (Steinberg 2012; Mollick 2014). Based on analyses reported in our extended working paper (Kuppuswamy and Bayus 2015), we do find that backer behavior in this subsample differs once a project reaches its funding goal—here, the coefficient estimate for *PostFunded* is positive and significant. Thus, there is strong evidence that successfully funded projects in the Design, Games, and Technology categories receive even more contributors before their funding cycle ends. Once a project offering product pre-orders is successfully funded, the risk for other "consumers" is reduced since the project creator will receive all the pledged funds. Although our data do not allow us to determine whether this represents rational or irrational herding behavior, it is interesting to speculate that this herding behavior for successfully funded projects may be responsible for the product rewards delivery delays reported by Mollick (2014). Successfully funded projects offering product pre-orders may actually be suffering from their own success! This will especially be the case for projects that dramatically exceed their original goal. For example, Eric Migicovsky's Pebble E-Paper Watch, one of the largest funded Kickstarter projects, received almost 69,000 backers—well over the 1000 backers expected with their original goal of USD 100,000. While the promised watches were shipped more than three months after the promised delivery date, all of their backers (including the authors) did not receive their watches for several more months.

Additional studies are needed to more completely understand the possible herding behavior of consumer-investors in crowdfunding communities. For example, an obvious recommendation might be to establish a restriction on the number of additional new backers that can support a project once it reaches its goal. Here, the thinking would be that small start-up businesses with limited resources and connections should not be stressed beyond their real capabilities. Such a restriction, however, could also change the dynamics of backer behavior—potential backers may be even more interested in contributing to projects with a lot of past project support because the project (and its product rewards) may not be available once it meets its target. Thus, herding and goal-gradient behaviors may be extreme if project backers are limited. Further research should tackle these topics more deeply by considering backer motivations and behavior in supporting projects that have already reached their goal.

Acknowledgments Comments from participants in research workshops at the University of North Carolina at Chapel Hill, Duke, University of Illinois, University of Utah, DRUID 2013, Emory, HEC Paris, and University of California at Berkeley helped to improve this chapter. We also thank Atul Nerkar, Page Ouimet, Avi Goldfarb, Tarun Kushwaha, Sri Venkataraman, Rich Bettis, Jennifer Conrad, Amin Sayedi, the book co-editors, for helpful comments on an earlier draft.

Notes

1. Shortly after our data collection in March 2012, Kickstarter removed this information from their updated website design.
2. One project had a goal of over USD 21 million (Kickstarter's limit) to help reduce the national debt (http://www.kickstarter.com/projects/2116548608/help-erase-the-national-debt-of-the-usa?ref=search). This project only had eight backers who pledged USD 180.
3. The largest funded project in our sample received a little over USD 95,000. Since our data collection, several projects have received over USD 1 million in funding.
4. An alternate measure involving the number of competing projects in the same category as project *i* gives the same results across all our estimated models as those reported for *ActiveProjects*.
5. The consistent drop in the coefficient estimate for the very last day comes from the fact that projects end at various times during the last day, that is, many projects do not have a complete 24 hours of funding time on the last day.
6. Yan Budman, Director of Marketing at Indiegogo, reports a similar pattern of backer behavior for Indiegogo projects (Budman 2012).
7. Some of our preliminary analyses involving the Kickstarter (all-or-nothing) and Indiegogo (keep-it-all) communities suggest that the goal-gradient effect is robust across platforms.

References

Agrawal, Ajay, Christian Catalini, and Avi Goldfarb. 2015. Crowdfunding: Geography, Social Networks, and the Timing of Investment Decisions. *Journal of Economics and Management Strategy* 24: 253–274.

Allison, Paul D. 2005. *Fixed Effects Regression Methods for Longitudinal Data Using SAS*. Cary, NC: SAS Institute.

Allison, Thomas H., Blakley C. Davis, Jeremy C. Short, and Justin W. Webb. 2015. Crowdfunding in a Prosocial Microlending Environment: Examining the Role of Intrinsic Versus Extrinsic Cues. *Entrepreneurship Theory and Practice* 39: 53–73.

Ariely, Dan, and Itamar Simonson. 2003. Buying, Bidding, Playing, or Competing? Value Assessment and Decision Dynamics in Online Auctions. *Journal of Consumer Psychology* 13: 113–123.

Bakos, J. Yannis. 1997. Reducing Buyer Search Costs: Implications for Electronic Marketplaces. *Management Science* 43: 1676–1692.

Bayus, Barry L. 2013. Crowdsourcing New Product Ideas Over Time: An Analysis of the Dell IdeaStorm Community. *Management Science* 59: 226–244.

Belleflamme, Paul, Thomas Lambert, and Armin Schwienbacher. 2014. Crowdfunding: Tapping the Right Crowd. *Journal of Business Venturing* 29: 585–609.

Block, Jörn, Lars Hornuf, and Alexandra Moritz. 2017. Which Updates During an Equity Crowdfunding Campaign Increase Crowd Participation? *Small Business Economics*. Forthcoming.

Boyle, Katherine. 2013. Yes, Kickstarter Raises More Money for Artists than the NEA. *Washington Post*, July 27. http://www.washingtonpost.com/news/wonkblog/wp/2013/07/07/yes-kickstarter-raises-more-money-for-artists-than-the-nea-heres-why-thats-not-really-surprising/. Accessed 12 Sep 2014.

Budman, Yan. 2012. In a Crowdfunding Campaign, What is the Donation Pattern. *Quora Answer to Question*. http://www.quora.com/Crowdfunding/In-a-crowdfunding-campaign-what-is-the-donation-pattern-Peaks-and-valleys-vs-time-into-the-campaign. Accessed 7 Nov 2013.

Burtch, Gordon, Anindya Ghose, and Sunil Wattal. 2013. An Empirical Examination of the Antecedents and Consequences of Investment Patterns in Crowd-Funded Markets. *Information Systems Research* 24: 499–519.

Cameron, A. Colin, and Pravin K. Trivedi. 2009. *Microeconometrics: Methods and Applications*. New York: Cambridge University Press.

Ceyhan, Simla, Xiaolin Shi, and Jure Leskovec. 2011. Dynamics of Bidding in a P2P Lending Service: Effects of Herding and Predicting Loan Success. In *Proceedings of the 20th International Conference on World Wide Web*: 547–556. http://dl.acm.org/citation.cfm?id=1963483. Accessed 27 Nov 2013.

Colombo, Massimo G., Chiara Franzoni, and Cristina Rossi-Lamastra. 2015. Internal Social Capital and the Attraction of Early Contributions in Crowdfunding Projects. *Entrepreneurship Theory and Practice* 39: 75–100.

Cosh, Andy, Douglas Cumming, and Alan Hughes. 2009. Outside Entrepreneurial Capital. *The Economic Journal* 119: 1494–1533.

Cryder, Cynthia E., George Loewenstein, and Howard Seltman. 2013. Goal Gradient in Helping Behavior. *Journal of Experimental Social Psychology* 49: 1078–1083.

Cumming, Douglas, and Sofia A. Johan. 2009. *Venture Capital and Private Equity Contracting: An International Perspective*. New York: Academic Press.

Cumming, Douglas, Gaël Leboeuf, and Armin Schwienbacher. 2015. Crowdfunding Models: Keep-It-All Versus All-Or-Nothing. *Social Science Research Network*. https://papers.ssrn.com/abstract=2828919. Accessed 28 Feb 2017.

Devenow, Andrea, and Ivo Welch. 1996. Rational Herding in Financial Economics. *European Economic Review* 40: 603–615.

Dushnitsky, Gary, and Dan Marom. 2013. Crowd Monogamy. *Business Strategy Review* 24: 24–26.

Falkinger, Josef. 2008. Limited Attention as a Scarce Resource in Information-Rich Economies. *The Economic Journal* 118: 1596–1620.

Fishbach, Ayelet, Marlone D. Henderson, and Minjung Koo. 2011. Pursuing Goals with Others: Group Identification and Motivation Resulting From Things Done Versus Things Left Undone. *Journal of Experimental Psychology: General* 140: 520–534.

Flood, Alsion. 2012. Kickstarter Becomes the Fourth Biggest Publishers of Graphic Novels. *The Guardian*. http://www.theguardian.com/books/2012/jul/11/kickstarter-fourth-biggest-publisher-graphic-novels. Accessed 12 Sep 2014.

Galinsky, Michael. 2010. The Kickstarter Effect: Fundraising as Game Theory. *International Documentary Association*. http://www.documentary.org/content/kickstarter-effect-fundraising-game-theory. Accessed 7 Oct 2013.

Goninon, Mark. 2013. Is Kickstarter Fatgiue Starting to Kick In? *Choicest Games*, July 24. http://www.choicestgames.com/2013/07/is-kickstarter-fatigue-starting-to-kick.html. Accessed 8 Oct 2013.

Gorbatai, Andrea Daniela, and Laura Nelson. 2015. Gender and the Language of Crowdfunding. *Academy of Management Proceedings* 1: 15785.

Herzenstein, Michal, Uptal M. Dholakia, and Rick L. Andrews. 2011a. Strategic Herding Behaviors in Peer-to-Peer Loan Auctions. *Journal of Interactive Marketing* 25: 27–36.

Herzenstein, Michal, Scott Sonenshein, and Uptal M. Dholakia. 2011b. Tell Me a Good Story and I May Lend You Money: The Role of Narratives in Peer-to-Peer Lending Decisions. *Journal of Marketing Research* 48: 138–149.

Hodas, Nathan O., and Kristina Lerman. 2013. Attention and Visibility in an Information-Rich World. *Second International (ICME) Workshop on Social Multimedia Research* arXiv: 1307.4798 [cs.SI].

Hornuf, Lars, and Armin Schwienbacher. 2017. Market Mechanisms and Funding Dynamics in Equity Crowdfunding. *Journal of Corporate Finance*. http://www.sciencedirect.com/science/article/pii/S0929119916302450. Accessed 20 Feb 2017.

Hull, Clark. 1932. The Goal-Gradient Hypothesis and Maze Learning. *Psychological Review* 39: 25–43.

Kickstarter. 2013. *Blockbuster Effects*. Accessed October 15, 2013. http://www.kickstarter.com/blog/blockbuster-effects

———. 2016. *Kickstarter Stats*. https://www.kickstarter.com/help/stats. Accessed 28 Oct 2016.

Kivetz, Ran, Oleg Urminsky, and Yuhuang Zheng. 2006. The Goal-Gradient Hypothesis Resurrected: Purchase Acceleration, Illusionary Goal Progress, and Customer Retention. *Journal of Marketing Research* 43: 39–58.

Kuppuswamy, Venkat, and Barry L. Bayus. 2015. Crowdfunding Creative Ideas: The Dynamics of Project Backers in Kickstarter, *Social Science Research Network*. http://ssrn.com/abstract=2234765. Accessed 20 Feb 2017.

———. 2017. A Review of Crowdfunding Research and Findings. In *Handbook of New Product Development Research*, ed. P. Golder, and D. Mitra. Northhampton, MA: Edward Elgar.

———. 2017. Does My Contribution to Your Crowdfunding Project Matter? *Journal of Business Venturing* 32: 72–89.

Liberman, Nira, and Jens Forster. 2008. Expectancy, Value and Psychological Distance: A New Look at Goal Gradients. *Social Cognition* 26: 515–533.

Lin, Yan, Wai F. Boh, and Kim H. Goh. 2014. How Different are Crowdfunders? Examining Archetypes of Crowdfunders and Their Choice of Projects. *Academy of Management Proceedings*. http://proceedings.aom.org/content/2014/1/13309.short. Accessed 4 Jan 2016.

Marom, Dan, Alicia Robb, and Orly Sade. 2015. Gender Dynamics in Crowdfunding (Kickstarter): Evidence on Entrepreneurs, Investors, Deals and Taste Based Discrimination. *Social Science Research Network*. http://ssrn.com/abstract=2442954. Accessed 20 Feb 2017.

Maxwell, Brian. 2013. Kickstarter Fatigue a Myth, Says Richard Garriott. http://www.edge-online.com/news/kickstarter-fatigue-a-myth-says-richard-garriott/. Accessed 10 Oct 2013.

Mollick, Ethan. 2014. The Dynamics of Crowdfunding: An Exploratory Study. *Journal of Business Venturing* 29: 1–16.

Mollick, Ethan, and Ramanda Nanda. 2016. Wisdom or Madness? Comparing Crowds with Expert Evaluation in Funding the Arts. *Management Science* 62: 1533–1553.

Moritz, Alexandra, and Jörn Block. 2016. Crowdfunding: A Literature Review and Research Directions. In *Crowdfunding in Europe: State of the Art in Theory and Practice*, ed. D. Bruntje and O. Gajda, 25–53. Cham: Springer International Publishing.

Nelson, S.. 2013. The Kickstarter Effect (Or How I Learned to Stop Worrying and Love Crowdfunding). *Kickstarteradventure*. http://www.kickstartadventure.com/home/the-kickstarter-effect-or-how-i-learned-to-stop-worrying-and-love-crowdfunding/. Accessed 7 Oct 2013.

Pope, Devin G., and Justin R. Sydnor. 2011. What's in a Picture? Evidence of Discrimination from Prosper.com. *Journal of Human Resources* 46: 53–92.

Qiu, Calvin. 2013. Issues in Crowdfunding: Theoretical and Empirical Investigation on Kickstarter. *Social Science Research Network*. http://ssrn.com/abstract=2345872. Accessed 20 Feb 2017.

Schwienbacher, Armin, and Benjamin Larralde. "Crowdfunding of Entrepreneurial Ventures." In *The Oxford Handbook of Entrepreneurial Finance*, by D. Cumming (ed.), 369-391. Oxford: Oxford University Press, 2012.

Simon, Herbert. 1971. Designing Organizations for an Information-Rich World. In *Computers, Communications, and the Public Interest*, ed. M. Greenberger, 38–52. John Hopkin: Baltimore.

Smith, Sarah, Frank Windmeijer, and Edmund Wright. 2014. Peer Effects in Charitable Giving: Evidence from the (Running) Field. *The Economic Journal* 125: 1053–1071.

Steinberg, Don. 2012. *The Kickstarter Handbook*. Philadelphia, PA: Quirk Books.

Stemler, Abbey R. 2013. The JOBS Act and Crowdfunding: Harnessing the Power—and Money—of the Masses. *Business Horizons* 56: 271–275.

Strickler, Yancey. 2011. Shortening the Maximum Project Length. *Kickstarter*, June 17. http://www.kickstarter.com/blog/shortening-the-maximum-project-length. Accessed 17 Oct 2013.

Toure-Tillery, Maferima, and Ayelet Fishbach. 2011. The Course of Motivation. *Journal of Consumer Psychology* 21: 414–423.

Vismara, Silvio. 2015. Information Cascades Among Investors in Equity Crowdfunding. *Social Science Research Network*. https://ssrn.com/abstract=2589619. Accessed 20 Feb 2017.

Webb, Eugene, and Karl E. Weick. 1979. Unobtrusive Measures in Organizational Theory: A Reminder. *Administrative Science Quarterly* 24: 650–659.

de Witt, Nelson. 2012. A Kickstarter's Guide to Kickstarter. *Kickstarterguide*. http://kickstarterguide.com/files/2012/07/A-Kickstarters-Guide.pdf. Accessed 15 Nov 2012.

Wooldridge, Jeffrey M. 1999. Distribution-Free Estimation of Some Nonlinear Panel Data Models. *Journal of Econometrics* 90: 77–97.

Wu, Fang, and Bernardo A. Huberman. 2007. Novelty and Collective Attention. *Proceedings of the National Academy of Sciences* 104: 17599–17601.

Zhang, Juanjuan, and Peng Liu. 2012. Rational Herding in Microloan Markets. *Management Science* 58: 892–912.

Zheng, Haichao, Dahui Li, Jing Wu, and Xu. Yun. 2014. The Role of Multidimensional Social Capital in Crowdfunding: A Comparative Study in China and US. *Information and Management* 51: 488–496.

Venkat Kuppuswamy is Assistant Professor of Strategy & Entrepreneurship at the University of North Carolina at Chapel Hill and a board member of NCGrowth at the Kenan Institute of Private Enterprise. His research has appeared in prestigious scholarly journals in addition to popular press outlets, such as *The Atlantic*, *Forbes*, *Washington Post*, *Huffington Post*, and *National Public Radio (NPR)*. His research focuses on understanding when and why the crowd contributes to crowdfunding campaigns, as well as the benefits of crowdfunding campaigns for entrepreneurs. More recently, he has explored whether crowdfunding truly represents a discrimination-free platform for minority entrepreneurs to raise capital.

Barry L. Bayus is the Roy O. Rodwell Distinguished Professor of Marketing at the Kenan-Flagler Business School, University of North Carolina. His current research focuses on crowdsourcing and crowdfunding innovative ideas, as well as design thinking. He is part of a National Institutes of Health (NIH)-sponsored research team studying the effectiveness of crowdsourced health messages. Bayus has written over 50 research papers in academic and business journals. The *Journal of Product Innovation Management* cited him as one of the world's top five scholars in innovation management (2007 and 2012) and *Management Science* named him as one of the top researchers in the field of innovation (2004).

Part IV

Recent Regulatory Efforts

9

The Regulation of Crowdfunding in the United States

C. Steven Bradford

9.1 Introduction

The regulation of crowdinvesting involves a trade-off between small business capital formation and investor protection. Offerings of securities in the United States, including both equity and debt securities, must ordinarily be registered with the Securities and Exchange Commission (SEC). This registration process involves extensive mandatory disclosure and complicated limits on the offer and sale of the securities. These requirements, designed to protect investors, are too expensive for the small capital offerings typically attracted to crowdinvesting.

The registration requirements do not apply to donation- and reward-based crowdfunding, and these types of crowdfunding have been very popular in the United States. But sales of equity through crowdinvesting and sales of debt securities through crowdlending are subject to the SEC registration requirements; because of the high cost of registration,

C. Steven Bradford (✉)
University of Nebraska-Lincoln College of Law, Lincoln, NE, USA

D. Cumming, L. Hornuf (eds.), *The Economics of Crowdfunding*,
https://doi.org/10.1007/978-3-319-66119-3_9

these types of offerings can succeed in the United States only if they are exempted from these requirements.

Four different exemptions are available for crowdinvesting in the United States. Two of these exemptions—federal Rules 506(b) and 506(c)—limit sales to sophisticated or wealthy investors, and therefore are probably not accurately described as crowdinvesting exemptions. They do not allow sales to the "crowd" of public investors. However, Regulation Crowdfunding, finalized by the SEC in 2015 to implement an exemption in section 4(a)(6) of the Securities Act, is specifically aimed at retail crowdinvesting by the general public. In addition, many US states have adopted state crowdfunding exemptions that allow debt and equity offerings limited to the residents of a particular state. These state exemptions are coordinated with a federal intrastate offering exemption, so, like the other exemptions discussed, they provide a coordinated exemption from both federal and state securities law.

There are three different groups involved in crowdinvesting, and thus three different possible loci for any crowdinvesting regulation: the issuers who sell securities to raise capital; the intermediaries who operate the platforms through which these securities are sold; and the investors buying the securities. The Rules 506(b) and 506(c) exemptions focus their regulation almost exclusively on investors, limiting who may invest. The policy idea is to limit investment to those who can protect themselves and therefore do not need mandatory disclosure or other regulation. The absence of other significant restrictions reduces the regulatory cost, but it is not clear that the basic premise of these rules is sound. Many of the investors who qualify for these offerings are not sophisticated investors.

Regulation Crowdfunding and the state exemptions broadly regulate all three groups, imposing substantial regulatory requirements on issuers, intermediaries, and investors. The investor protection motive underlying these extensive regulatory requirements may be admirable, but the cost may be too high for many small business offerings. It is not clear that any of the US exemptions has found the appropriate balance between capital formation and investor protection.

This chapter discusses the various exemptions available for crowdfunding and the policy underlying them. Section 9.2 briefly describes the US registration requirement, its scope, and the problem it poses for crowdfunding. Section 9.3 discusses the Rule 506(b) and 506(c) exemptions. Section 9.4 discusses the crowdfunding exemption in section 4(a)(6) of the Securities Act, and Regulation Crowdfunding adopted to implement it. Section 9.5 discusses the intrastate crowdfunding exemptions. Section 9.6 provides a brief comment on the scope of these exemptions.

9.2 Applicable Regulation in the Absence of a Crowdfunding-Specific Exemption

9.2.1 The Registration and Prospectus Requirements

In the United States, companies selling securities must register their offerings with the SEC unless an exemption is available.[1] The offering company must file an extensive disclosure document known as a registration statement with the SEC and must provide most of that disclosure to investors in a document known as the prospectus. There are also complicated limits on communications with potential investors, including posting on websites, before and during the offering.

The registration process for first-time registrants often takes months (SEC 1996, 88,439; Cohn and Yadley 2007, 7), and the direct cost to prepare and file the registration statement—including legal fees, accounting fees, registration fees, and printing costs—can be hundreds of thousands of dollars (U.S. Government Accountability Office 2000, 23; Prifti 2010, § 1A-17; Sjostrom 2001, 575–576). This cost is simply too high for the smaller amounts entrepreneurial capital start-ups and other small businesses want to raise through crowdinvesting and crowdlending. Because of economies of scale, registration expenses that might be manageable for large offerings are not feasible for smaller offerings (Bradford 2001, 25–27). And the United States, unlike some countries, has no general exemption for smaller offerings.

Registration, however, is not impossible. Two US crowdlending sites, Prosper and Lending Club, register the notes they offer, but they had to completely restructure their business models to make it work (Bradford 2012a, 43–44). The model they use would not work for crowdinvesting.

9.2.2 What Is a Security?

The US registration requirement applies only when a company is selling "securities." The definition of "security" in section 2(a)(1) of the Securities Act[2] is a little vague, but it is reasonably clear that certain kinds of crowdfunding do not involve securities for purposes of federal law.

Donation- and reward-based crowdfunding, including pre-purchases, do not involve the sale of securities (Bradford 2012a, 31–32). Therefore, federal securities law, including the registration requirement, does not apply to them. Donation- and reward-based crowdfunding are essentially unregulated, except for the prohibitions on fraud and false advertising that would apply to any commercial transaction. Neither the federal government nor the states have imposed any special regulation on non-securities crowdfunding.

Crowdlending probably involves a security, and therefore is subject to US securities regulation, unless, as on the Kiva website, lenders do not receive interest. If lenders are entitled only to a return of their principal, with no interest, a security is probably not involved (Bradford 2012a, 34–42). Crowdinvesting, where investors receive equity in the company or any participation in the company's profits, almost certainly involves the sale of a security (Bradford 2012a, 33–34).

9.3 Accredited Investor Crowdfunding

Two US exemptions allow unregistered Internet offerings limited to "accredited investors," or, in the case of one of the exemptions, also sophisticated investors who are not accredited investors. One of these exemptions, Securities Act Rule 506(b),[3] has been in place for many years. The other, Rule 506(c),[4] was added by the SEC in 2013 in response to Congressional direction in the ambitiously titled Jumpstart Our Business Startups (JOBS) Act.[5]

The term "accredited investor" is defined to include, among others, institutional investors such as banks, brokers, insurance companies, professionally directed employee benefit plans, and, more generally, any business entity with more than USD 5 million in assets.[6] But it also includes individual investors with either (1) a net worth of at least USD 1 million (excluding the value of their home and related mortgage indebtedness up to the value of the home)[7] or (2) an annual income of more than USD 200,000 (or joint income with a spouse of at least USD 300,000).[8]

The argument for exempting offers to sophisticated investors such as brokers and insurance companies is apparent: these investors can fend for themselves and do not need the regulatory protection that registration provides.[9] The extension of this argument to wealthy, unsophisticated investors is more controversial. Wealth is a very imperfect proxy for investor sophistication; the person who wins USD 5 million in a lottery, for example, may know absolutely nothing about investing. One might argue that wealthy people can afford to lose the money they are investing, and do not need as much protection for that reason. But the wealth and income levels necessary to qualify as an accredited investor are relatively low; many of these people do not have money to burn. In addition, there are no limits on how much of their wealth accredited investors may invest. An investor who has a net worth of USD 1 million and invests the entire USD 1 million in a single offering certainly cannot afford to lose that money. There has been some discussion at the SEC about restructuring the definition of accredited investor or limiting how much accredited investors may invest (SEC 2015c), but the SEC has not yet taken any action on these proposals.

Because of the limits on who may purchase, securities cannot be sold to the general public in Rule 506(b) and 506(c) offerings. Since the issuer is not selling to the "crowd," it is probably inappropriate to call these offerings crowdinvesting or crowdfunding. But these terms have been applied to Rule 506 offerings, and therefore these offerings are discussed here.

Rule 506(b) and Rule 506(c) share some common requirements. First, they contain so-called bad actor disqualifications barring issuers from using the exemption if they or certain related persons have been found to have engaged in various types of wrongdoing in the past.[10] The theory is that companies and individuals who have been involved in past wrongdoing are more likely to engage in similar behavior now; barring them helps to protect investors in the current offering. There are no other limits on the companies that may use the Rule 506(b) and 506(c) exemptions; any company not barred by the "bad actor" disqualifications is eligible.

The two exemptions also share resale restrictions. Securities acquired in a Rule 506(b) or (c) offering may not be resold without registration or an exemption for the resale.[11] The most commonly applicable resale exemption in the United States would allow resale after a 6- or 12-month holding period.[12]

9.3.1 The Rule 506(b) Exemption

To qualify for the Rule 506(b) exemption, sales must be made only to accredited investors or up to 35 non-accredited investors who satisfy a sophistication requirement.[13] Each *non-accredited* investor must "either alone or with his purchaser representative(s) … [have] … such knowledge and experience in financial and business matters that he is capable of evaluating the merits and risks of the prospective investment."[14] Accredited investors are not required to meet this standard. Even if a particular purchaser does not fall within one of these two categories, the issuer's exemption is still protected as long as the issuer reasonably believed the purchaser qualified.[15]

Otherwise, Rule 506(b) offerings are lightly regulated. Rule 506(b) does not limit either the size of the offering or the amount each investor may invest. The issuer is not required to use an intermediary and, if it does sell through an intermediary, Rule 506(b) imposes almost no requirements on that intermediary. However, if an intermediary is involved, depending on how the intermediary operates, there is a risk that it could be a securities broker or investment adviser, and in violation of federal securities law if it is not registered as such (Bradford 2012a, 51–80).

No mandatory disclosure is required if the issuer sells only to accredited investors. If, however, the issuer also sells to non-accredited, sophisticated investors, it must furnish those investors with detailed information about the issuer, including financial statements.[16] The balance sheet must generally be audited and, in larger offerings, the issuer's other financial statements must also be audited.[17] Because of that and because of the uncertainty of the sophistication standard, Rule 506(b) offerings are typically limited to accredited investors only (Ivanov and Bauguess 2012, 6).

The biggest problem with using Rule 506(b) for crowdinvesting is that the rule prohibits "any form of general solicitation or general advertising," including "[a]ny advertisement, article, notice or other communication, published in any newspaper, magazine, or similar media or broadcast over television or radio."[18] The SEC staff has read this broadly to prohibit any offers to investors with whom the issuer or its sales agents do not have a preexisting relationship (Sjostrom 2004, 13).

This interpretation has two important implications for crowdinvesting. First, although Rule 506(b) does not require the use of an intermediary, an issuer using an intermediary can take advantage of the intermediary's customer base—the intermediary already has a preexisting relationship with those investors. Second, the staff interpretation effectively prohibits putting information about an offering on a website accessible to the general public because the posting would reach investors with whom the issuer and its intermediary have no preexisting relationship (SEC 2000, 25,851–25,852). The issuer could sell through a website, but the offering materials would have to be placed behind a gateway through which only investors with a preexisting relationship could pass.

However, SEC staff interpretations make the general solicitation restriction slightly less draconian and slightly more amenable to crowdinvesting. The SEC staff has allowed intermediary brokers to solicit potential investors publicly, qualify them as eligible for Rule 506(b) offerings, and then allow them access to Rule 506(b) offerings—but only to offerings that postdate their initial solicitation.[19] This interpretation allows Rule 506(b) to be used for what some people call "crowdfunding," but it is crowdfunding in a very limited sense. Public websites advertise for investors without mentioning any specific offering, and offering materials appear behind a firewall that only accredited or sophisticated investors are allowed through.

9.3.2 The Rule 506(c) Exemption

Rule 506(c) is much more amenable to crowdinvesting than Rule 506(b). General solicitation and advertising are allowed, so the offering may be posted on a publicly accessible website. However, actual sales are limited to accredited investors, and Rule 506(c) enforces this requirement a little more stringently than Rule 506(b). The issuer must "take reasonable steps to verify that purchasers ... are accredited investors."[20] If it does not do so, the exemption is lost, even if it turns out that all of the investors actually were accredited. Rule 506(c) does not mandate any particular steps to verify accredited investor status, but it does provide some non-exclusive alternatives, such as looking at tax forms to verify income.[21]

These are the only significant limitations in Rule 506(c). There are no mandatory disclosure requirements, limits on the size of the offering or the amount each investor may invest, or restrictions on the web portal hosting the offering. As with Rule 506(b), the issuer is not even required to use an intermediary. It could post the offering on its own website.

9.4 Section 4(a)(6) and Regulation Crowdfunding

The Section 4(a)(6) crowdfunding exemption was added to the Securities Act by the JOBS Act in 2012.[22] However, the SEC did not adopt the required implementing regulations, known as Regulation Crowdfunding, until November 2015; these regulations became effective on May 16, 2016 (SEC 2015b). The statutory requirements of the crowdfunding exemption lie primarily in sections 4(a)(6) and 4A of the Securities Act.[23] Regulation Crowdfunding incorporates these requirements and adds additional ones.[24] For convenience, I will refer to the exemption as the section 4(a)(6) exemption, even though one must look to the regulation to see the full set of requirements.

The section 4(a)(6) exemption, unlike the Rule 506(b) and 506(c) exemptions, is designed for and limited to crowdfunded securities offerings. Section 4(a)(6) is also much more regulatory than those other exemptions, imposing significant restrictions on all three groups involved in crowdinvesting: the issuers selling securities; the intermediaries through whom the securities are sold; and the investors purchasing the securities. Section 4(a)(6) also imposes structural requirements on the offerings themselves.

Section 4(a)(6) offerings are open to the general public, and many of these requirements are designed to protect unsophisticated investors. But the cost to comply with these regulatory requirements, although less than the cost of registration, is significant. Crowdfunding regulation requires a careful balancing of cost and investor protection, and the section 4(a)(6) exemption may have tilted too far to the investor protection side. Hence, many small business issuers may find section 4(a)(6) too expensive, and it is unlikely to be the capital formation panacea many of its supporters hoped for.

9.4.1 Restrictions on Investors

Section 4(a)(6) offerings are open to the general public. Anyone—from the most sophisticated institutional investor to the financially illiterate—may invest in a section 4(a)(6) offering. But section 4(a)(6) restricts investors in other ways. The amount they may invest in crowdfunded offerings is limited; they must be provided with "investor education"; and there are restrictions on the resale of the securities they purchase.

9.4.1.1 Investment Limits

Section 4(a)(6) limits how much each investor may invest; the limit depends on each investor's net worth and annual income, and there are special rules for calculating these.[25] Net worth may be calculated jointly with the investor's spouse, as long as the aggregate investment of the two does not exceed the limits that would apply to the two of them individually.[26] Generally, the investor's principal residence, and related mortgage indebtedness up to the value of that residence, is excluded from the net worth calculation.[27]

If the investor's annual income and net worth each exceed USD 100,000, the investor's investment limit is 10 percent of annual income or net worth, whichever is less. If not, then the limit is 5 percent of annual income or net worth, whichever is less. However, there is a USD 2000 minimum and a USD 100,000 maximum. Every investor may invest USD 2000, no matter how small their annual income and net worth. And no one may invest more than USD 100,000, no matter how great their annual income and net worth.

These are annual investment limits; an investor may not exceed his or her limit in any 12-month period. But there are no limits on the total investment in his or her portfolio. For example, an investor whose limit is USD 7000 could invest USD 7000 now and an additional USD 7000 12 months later, even if he or she still owns the prior investment.

However, the limits are applied collectively to all section 4(a)(6) investments, not just on a per-offering basis. The total amount an investor invests annually in *all* section 4(a)(6) offerings cannot exceed the investor's limit. Assume again that the investor's limit is USD 7000. If the investor, in a single 12-month period, invests in section 4(a)(6) offerings by issuers A, B, and C, the total of the investments in A, B, and C may not exceed USD 7000.

The intermediary must disclose these limits to the investor when the investor opens an account.[28] The intermediary is also required to enforce these limits at the time of any investment. Before accepting any investment commitment, the intermediary must "have a reasonable basis for believing that the investor satisfies … [these] … limitations."[29] The intermediary usually will not know what amounts the investor has invested through other intermediaries, of course. But the intermediary is allowed to rely on the investor's representations as to annual income, net worth, and the amount of the investor's other section 4(a)(6) investments unless the intermediary has some reason to question those representations.[30] Therefore, the intermediary's burden is nominal.

The policy argument for these investment limits is straightforward. They limit each investor's risk so that, even if the investor loses the entire amount invested, the loss will be less than catastrophic. Of course, even a USD 2000 loss will be catastrophic to many poorer investors, and it is not clear whether more sophisticated investors need this paternalistic protection. Moreover, investors can easily circumvent these limits by lying about their net worth or annual income. Hence, the limits might not be very effective.

9.4.1.2 Investor "Education" Requirements

The crowdfunding regulation also includes a series of "education" requirements, but these are really only glorified risk disclosure. To invest in an offering pursuant to the crowdfunding exemption, investors must open an account with the intermediary. When an investor opens such an account, the intermediary must provide materials that explain various aspects of crowdinvesting to the investor "in plain language."[31] These educational materials must disclose the following:

- how the section 4(a)(6) process works and the risks associated with section 4(a)(6) crowdfunding;
- the types of securities offered on the intermediary's platform and the risks associated with each type of security, including the risk of dilution in voting power;
- the restrictions on the resale of securities purchased in section 4(a)(6) offerings;
- the types of information the issuer is required to provide, including annual reports, and the possibility that these disclosure obligations might terminate in the future, leaving the investor without current financial information about the issuer;
- the limits on how much investors may invest;
- the rules regarding cancellation of an investment commitment, either by the investor or by the issuer;
- the need for the investor to consider whether the investment is appropriate for the investor; and
- the fact that the relationship between the issuer and the intermediary might terminate after the offering.

The intermediary must keep this disclosure posted on its platform at all times, and, if it materially revises this disclosure, it must make the revisions available to all investors before accepting any additional investment commitments.[32]

In addition, each time before an investor invests in an offering, the intermediary must obtain a representation from the investor that the investor has reviewed this educational material, understands that his or her entire investment may be lost, and can bear the loss.[33] The intermediary must also, again each time before an investor invests, require the investor to complete a questionnaire that shows the investor understands that

- the investor's ability to cancel an investment commitment and get his or her money back is limited;
- it may be difficult for the investor to resell the securities;
- the investment is risky and the investor should not invest unless he or she can afford to lose the entire amount invested.[34]

It is unlikely that these requirements will result in any serious education of investors. The regulation does not mandate the format or wording of the required questionnaire, so intermediaries may just ask leading questions directing investors to the required response. The rest of the "education" requirement is essentially just a risk disclosure document. None of this will make unsophisticated investors sophisticated, but it will at least expose them to warnings about the risks of investing in these offerings. Whether they will benefit from such an exposure is a separate question.

9.4.1.3 Restrictions on Resale

Investors who purchase securities in a section 4(a)(6) offering generally may not resell or otherwise transfer these securities for one year.[35] However, there are a number of exceptions. The securities may be transferred within the one-year holding period (1) to the issuer; (2) to any accredited investor; (3) to anyone, in a registered offering; (4) to a family member, broadly defined; (5) to a trust controlled by the transferor or created for the benefit of a family member; or (6) in connection with the transferor's death, divorce, or similar circumstances.[36]

Resale restrictions such as these are commonly applied to exempted offerings in the United States (Campbell 1995, 1331–1384). But, in this case, they seem counterproductive, hurting investors rather than protecting them in any way. The resale restrictions make these small business investments even less liquid than they already are, with one additional risk—the risk of illiquidity—added to what is already a very risky investment.

9.4.2 Restrictions on Issuers

Section 4(a)(6) limits the companies that may use the exemption and the amount of money these companies may raise. It also imposes significant disclosure requirements on these issuers. Issuers must provide extensive disclosure, including in some cases audited or certified financial statements, to potential investors and to the SEC at the time of the offering. In addition, issuers who successfully complete a section 4(a)(6) offering must subsequently file annual reports that include audited or certified financial statements. These disclosure requirements may prove too costly for many of these small offerings, reducing the usefulness of the section 4(a)(6) exemption.

9.4.2.1 Who May Use the Exemption

There are a number of limits on the issuers that may use the crowdfunding exemption. The issuer must be incorporated or organized under US law.[37] It cannot be a public company already subject to the reporting requirements of the Securities Exchange Act of 1934,[38] and certain other types of companies are also excluded.[39]

Finally, the crowdfunding rules contain an extensive list of what are known as "bad actor" disqualifications. The exemption is not available if the issuer, or specified parties related to the issuer, have been found to have engaged in any of a long list of violations in the past.[40] These disqualifications apply to the issuer; any predecessor or affiliated issuer; any director, officer, general partner, or managing member of the issuer; anyone who beneficially owns at least 20 percent of the issuer's voting securities; any promoter connected with the issuer; any person who will be compensated for soliciting purchasers in the offering; or any general partner, director, officer, or managing member of any such solicitor.[41] The policy basis for these "bad actor" disqualifications is obvious: one of the best ways to protect investors is to exclude past violators.

9.4.2.2 Offering Amount

The total amount of securities sold by the issuer pursuant to the crowdfunding exemption cannot exceed USD 1 million in any 12-month period.[42] There is no cumulative limit; nothing would keep the issuer from using the crowdfunding exemption to sell securities again and again, as long as the amount raised in any 12-month period never exceeds USD 1 million.

9.4.2.3 Disclosure Requirements

The crowdfunding exemption imposes disclosure obligations on issuers at two points: (1) when the issuer makes the offering; and (2) on an annual basis after the offering is successfully completed. There is no general obligation to promptly disclose material information at other times. US securities law does not ordinarily impose such a duty and the crowdfunding exemption does not create any special duty of this sort just for crowdfunding issuers.

Some of the crowdfunding exemption's disclosure requirements are complicated; a lawyer will probably be necessary to avoid violations. Preparing and verifying this information will significantly add to the cost of using the exemption.

Offering-Related Disclosure

The issuer must provide detailed disclosure about the company, the securities being offered, and the offering process. If, during the course of the offering, the issuer makes any material changes to its disclosure or the terms of its offering, it must notify all investors who have already committed to invest.[43] All investment commitments are automatically canceled unless the investor reconfirms the commitment within five business days after the notice.[44] If a material change occurs within five business days of the end of the offering, the offering deadline must be extended to allow investors the full five business days.[45]

Information About the Issuer

The issuer must provide detailed disclosure about itself and its principals, including:

- Its name, legal status (including its form of organization, jurisdiction in which it is organized, and date of organization), physical address, and web site[46]
- How many employees it has[47]
- A description of its business and its anticipated business plan[48]
- The names of its directors and officers, all the positions those people hold with the company, and when they have served in those positions[49]
- The business experience of its directors and officers in the last three years, including details on their employment by other companies[50]
- The name of each person who is a beneficial owner of equity securities holding 20 percent or more of the voting power, and the ownership level of each such person[51]
- A description of recent transactions or proposed transactions with various related parties (including officers, directors, and 20 percent equity owners) that exceed 5 percent of the amount raised under the crowdfunding exemption[52]
- A description of the issuer's ownership and capital structure, including
  - the terms of the securities being offering and every other class of securities, including how the rights of the securities being offered might be limited or diluted by the rights of other classes[53]
  - how the securities being offered are being valued and how they might be valued by the issuer in the future[54]
  - the risks to purchasers of minority ownership and the risks associated with corporate actions the issuer might take in the future[55]

  - the restrictions on transfer of the securities[56] and
  - a description of how the exercise of rights held by the principal shareholders could affect the purchasers of the securities being offered[57]

- A discussion of the material factors that make an investment in the issuer speculative or risky[58]
- The material terms of any indebtedness of the issuer, including the amount of the indebtedness, interest rates, and maturity dates[59]
- A description of any exempt securities offerings the issuer has conducted within the past three years[60]
- Any matters that would have disqualified the issuer from using the exemption, but which occurred before the effective date of the exemption[61]
- Where on the issuer's website investors will be able to find the annual report required by the exemption (discussed later) and when that report will be available[62]
- Whether the issuer or its predecessors previously failed to comply with the annual reporting requirement of the exemption[63]

Financial Information

The issuer is required to discuss its financial condition, including, to the extent material, its liquidity, capital resources, and historical results of operations.[64] Some of this discussion is clearly intended to be forward-looking. If the issuer has no operating history, its discussion must focus on "financial milestones and operational, liquidity and other challenges."[65] If it has an operating history, it should focus on "whether historical results and cash flows are representative of what investors should expect in the future."[66] The discussion must include how the proceeds from the offering will affect liquidity and other available sources of capital.[67]

The amount of additional financial disclosure required depends on the target amount of the offering.[68]

- *USD 100,000 or less.* If the target amount is USD 100,000 or less, the issuer must disclose the total income, taxable income, and total tax reported on its most recent federal income tax returns. The chief executive officer (CEO) must certify the accuracy of these figures. However, if certified or audited financial statements are available, the issuer must provide those instead.

- *USD 100,000–USD 500,000.* If the target amount is more than USD 100,000 but not more than USD 500,000, the issuer must furnish financial statements reviewed by an independent public accountant. However, if audited financial statements are available, the issuer must provide those instead.
- *More than USD 500,000.* If the target amount of the offering is more than USD 500,000, the issuer must furnish audited financial statements, unless this is its first section 4(a)(6) offering. In that case, financial statements reviewed by an independent public accountant are sufficient (unless it already has audited financial statements available).

Information About the Offering

The issuer must also include detailed disclosure about the offering and the offering process:

- The purpose and intended use of the offering proceeds[69]
- The offering price, or the method of determining the price[70]
- The name and identification of the intermediary through which the offering is being conducted[71]
- A description of the intermediary's financial interest in the offering, including the compensation the intermediary is to receive, and any financial interest the intermediary has, or is expected to acquire, in the issuer[72]
- The target amount of the offering and the deadline to reach that target[73]
- Whether the issuer will accept investments in excess of the target amount and, if so, how much and how any oversubscriptions will be allocated[74]
- A description of the offering process, including how and when investors can cancel investment commitments[75]
- A statement that, if an investor does not reconfirm his or her commitment after a material change to the offering, the commitment will be canceled[76]

The issuer must also post updates on its progress in meeting the target offering amount.[77] At a minimum, it must disclose when it reaches 50 percent of its target offering amount and when it reaches 100 percent of its target offering amount.[78] If it sells more than its target amount, it must within five business days of the offering deadline disclose the total amount of securities it sold.[79]

Catch-All Disclosure Provision

The disclosure requirements also include a catch-all provision requiring disclosure of any additional material information necessary to keep the statements made in the issuer's disclosure from being misleading.[80]

Annual Reports

Issuers which have successfully sold securities using the section 4(a)(6) exemption are required to provide subsequent annual reports. These annual reports must be filed with the SEC no later than 120 days after the end of the issuer's fiscal year, and must be posted on the issuer's website, but they are not required to be provided directly to investors.[81]

If the issuer has available financial statements that have been reviewed or audited by an independent public accountant, these financial statements must be included in the annual report. If not, the issuer must provide financial statements that its CEO certifies are true and complete in all material respects.[82] These annual reports must also include much of the disclosure that was required at the time of the offering, except for the disclosures related to the offering and the offering process.[83]

The issuer's annual reporting obligation generally continues until it becomes a reporting company required to file reports under the Securities Exchange Act; it (or someone else) repurchases all of the securities it sold pursuant to the crowdfunding exemption; or it liquidates or dissolves its business.[84] There are also two size-based exceptions to the annual reporting requirement. The issuer no longer has to provide annual reports if (1) after it has filed at least one annual report, it has fewer than 300 record shareholders[85]; or (2) if it has filed annual reports for the past three years and has total assets of less than USD 10 million.[86]

9.4.3 Restrictions on Intermediaries and the Manner of the Offering

One way that section 4(a)(6) attempts to protect investors is to require that offerings be conducted through a neutral intermediary, which has an enforcement role. Section 4(a)(6) also imposes requirements on the conduct of the offerings on the intermediary's platform.

9.4.3.1 The Intermediary Requirement

The offering must be conducted through a web platform operated by a registered securities broker or a registered funding portal.[87] Funding portals are a new type of regulated entity limited to operating section 4(a)(6) crowdfunding platforms; they may not engage in many of the other activities that ordinary securities brokers engage in.[88]

Neither the intermediary nor its directors, officers, or partners may have any financial interest in the issuer.[89] This requirement is designed to protect investors from conflicts of interests that might arise if the intermediary had a financial stake in the outcome of the offering (SEC 2013, 66,461). The intermediary may, however, receive some of the same securities being sold on the platform as compensation for its services.[90] The intermediary must disclose to investors establishing accounts on its platform how it is being compensated.[91]

9.4.3.2 Off-Platform Activities

The issuer must sell the crowdfunded securities through the crowdfunding platform. The issuer and its representatives may not even advertise the offering off-platform.[92] Nor may the issuer compensate anyone else for promoting an offering off the intermediary's platform.[93] The issuer may, however, publish a brief notice that directs investors to the intermediary's platform and contains limited information about the issuer and the offering, including the type and amount of securities being offered, the price, and the closing date.[94]

9.4.3.3 Communications Channels

The crowdfunding regulation requires the intermediary to establish communications channels on its platform that allow potential investors to communicate with the issuer, and with each other, about the offering.[95] These communications channels must be publicly accessible, but only investors who have opened an account with the intermediary may post comments.[96] The issuer and persons acting on its behalf may post comments, but only if they disclose their affiliation in each such communication.[97] The issuer may compensate people to promote its offering on the intermediary's communications channels, but only if it takes reasonable steps to ensure that the compensation is disclosed in each communication the promoter posts.[98]

These communications channels are an attempt to take advantage of the "wisdom of the crowd," the idea that the collective decision-making of a group of people is better than individual decision-making and, sometimes, even better than expert decision-making (Surowiecki 2004). Surowiecki (2004) argues that crowds can be collectively wiser than individual decision-makers, but only when their decisions are independently made. Communications channels eliminate this independence and could lead to irrational herding behavior. Nevertheless, these communications channels do allow investors to share information they might have about the issuer and its business, reducing the risk of fraud (Bradford 2012b, 219).

9.4.3.4 The Intermediary's Enforcement Role

The crowdfunding intermediary has an enforcement role under the exemption. As indicated earlier, the issuer is subject to mandatory disclosure requirements. The intermediary is required to make the issuer's disclosure available to the general public on its platform; that disclosure must remain publicly available until the offering is completed or canceled.[99] The intermediary must also have a reasonable basis for believing that various requirements of the exemption are satisfied:

- *Investment Limits*. The intermediary must have a reasonable basis for believing that each investor satisfies the investment limits of the exemption. However, the intermediary may rely on the investor's representations concerning compliance unless the intermediary has reason to question the reliability of those representations.[100]
- *Issuer's Compliance*. The intermediary must have a reasonable basis for believing that the issuer is in compliance with the requirements of the exemption. However, the intermediary may rely on the issuer's representations to that effect unless the intermediary has reason to question the reliability of the issuer's representations.[101]
- *Issuer's Record-Keeping*. The intermediary must have a reasonable basis for believing that the issuer has established means to keep accurate records of the holders of the securities it is offering through the intermediary's platform. However, the intermediary may rely on the issuer's representations to that effect unless the intermediary has reason to question the reliability of those representations.[102]

In satisfying these requirements, the intermediary can usually rely on others' statements; no independent investigation is required. However, at least one enforcement requirement requires an independent check by the intermediary. The intermediary must deny an issuer access to its platform if it has a reasonable basis for believing that the "bad actor" disqualifications, discussed earlier, apply.[103] To satisfy this requirement, the intermediary must, "at a minimum," conduct a background and securities enforcement regulatory check on the issuer and on each officer, director, and 20 percent beneficial owner of the issuer's voting securities.[104]

The issuer must also deny access to its platform if it believes the issuer or the offering "presents the potential for fraud or otherwise raises concerns about investor protection."[105] This requirement raises more questions than it answers. When exactly is a "potential" for fraud present? And when does a non-fraudulent offering otherwise raise concerns about investor protection? Most importantly, does this provision require an intermediary to investigate each offering or is it enough that the intermediary is unaware of any facts that might raise suspicion? The answer to all of these questions is unclear (Bradford 2015, 376–377), and their resolution will have an important impact on the investor protection/capital formation trade-off made by the exemption. The stronger the intermediary's due diligence role, the more protection the intermediary's presence provides to investors. But stronger due diligence requirements also increase the intermediary's compliance costs, and thus the cost of using the exemption.

9.4.3.5 Conduct of the Offering

Section 4(a)(6) contains specific requirements as to how offerings are to be conducted. The issuer, in its disclosure, must specify a target amount it wants to raise in the offering and a deadline for raising that amount.[106] The offering must be open for at least 21 days.[107] Investors may cancel their investment commitments until 48 hours prior to the specified deadline.[108]

The issuer cannot access any investor funds until the target amount is reached. If the offering does not reach the target amount by the deadline, or the offering is not completed for some other reason, the intermediary must, within five business days, direct the return of investors' funds.[109] If the issuer reaches the target amount prior to the deadline, it may close the offering early, as long as the offering has been open for at least 21 days.[110] However, the issuer must notify investors of the new closing deadline and the new deadline must be at least five business days after the notice.[111]

9.5 Intrastate Crowdfunding

Securities offerings in the United States are regulated by both the federal government and the individual states in which the offerings occur. However, the Securities Act of 1933 exempts purely intrastate offerings from the federal registration requirement, essentially relegating these offerings to regulation by the particular state in which they occur.[112] The exact outlines of that statutory exemption are uncertain, but the SEC has adopted a safe harbor rule, Securities Act Rule 147,[113] that provides more certainty. To qualify for that intrastate offering safe harbor, all of the *offerees* (not just the ultimate purchasers) must be residents of the same state as the issuer. The issuer must be organized or incorporated under that state's laws and have its principal office in the state.[114]

Until recently, the issuer also had to meet several other requirements: (1) at least 80 percent of its gross revenues had to be from operations in that state; (2) at least 80 percent of its assets had to be located in the state; and (3) at least 80 percent of the offering proceeds had to be used in connection with operations in that state.[115] *All* of these requirements had to be met. However, the SEC amended Rule 147 in 2016 (effective in 2017) to phrase these requirements in the alternative. Now, *only one* of these requirements *or* a new fourth requirement—that a majority of the issuer's employees be based in the state—must be met (SEC 2016, 197). The SEC (2016, 202–207) also adopted a new intrastate exemption, Rule 147A, that does not require the issuer to be incorporated in the state and allows *offers* to non-residents, as long as the securities are *sold* only to residents.

The intrastate offering exemption, as I indicated, is only from *federal* registration requirements; it does not free issuers from the registration requirements imposed by the law of the state in which the offering occurs. However, many states have adopted crowdfunding exemptions under state law that free intrastate crowdfunded offerings of securities from *state* registration requirements as well. The exact requirements of these state crowdfunding exemptions vary from state to state, but they generally mimic many of the requirements of the federal crowdfunding exemption (Pei 2014, 869–876). They limit the amount of the offering; limit the amounts investors may invest; require risk disclosures; require disclosure by the issuer; require that the offering be conducted through a state-regulated portal; and restrict how these portals operate.[116] However, there is considerable variation among the states. Some state exemptions remove investment limits for certain categories of investors; some of them allow advertising; and some of them do not even require the use of an intermediary (Pei 2014, 869–876).

It is not clear how successful these intrastate provisions will be. The requisite connections to a single state may be too restrictive, particularly in smaller states, although the recent amendments to Rule 147 ease these restrictions a bit. The SEC staff has also provided some relief, indicating that an offer is not made to out-of-state offerees merely because it appears on a web platform accessible from out of state. According to the SEC (2015a), the offering would be intrastate as long as the portal makes it clear that the offering is limited to residents of a particular state; the offeree confirms his or her residence before accessing the offering materials; and sales are made only to residents of the state. New Rule 147A makes it even easier, completely eliminating the requirement that all offerees be residents, but many of the state exemptions will have to be amended to take advantage of that new rule.

9.6 The Extent of the Exemptions

The exemptions discussed in this chapter free crowdinvesting and crowdlending from both state and federal securities registration requirements. They do not, however, completely exempt these offerings from securities regulation. Federal and state antifraud provisions would still apply.

9.6.1 State and Federal Registration Requirements

All of the exemptions discussed in this chapter exempt offerings from the registration and prospectus requirements of both federal and state law.

Securities offered and sold pursuant to the Rule 506(b) or 506(c) exemptions are "covered securities" as defined in section 18 of the Securities Act of 1933.[117] Securities sold pursuant to the crowdfunding exemption in § 4(a)(6) of the Securities Act are also covered securities.[118] Section 18(a) of the Securities Act expressly excludes offerings involving covered securities from state registration, offering, and prospectus requirements.[119]

The state crowdfunding exemptions are, by definition, exemptions from state registration and prospectus requirements. But since these state exemptions require that the offering also be in compliance with the federal intrastate offering exemption, these offerings would also be exempted from the federal registration requirement.[120]

9.6.2 Antifraud Rules

Issuers selling securities pursuant to one of the exemptions discussed in this chapter would still be subject to federal and state securities law rules prohibiting fraud. The crowdfunding exemptions only exempt offerings from the registration and prospectus delivery requirements, not the antifraud rules.

US securities law includes a number of general antifraud provisions that could apply to crowdinvesting and crowdlending[121] and one new antifraud rule, section 4A(c) of the Securities Act, that applies specifically to section 4(a)(6) crowdfunding.[122] Rule 10b-5, for example, makes it unlawful, in connection with the sale of any securities, "[t]o make any untrue statement of a material fact or to omit to state a material fact necessary in order to make the statements made … not misleading."[123] State securities laws contain similar prohibitions on securities fraud (Long 2015, ch. 9).

Issuers making materially false statements in selling securities to crowdinvestors could be liable under these antifraud provisions. Crowdfunding intermediaries might also be liable for false statements made by issuers, although their liability risk is less clear (Bradford 2015, 371–410).

The existence of an antifraud remedy does not mean that it will be used, however. Crowdinvesting typically involves relatively small investments by each investor; the section 4(a)(6) exemption even limits how much each investor may invest. Hence, the cost of bringing a private antifraud action would often exceed the potential recovery (Palmiter 2012, 416). Given the relatively small amount raised, even class actions brought on behalf of all the investors in an offering might not be feasible (416–417). Thus, private enforcement actions are unlikely in many cases.

The SEC and state securities regulators can bring actions against issuers engaged in fraudulent crowdinvesting and crowdlending offerings, but these regulators are unlikely to focus their limited resources on such relatively low-profile offerings. Therefore, even public enforcement of the antifraud provisions could be limited (Palmiter 2012, 375).

9.7 Conclusion

The regulation of crowdinvesting and crowdlending involves a trade-off between capital formation and investor protection. Disclosure requirements, structural limitations on crowdfunded offerings, investment limits, and other regulatory requirements designed to protect investors increase the cost of crowdinvesting and crowdlending. As the regulatory cost increases, crowdfunding become a less viable option for small business capital formation. But, absent adequate investor protection, losses due to fraud and manipulation may drive investors away from crowdfunded securities offerings.

The two federal exemptions limited to accredited or sophisticated investors—Rule 506(b) and Rule 506(c)—impose the least regulatory cost. Issuers can avoid mandatory disclosure requirements, limits on the structure of their offerings, and offering and investment amount limits. But these two exemptions essentially take the "crowd" out of crowdinvesting. Issuers may sell only to sophisticated or wealthy investors and, in the case of Rule 506(b), may not even advertise the offering on a publicly accessible Internet site.

These exemptions also raise investor protection concerns. Their basic premise—that investors who meet the wealth and income requirements to qualify as accredited investors do not need regulatory protection—is questionable, particularly since the amounts these investors may invest is unlimited.

The Section 4(a)(6) crowdfunding exemption and the many intrastate crowdfunding exemptions widen the scope of permissible investors. The intrastate exemptions still limit the investors to the residents of a particular state, a troublesome, perhaps archaic restriction in the global Internet age. But all of the crowdinvesting-specific exemptions, state and federal, allow the general public to invest, without any restrictions based on wealth or sophistication.

That breadth comes at a regulatory price. The federal and state regulators have imposed significant regulatory costs on these offerings—investment limits, sales through neutral intermediaries, limits on the structure of offerings, and, probably the costliest part of these rules, substantial mandatory disclosure requirements. The regulatory price paid to access non-accredited investors is significant.

It is too early to say whether any of these four possibilities has struck the right balance. The Rule 506 exemptions may prove too limited. The Section 4(a)(6) exemption may prove too costly. The intrastate offering exemptions may be both too limited and too costly. On the other hand, one of these exemptions may allow crowdinvesting to explode, substantially expanding small business capital formation opportunities and providing investors with significant new opportunities to invest in small entrepreneurial enterprises.

Notes

1. Section 5(c) of the Securities Act of 1933 provides that no one may offer securities until a registration statement has been filed with the SEC. 15 U.S.C. § 77e(c). Section 5(a)(1) of the Act prohibits sales of those securities until the registration statement has become effective. 15 U.S.C. § 77e(a)(1).
2. 15 U.S.C. § 77b(a)(1). Hazen (2016, §§ 1:49–1:79) provides a good general discussion of the interpretation of that definition.
3. 17 C.F.R. § 230.506(b). Before 2013, when the Rule 506(c) exemption was added, this exemption was known simply as the Rule 506 exemption.
4. 17 C.F.R. § 230.506(c).
5. Pub. L. 112–106, 126 Stat. 306 (2012).
6. See Securities Act Rule 501(a), 17 C.F.R. § 230.501(a).
7. Securities Act Rule 501(a)(5), 17 C.F.R. § 230.501(a)(5). A spouse's net worth may also be included to reach the USD 1 million limit. *Id.*
8. Securities Act Rule 501(a)(6), 17 C.F.R. § 230.501(a)(6).
9. See, for example, SEC v. Ralston Purina Co., 346 U.S. 119 (1953). In *Ralston Purina*, the court held that the US private offering exemption (now in section 4(a)(2) of the Securities Act) applies to offerings to those who are "able to fend for themselves" and therefore do not need the protection of registration. *Id.*, at 125.
10. Securities Act Rule 506(d), 17 C.F.R. § 230.506(d).
11. Securities Act Rule 502(d), 17 C.F.R. § 230.502(d).

12. See Securities Act Rule 144, 17 C.F.R. § 230.144.
13. Securities Act Rule 506(b)(2)(ii), 17 C.F.R. § 230.506(b)(2)(ii).
14. *Id.*
15. Securities Act Rules 501(a), 506(b)(2)(ii), 17 C.F.R. §§ 230.501(a), 230.506(b)(2)(ii).
16. Securities Act Rule 502(b), 17 C.F.R. 230.502(b).
17. See Securities Act Rule 502(b)(2), 17 C.F.R. § 230.502(b)(2).
18. Securities Act Rule 502(c), 17 C.F.R. § 230.502(c).
19. See, for example, *IPOnet*, SEC No-Action Letter (July 26, 1996).
20. Securities Act Rule 506(c)(2)(ii), 17 C.F.R. § 230.506(c)(2)(ii).
21. Securities Act Rule 506(c)(2)(ii)(A)–(B), 17 C.F.R. § 230.506(c)(2)(ii)(A)–(B).
22. See 15 U.S.C. § 77d(a)(6).
23. 15 U.S.C. §§ 77d(a)(6), 77d-1.
24. See 17 C.F.R. § 227.10 *et seq.*
25. 17 C.F.R. § 227.100(a)(2)(i),(ii).
26. 17 C.F.R. § 227.100, Instruction 2 to paragraph (a)(2).
27. 17 C.F.R. § 227.100, Instruction 1 to paragraph (a)(2); 17 C.F.R. § 230.501(a)(5)(i).
28. 17 C.F.R. § 227.302(b)(1)(v).
29. 17 C.F.R. § 227.303(b)(1).
30. *Id.*
31. 17 C.F.R. § 227.302(b)(1).
32. 17 C.F.R. § 227.302(b)(2).
33. 17 C.F.R. § 227.303(b)(2)(i).
34. 17 C.F.R. § 227.303(b)(2)(ii).
35. 17 C.F.R. § 227.501.
36. *Id.*
37. 17 C.F.R. § 227.100(b)(1).
38. 17 C.F.R. § 227.100(b)(2).
39. Investment companies and companies that would be investment companies except for certain statutory exemptions are excluded. 17 C.F.R. § 227.100(b)(3). Also excluded are companies that have no specific business plan or whose business plan is to engage in a merger or acquisition with an unspecified company. 17 C.F.R. § 227.100(b)(6). Companies that have used the crowdfunding exemption in the past and have not filed the required annual reports in the past two years are also excluded. 17 C.F.R. § 227.100(b)(5).
40. See 17 C.F.R. §§ 227.100(b)(4); 227.503.

41. 17 C.F.R. § 503(a).
42. 17 C.F.R § 227.100(a)(1).
43. 17 C.F.R. § 304(c).
44. *Id.*
45. *Id.*
46. 17 C.F.R. § 227.201(a).
47. 17 C.F.R. § 227.201(e).
48. 17 C.F.R. § 227.201(d).
49. 17 C.F.R. § 227.201(b).
50. 17 C.F.R. § 227.201(b).
51. 17 C.F.R. §§ 227.201(c); 227.201(m)(3).
52. 17 C.F.R. § 227.201(r).
53. 17 C.F.R. § 227.201(m)(1).
54. 17 C.F.R. § 227.201(m)(4).
55. 17 C.F.R. § 227.201(m)(5).
56. 17 C.F.R. § 227.201(m)(6).
57. 17 C.F.R. § 227.201(m)(2).
58. 17 C.F.R. § 227.201(f).
59. 17 C.F.R. § 227.201(p).
60. 17 C.F.R. § 227.201(q).
61. 17 C.F.R. § 227.201(u).
62. 17 C.F.R. § 227.201(w).
63. 17 C.F.R. § 227.201(x).
64. 17 C.F.R. § 227.201(s).
65. 17 C.F.R. § 227.201(s), Instruction 2.
66. *Id.*
67. *Id.*
68. See 17 C.F.R. § 227.201(t).
69. 17 C.F.R. § 227.201(i).
70. 17 C.F.R. § 227.201(l).
71. 17 C.F.R. § 227.201(n).
72. 17 C.F.R. § 227.201(o).
73. 17 C.F.R. § 227.201(g).
74. 17 C.F.R. § 227.201(h).
75. 17 C.F.R. § 227.201(j).
76. 17 C.F.R. § 227.201(k).
77. 17 C.F.R. § 227.201(v)
78. 17 C.F.R. § 227.203(a)(3)(i).
79. 17 C.F.R. § 227.203(a)(3)(ii).

80. 17 C.F.R. § 227.201(y).
81. 17 C.F.R. § 227.202(a).
82. 17 C.F.R. § 227.202(a).
83. See 17 C.F.R. § 227.202(a).
84. 17 C.F.R. § 227.202(b)(1),(4),(5).
85. 17 C.F.R. § 227.202(b)(2).
86. 17 C.F.R. § 227.202(b)(3).
87. 17 C.F.R. § 227.300(a).
88. See Securities Exchange Act of 1934 § 3(a)(80), 15 U.S.C. § 78c(a)(80); 17 C.F.R. §§ 227.401–227.402.
89. 17 C.F.R. § 227.300(b).
90. 17 C.F.R. § 227.300(b)(1),(2).
91. 17 C.F.R. § 227.302(d).
92. 17 C.F.R. § 227.204(a).
93. 17 C.F.R. § 227.205(b).
94. 17 C.F.R. § 227.204(b).
95. 17 C.F.R. § 227.303(c).
96. 17 C.F.R. § 227.303(c)(2),(3).
97. 17 C.F.R. §§ 227.204(c), 227.303(c)(4).
98. 17 C.F.R. § 227.205(a).
99. 17 C.F.R. § 227.303(a)(1),(3).
100. 17 C.F.R. § 227.303(b)(1).
101. 17 C.F.R. § 227.301(a).
102. 17 C.F.R. § 227.301(b).
103. 17 C.F.R. § 227.301(c)(1).
104. *Id.*
105. 17 C.F.R. § 227.301(c)(2).
106. 17 C.F.R. § 227.201(g).
107. 17 C.F.R. § 227. 303(a)(2).
108. 17 C.F.R. § 227.304(a).
109. 17 C.F.R. § 227.304(d).
110. 17 C.F.R. § 227.304(b).
111. 17 C.F.R. § 227.304(b)(2),(3).
112. Section 3(a)(11) of the Securities Act exempts "[a]ny security which is a part of an issue offered and sold only to persons resident within a single State or Territory, where the issuer of such security is a person resident and doing business within, or, if a corporation, incorporated by and doing business within, such State or Territory" 15 U.S.C. § 77c(a)(11).

113. 17 C.F.R. § 230.147.
114. 17 C.F.R. § 230.147(c)(1).
115. 17 C.F.R. § 230.147(c)(2).
116. For a fairly typical example of such a state exemption, see NEB. REV. STAT. § 8-1111(24).
117. Securities Act of 1933 § 18(b)(4)(E), 15 U.S.C. § 77r(b)(4)(E).
118. Securities Act of 1933 § 18(b)(4)(C), 15 U.S.C. § 77r(b)(4)(C).
119. Securities Act of 1933 § 18(a), 15 U.S.C. § 77r(a).
120. See Securities Act of 1933 § 3(a)(11), 15 U.S.C. § 77c(a)(11); Securities Act Rule 147, 17 C.F.R. § 230.147.
121. See Securities Act of 1933 § 12(a)(2), 15 U.S.C. § 77l(a)(2); Securities Act of 1933 § 17(a), 15 U.S.C. § 77q(a); Exchange Act Rule 10b-5, 17 C.F.R. § 240.10b-5.
122. Securities Act of 1933 § 4A(c), 15 U.S.C. § 77d-1(c).
123. Exchange Act Rule 10b-5, 17 C.F.R. § 240.10b-5.

References

Bradford, C. Steven. 2001. Securities Regulation and Small Business: Rule 504 and the Case for an Unconditional Exemption. *The Journal of Small and Emerging Business Law* 5: 1–47.

———. 2012a. Crowdfunding and the Federal Securities Laws. *Columbia Business Law Review*, 1–150.

———. 2012b. The New Federal Crowdfunding Exemption: Promise Unfulfilled. *Securities Regulation Law Journal* 40: 195–250.

———. 2015. Shooting the Messenger: The Liability of Crowdfunding Intermediaries for the Fraud of Others. *University of Cincinnati Law Review* 83: 371–410.

Campbell, Rutheford B., Jr. 1995. Resales of Securities under the Securities Act of 1933. *Washington & Lee Law Review* 52: 1331–1384.

Cohn, Stuart R., and Gregory C. Yadley. 2007. Capital Offense: The SEC's Continuing Failure to Address Small Business Financing Concerns. *N.Y.U. Journal of Law and Business* 4: 1–87.

Hazen, Thomas Lee. 2016. *Treatise on the Law of Securities Regulation*. 7th ed. St. Paul, Minn: Thomson Reuters.

Ivanov, Vlad, and Scott Bauguess. 2012. Capital Raising in the U.S.: The Significance of Unregistered Offerings Using the Regulation D Exemption.

Securities and Exchange Commission (SEC). https://www.sec.gov/info/smallbus/acsec/acsec103111_analysis-reg-d-offering.pdf. Last modified Feb 2012.

Long, Joseph C. 2015. *Blue Sky Law*. St. Paul, Minn.: Thomson/West Group.

Palmiter, Alan R. 2012. Pricing Disclosure: Crowdfunding's Curious Conundrum. *Ohio State Entrepreneurial Business Law Journal* 7: 373–427.

Pei, Matthew A. 2014. Intrastate Crowdfunding. *Columbia Business Law Review*: 854–898.

Prifti, William M. 2010. *Securities: Public and Private Offerings*. 2nd ed. Eagan, Minn.: Thomson/West Group.

Securities and Exchange Commission (SEC). 1996. Report of the Advisory Committee on the Capital Formation and Regulatory Processes. http://www.sec.gov/news/studies/capform.htm. Last modified 24 July 1996.

———. 2000. Use of Electronic Media. *Securities Act Release No. 7856, Federal Register* 65: 25843–25855.

———. 2013. Crowdfunding. *Securities Act Release No. 9470, Federal Register* 78: 66428–66602.

———. 2015a. Compliance and Disclosure Interpretations: Securities Act Rules. www.sec.gov/divisions/corpfin/guidance/securitiesactrules-interps.htm. Last modified 8 Dec 2016.

———. 2015b. Crowdfunding. *Securities Act Release No. 9974, Federal Register* 80: 71388–71615.

———. 2015c. Report on the Review of the Definition of 'Accredited Investor'. https://www.sec.gov/corpfin/reportspubs/special-studies/review-definition-of-accredited-investor-12-18-2015.pdf. Last modified 18 Dec 2015.

———. 2016. Exemptions to Facilitate Intrastate and Regional Securities Offerings. *Securities Act Release No. 10238*. https://www.sec.gov/rules/final/2016/33-10238.pdf. Last modified 26 Oct.

Sjostrom, William K., Jr. 2001. Going Public through an Internet Direct Public Offering: A Sensible Alternative for Small Companies? *Florida Law Review* 53: 529–594.

———. 2004. Relaxing the Ban: It's Time to Allow General Solicitation and Advertising in Exempt Offerings. *Florida State University Law Review* 32: 1–50.

Surowiecki, James. 2004. *The Wisdom of Crowds: Why the Many Are Smarter than the Few and How Collective Wisdom Shapes Business, Economics, Societies, and Nations*. New York: Anchor Books.

U.S. Government Accountability Office. 2000. *Small Business Efforts to Facilitate Equity Capital*. Washington, D.C.: U.S. Government Printing Office.

C. Steven Bradford is the Henry M. Grether, Jr. Professor of Law at the University of Nebraska-Lincoln College of Law. He has written numerous articles on US securities law, including several articles on crowdfunding and the regulation of small business securities offerings. He has testified on crowdfunding issues before the US Congress and the Nebraska State Legislature. He has made crowdfunding presentations to numerous groups, including the SEC Government-Business Forum on Small Business Capital Formation, the New York State Bar Association, and the Practising Law Institute.

10

The Regulation of Crowdfunding in Europe

Lars Klöhn

10.1 The Capital Markets Union and the European Institutions' Work on Crowdfunding

On September 30, 2015, the European Commission published its Capital Markets Union (CMU) Action Plan.[1] The plan aims to tackle investment shortage by increasing and diversifying the funding sources for European businesses—especially small and medium-sized enterprises (SMEs)—and long-term projects and to provide more options and better returns for savers and investors. Crowdfunding is a cornerstone of the CMU Action Plan. The Commission conducted a public consultation on crowdfunding, set up a website on which it informs market participants on its ongoing work,[2] and established a European Crowdfunding Stakeholder Forum (ECSF), which at the time of writing, has held four meetings since its creation.[3]

L. Klöhn (✉)
Faculty of Law, Humboldt University of Berlin, Berlin, Germany

D. Cumming, L. Hornuf (eds.), *The Economics of Crowdfunding*,
https://doi.org/10.1007/978-3-319-66119-3_10

The Commission's work on crowdfunding had begun earlier. Building on its Green Paper on Long Term Financing of the European Economy,[4] the European Commission held a public consultation on crowdfunding between October and December 2013 and subsequently published a programmatic communication paper to the other European institutions on March 27, 2014, titled "Unleashing the potential of Crowdfunding in the European Union."[5]

In May 2016 the European Commission published a Commission Staff Working Document, reporting on the Commission's work on crowdfunding since its publication of 2014.[6] The report states that "crowdfunding remains relatively small in the EU but is developing rapidly. It has the potential to be a key source of financing for SMEs over the long term."[7] The Commission asserts that "[g]iven the predominantly local nature of crowdfunding, there is no strong case for EU level policy intervention at this juncture. Crowdfunding is still relatively small and needs space to innovate and develop."[8] However, "[g]iven the dynamism of crowdfunding and the potential for future cross border expansion, it will be important to monitor the development of the sector and the effectiveness, and degree of convergence of, national regulatory frameworks."[9] The Commission therefore intends to "maintain regular dialogue (…) with the European Supervisory Authorities, Member States, and the crowdfunding sector to promote convergence, sharing of best practice and keep developments under review." The aim is to be able to act in a timely manner if further steps become necessary to support convergence of regulatory approaches in the member states, "both to promote the development of the sector and to ensure appropriate investor protection."[10]

The European Parliament stated in 2015 that "the CMU should create an appropriate regulatory environment that enhances cross-border access to information on the companies looking for credit, quasi-equity and equity structures, in order to promote growth of non-bank financing models, including crowdfunding and peer-to-peer lending."[11] The European Parliament resolution of January 19, 2016, underlines the potential of innovative market-based funding and stresses the need to streamline regulatory regimes. At the same time, it—quite notably—asks the Commission to give "breathing space for the emergence of these new models and to explore and promote them, giving priority to their cross-border dimension and ensuring the reduction of market entry barriers."[12]

10.2 Aim and Scope of This Chapter

The aim of this chapter is to give an overview of the regulation of crowdfunding in Europe on the level of the member states as well as on the supranational EU level and to assess whether there is need for more supranational regulation.[13] As such regulation should take into account whether platforms have an incentive to provide investors with optimal financing contracts and develop other market-based solutions for the various risks faced by investors (regarding these risks compare Armour and Enriques, Chap. 12 sub 12.2.; Dehner and Kong 2014, 441; Gabison 2015, 369 et seq.; Wilson and Testoni 2014, 7), this chapter also tries to shed light on the contractual terms, under which crowdinvesting is taking place in Europe, and investor protection mechanisms crowdinvesting platforms have developed in the absence of regulatory requirements.

The focus of this chapter is on crowdinvesting rather than crowdlending or reward-based or donation-based crowdfunding.[14] While there is a vibrant crowdlending market in Europe, it does not seem to be frequented by start-ups, perhaps due to the fact that debt financing is unsuitable for firms without hard assets (Armour and Enriques 2017, 11). The European market for reward-based or donation-based crowdfunding appears rather insignificant, especially when compared to the US. A regulatory reason seems to be the Directive on Consumer Rights,[15] which grants consumers purchasing under a distance sales contract a right of withdrawal without justification within 14 days of receipt of the goods (Armour and Enriques 2017, 30 et seq.). Finally, this chapter will be limited to "hard" law, which means it will not cover the various soft law regimes that have been established, for example, by the European Crowdfunding Network.[16]

10.3 EU Law

10.3.1 Overview

Currently there is no specific crowdfunding regulation at the EU level. There are, however, several legal acts which set the general regulatory framework for crowdinvesting, such as the prospectus requirement and conduct of business regulation for financial intermediaries. Note, however, that these acts apply only if the crowdinvesting model falls within the scope of application of these acts. As a general rule, this requires the distribution of transferable securities such as stocks or mini bonds. As the German market shows, crowdfunding can take place on the basis of investment contracts not covered by current European regulation (see below Sect. 10.4.3.1).

10.3.2 Prospectus Requirement

The standard tool of Securities Regulation to mitigate information asymmetries between investors and issuers prior to the investment decision is the issuer's duty to disclose all relevant information in a document known as the prospectus (on information asymmetries in crowdinvesting see Hornuf and Schwienbacher 2016, sub 4.5; Ibrahim 2015, 573 et seq., 591 et seq.). Usually this obligation is enforced publicly (i.e. by the state) by requiring issuers to submit the prospectus or an equivalent document with the competent authority before offering or marketing the securities ("gun jumping laws"). Moreover, securities laws around the world have chosen to supplement this regime by means of private law because no regulator has—and probably should not have—the manpower and the resources to verify all information contained in a prospectus before approving the offering within a reasonable period of time. The cornerstones of this supplementary private law enforcement regime are the rules on prospectus liability, that is liability for material omissions or misstatements contained in a prospectus or for the complete failure to submit a prospectus with the competent authority prior to the offer.

The EU Prospectus Directive[17] and the accompanying Prospectus Regulation[18] regulate the public law side of the above-mentioned regime and set out some rudimentary rules for the private law side. The Prospectus Directive is a legal act which is not directly applicable. It must be implemented by the member states, which means it obliges the member states to pass domestic law implementing the rules contained in the Directive. The Prospect Regulation is directly applicable in all member states and thus does not need to be implemented by the member states.

Under Art. 3(1) Prospectus Directive member states shall not allow any offer of securities to be made to the public within their territories without prior publication of a prospectus. Art. 13(1) Prospectus Directive states that no prospectus shall be published until it has been approved by the competent authority of the home member state. The prospectus shall contain all information which, according to the particular nature of the issuer and of the securities offered, is necessary to enable investors to make an informed assessment of the assets and liabilities, financial position, profit and losses, and prospects of the issuer and of any guarantor, and of the rights attaching to such securities, Art. 5(1) Prospectus Directive. The Prospectus Regulation sets minimum requirements with regard to what information must be included in a prospectus, the format of the prospectus, the modalities of disclosure, and the methods of publication and dissemination of the prospectus. Once a prospectus has been approved by the competent authority of the home member state, it shall be valid for public offer in any number of host member states, Art. 17(1) Prospectus Directive. This scheme of mutual recognition in the EU is commonly referred to as the "European Passport".

The Prospectus Directive contains several exemption clauses. Under Art. 3(2)(a), (b) Prospectus Directive, the prospectus requirement does not apply to offers addressed solely to qualified investors and to offers addressed to fewer than 100 natural or legal persons per member state, other than qualified investors. Also, there is no prospectus requirement for offers of securities with a total consideration of less than EUR 100.000 which limit shall be calculated over a period of 12 months, Art.

3(2)(e) Prospectus Directive. Finally, the Prospectus Directive allows member states to refrain from imposing a prospectus requirement as long as the total consideration of the offer is less than EUR 5 million, Art. 1(2)(h) Prospectus Directive.[19] Thus, member states *must exempt* offers from the prospectus requirement if the total consideration is less than EUR 100.000 and they *must require* a prospectus if the total consideration is EUR 5 million or more. Within that range between EUR 100.000 and EUR 4.99 million member states can choose: They may impose a prospectus requirement, and they may choose to allow such offers without a prospectus.

Finally, the Prospectus Directive applies only to offerings of transferable securities as defined by Art. 4(1)(44) MiFID. The paradigm of such securities are stocks (common or preferred) and bonds, Art. 2(1) lit. a Prospectus Directive. The concept of security under EU law is much narrower than for example in the US.[20] Thus, there are several investment contracts not covered by the Prospectus Directive, especially subordinated profit participating loans (*partiarische Nachrangdarlehen*) which are issued on the German crowdinvesting market. Such offers must be accompanied by a prospectus only if member states' domestic securities laws require a prospectus to be published.

In conclusion, there is no single unified prospectus regime in Europe but a hotchpotch of different domestic regimes, partly harmonized by the EU Prospectus Directive. The main divide runs along the investment contracts that are being offered:

- If start-ups offer transferable securities as defined by MiFID, the harmonized EU prospectus regime applies, unless the total consideration is less than EUR 5 million and the member state, in which the offer is being made, has chosen to exempt the offer from the prospectus requirement. If the consideration is less than EUR 100.000, such exemption is mandatory.
- If start-ups offer investment contracts which do not qualify as transferable securities, the EU prospectus regime does not apply. Whether the start-up has to publish a prospectus is a question of (non-harmonized) domestic law.

10.3.3 Platform Regulation

10.3.3.1 Authorization, Organizational Requirements, and Conduct of Business Regulation

Overview

The major regulation of financial intermediaries is contained in the Markets in Financial Instruments Directive (MiFID)—a tight regulatory regime which has just been remolded in 2014 (therefore often referred to as MiFID II).[21] As a directive, MiFID is not directly applicable; its rules must be implemented by the member states. So, just like the Prospectus Directive, MiFID obliges the European member states to pass domestic law implementing the rules contained in the Directive.

Authorization and European Passport

MiFID establishes, among others, requirements in relation to the authorization and operating conditions of investment firms. Under Art. 5(1) MiFID each member state shall require that the provision of investment services be subject to prior authorization by the competent authority. If investment firms obtain authorization they may freely provide investment services within the territories of all EU member states, Art. 34(1) MIFID. Thus, authorization obtained under MiFID grants investment firms a "European Passport".

Organizational Requirements

Art. 16 MiFID establishes organizational requirements, for example with regard to the compliance structure of the investment firms or measures to be taken to prevent conflicts of interest. While Art. 16 MiFID contains the general organizational objectives and principles, the specific rules are contained in delegated or implementing regulations passed by the European Commission (so-called Level-2-acts).[22] Art. 24 to 30 MiFID contain the rules under which investment firms must conduct their business with regard to investor protection. As a general rule, Art. 24(1) MiFID obliges member states to make sure that, when providing investment services, an investment firm act honestly, fairly, and professionally in accordance with the best interests of its clients and comply with all principles set out in MiFID and the respective Level-2-acts. Specific aspects of this general duty to always act in good faith are the investment firm's information duties and know-your-customer-requirements.

Information Duties

Under Art. 24(4) MiFID appropriate information shall be provided in good time to clients or potential clients with regard to the investment firm and its services, the financial instruments and proposed investment strategies, execution venues, and all costs and related charges. The information must be provided in a comprehensible form in such a manner that clients or potential clients are reasonably able to understand the nature and risks of the investment service and of the specific type of financial instrument that is being offered and, consequently, to take investment decisions on an informed basis, Art. 24(5) MiFID. All information, including marketing communications, addressed by the investment firm to clients or potential clients shall be fair, clear, and not misleading. Market communications shall be clearly identifiable as such, Art. 24(3) MiFID.[23]

Know-Your-Customer-Rules

The requirements of the know-your-customer-rules depend on the nature of the investment service:

- If an investment firm provides investment advice, it must obtain the necessary information regarding the client's or potential client's knowledge and experience, that person's financial situation including the investor's ability to bear losses, and his or her investment objectives so as to enable the investment firm to recommend to the client or potential client the investment services and financial instruments that are *suitable* for him or her (*suitability test*), Art. 25(2) MiFID.

- If an investment firm provides other investment services such as the reception and transmission of orders in relation to financial instruments, the investment firm must ask the client or potential client to provide information regarding that person's knowledge and experience relevant to the specific type of product or service offered or demanded so as to enable the investment firm to assess whether the investment service or product envisaged is *appropriate* for the client (*appropriateness test*), Art. 25(3) MiFID.
- An investment firm is exempted from the appropriateness requirement, if it merely receives and transmits client orders with respect to non-complex financial instruments such as shares and bonds admitted to trading on a regulated market or on an equivalent third-country market or on a multilateral trading facility (MTF), Art. 25(4) MiFID. This exception, however, is not relevant for the European crowdinvesting market, because even if there is a secondary market, financial instruments offered by start-ups to the crowd are neither listed on a regulated or equivalent market nor on an MTF.

MiFID's Scope of Application

All of these rules apply only to investment firms within the meaning of Art. 4(1) MiFID, that is to firms providing *financial services* as defined by Section A of Annex I MiFID, relating to *financial instruments* as defined by Section C of Annex I MiFID. Therefore, the regulatory regime for crowdfunding platforms in Europe is just as divided as the prospectus regime:

- If crowdinvesting platforms broker investments in firms offering stocks, bonds, units in collective investment undertakings or other financial instruments listed in Section C of Annex I MiFID, they are governed by the national securities laws implementing MiFID.
- If crowdinvesting platforms broker other investment contracts not covered by MiFID, such as profit participating loans offered by

German crowdinvesting platforms, MiFID and its implementing rules of national law do not apply. Crowdinvesting platforms are governed by domestic bespoke regimes for investment firms operating outside the scope of MiFID.

- If crowdinvesting platforms merely provide the investment service of receiving and transmitting orders in transferable securities (such as stocks and bonds) and units in collective investment undertakings and/or of providing investment advice in relation to such financial instruments and are not allowed to hold client funds or client securities, member states can opt to exempt them from MiFID's rules if the unregulated investment firm is allowed to transmit orders only to investment firms authorized under MiFID, credit institutions authorized under the European Capital Requirements Directive (CRD), or certain other institutions (so-called Art. 3 exemption). If those firms are exempted under Art. 3 MiFID they may be governed by domestic bespoke regimes for investment firms operating outside the scope of MiFID (if such bespoke regimes exist).

10.3.3.2 Capital Requirements

MiFID investment firms are subject to EU-wide capital requirement regulation under Art. 15 MiFID, member states shall ensure that the competent authorities do not grant authorization unless the investment firm has sufficient initial capital. These requirements are governed by the EU Capital Requirement Directive (CRD)[24] and the EU Capital Requirements Regulation (CRR).[25] These requirements depend on the nature of the investment service.

- The default capital requirement is EUR 730,000, comprised only of certain so-called Equity Tier 1 items, Art. 28 CRD in connection with Art. 26(1)(a) to (e) CRR.
- If an investment firm merely receives and transmits orders for financial instruments and holds client money or securities, it shall have initial capital of EUR 125,000, Art. 29(1) CRD.

- If an investment firm merely receives and transmits orders for financial instruments and is not allowed to hold client money or securities, member states may reduce this amount to EUR 50,000, Art. 29(3) CRD.

10.3.3.3 Anti-Money Laundering Regulation

Crowdinvesting platforms that operate under MiFID are subject to anti-money laundering and anti-terrorist financing rules under the Anti-Money Laundering Directive.[26] If they operate outside MiFID, platforms can be subject to the Anti-Money Laundering Directive if they provide certain payment services within the meaning of the Payment Services Directive.[27]

10.3.3.4 Regulation under the Distance Marketing of Consumer Financial Services Directive

If the platform's activity qualifies as concluding a distance contract for financial services, its consumer clients have a right to obtain pre-contractual information as well as a right of withdrawal within 14 days without justification under the Distance Marketing of Consumer Financial Services Directive.[28]

10.3.3.5 Data Protection

If platforms or issuers process personal data they will be governed by EU data protection legislation, namely the European General Data Protection Regulation.[29]

10.4 Laws of the Member States

10.4.1 Overview

As evidenced above, there is no uniform legal framework for crowdinvesting in Europe. The investment contracts offered are the key differentiators for the applicable legal regimes. If start-ups offer investments in transferable securities, these offerings are subject to the prospectus requirement of Art. 3 Prospectus Directive unless an exemption applies. Platforms brokering such investments are regulated by MiFID, unless exempted under Art. 3 MiFID. If start-ups offer investment contracts not covered by MiFID, the offers are subject only to the domestic bespoke prospectus regimes. Investment firms brokering such investments are governed only by domestic financial intermediary regulation.

Thus, it is not surprising that there is a great variety of crowdinvesting regulatory regimes in the European member states. It is impossible to cover all those regimes, given the space constraints of this chapter. Furthermore, the European Commission has put together a comprehensive report on those regimes in its 2016 working document on crowdfunding.[30] Therefore, this chapter will be limited to the two member states which seem to have the most relevant crowdinvesting markets in Europe (as regards size), that is to the UK and to Germany. These two countries have chosen almost antagonistic approaches to regulating crowdinvesting, which makes them the ideal states to be featured in a report on European crowdinvesting regulation.

10.4.2 United Kingdom

10.4.2.1 Prospectus Requirement

In the UK, the legislator of the Financial Services and Markets Act (FSMA) has made use of the option provided by the Prospectus Directive to exempt all offerings of securities to the public from the prospectus requirement if the total consideration is less than EUR 5 million.[31] Therefore, start-ups can issue transferable securities such as stocks and bonds to the crowd without a prospectus as long as they raise less than EUR 5 million within 12 months. This generous exemption from the prospectus requirement reduces start-ups' and platforms' incentives for regulatory arbitrage by designing investment contracts which would fall outside the scope of the Prospectus Directive. Furthermore, crowdinvesting platforms do not seem to gain much from designing such contracts, because they would still be providing "financial promotions" covered by the FSMA 2000 [see below at Sect. 10.4.2.2]. This is why UK crowd investors usually obtain classic transferable securities, especially common and preferred stock. The exemption from the prospectus requirement applies regardless of whether securities are offered on a crowdinvesting platform or other financial intermediary or directly by the issuer. However, issuers may not market crowdinvesting securities directly to the public, they need to rely on an FCA authorized person such as a crowdinvesting platform.[32]

10.4.2.2 Platform Regulation

As start-ups offer transferable securities to the crowd, UK crowdinvesting platforms provide classic financial services—usually the receipt and transmission of orders—and therefore fall under the legislative provisions implementing MiFID, namely the authorization requirement[33] and the organizational and conduct of business requirements of FSMA 2000. Even if crowdinvesting platforms marketed only non-transferable securities or other investment contracts not covered by MiFID, they would most likely be subject to the same rules as their activities would be considered "financial promotions" (Armour and Enriques 2017, 23).

The Financial Conduct Authority (FCA), the UK financial markets regulator, issued a policy statement to specify those requirements for crowdinvesting platforms in 2014.[34] It has published a review of its regulatory regime in 2015[35] and is at the time of writing aiming to publish a second review in early 2017.[36]

As platform regulation in the UK follows MiFID, the law contains a general obligation to ensure financial promotions offered on the platform are fair, clear, and not misleading.[37] Platforms must ask their clients to provide information necessary to assess whether the securities are appropriate, that is whether the investors have the necessary knowledge and experience to understand the risks involved.[38] In practice, platforms require investors to answer a simple automated test about the characteristics of equity crowdfunding investments, for which they provide guidance (Armour and Enriques 2017, 23).

Statements by the FCA, however, suggest that platforms play a crucial role in securing a sufficient level of investor protection under the UK regime. In its 2015 review the FCA stated that "[w]e are particularly looking to see that platforms are disclosing *all relevant information* to enable potential investors to make informed decisions on whether or not to invest."[39] Compare this with the mandate by Art. 5(1) Prospectus Directive under which a prospectus shall contain "all information which (…) is necessary to enable investors to make an informed assessment of the assets and liabilities, financial position, profit and losses, and prospects of the issuer and of any guarantor, and of the rights attaching to such securities." It seems as if according to the FCA's interpretation, the platforms' disclosure duties under MiFID serve as a perfect functional equivalent to the missing prospectus requirement. Put differently, although start-ups are exempted from publishing a prospectus, the FCA's interpretation of MiFID (or the implementing provisions of the FSMA 2000) ultimately ensures investors are furnished with the same information, that is all information necessary to assess the value of the offered securities—however, not by issuers but by crowdinvesting platforms.

10.4.2.3 Investor Access

Investor access to crowdinvesting securities is restricted in the UK. Platforms may market non-readily realizable securities, that is securities for which no liquid secondary market exists, only to certain types of investors (see also Ridley 2016, 68 et seq.).[40] These are

- professional clients, or
- retail clients who confirm that, in relation to the investment promoted, they will receive regulated investment advice or investment management services from an authorized person ("advised investors"), or
- retail clients who are venture capital contacts or corporate finance contacts, or
- retail clients, who are certified or self-certify as sophisticated investors; or
- retail clients who are certified as high net worth investors, or

- retail clients who certify that they will not invest more than 10% of their net investible financial assets in unlisted equity and debt securities (i.e. they certify that they will only invest money that does not affect their primary residence, pensions, and life cover) ("restricted investors").

Note that, unlike in the US, the UK regulation knows no single-issuer limits but only an aggregate limit, that is for all non-readily realizable securities as an asset class. In addition, there is only a relative (percentage-wise) investment restriction, which means the absolute amount a single retail investor can invest depends on the amount of his or her overall investible financial assets. Finally, just like in the US, as a general rule, platforms may rely on the information provided by the investor in a "Restricted Investor Statement".[41] Therefore, investors seem to be able to avoid investment limits by lying about the amount of their investible financial assets.

10.4.3 Germany

10.4.3.1 Prospectus Requirement

Unlike in the UK, the German legislator has chosen not to make use of the Prospectus Directive's option to exempt all offerings with a consideration of less than EUR 5 million from the prospectus requirement. The small offer exemption provided by German law is available only to securities offerings of less than EUR 100,000 within a 12-month-period.[42] The same rule applies to firms offering investment contracts which do not qualify as securities.[43]

The strict prospectus requirement gave German crowdfunding platforms a strong incentive for regulatory arbitrage by designing investment contracts not covered by German prospectus regulation. In November 2012, crowdinvesting platforms in Germany therefore began to broker subordinated profit participating loans (*partiarische Nachrangdarlehen*) to the crowd. These are hybrid investment contracts which are loan-based but mimic features of equity. At the time of introduction to the crowdinvesting market profit participating loans were outside the scope of German prospectus regulation (Klöhn et al. 2016, 58 et seq.). They had been existent before their introduction to the crowd, although there is no reliable data about to what extent they had been used on the "grey", that is largely unregulated, German capital market. When the legislator introduced a prospectus requirement for investments sold on this market, profit participating loans were exempted for dubious reasons, never made explicit during the legislative process.

By switching to profit participating loans, crowdfunding platforms greatly increased their potential to earn fees. Before, they could collect a maximum amount of (less than) EUR 100,000 per offer without triggering a prospectus requirement. After the platforms had introduced profit participating loans, there was no limit as to the maximum amount to be collected.

For reasons unrelated to crowdinvesting, the German parliament introduced a prospectus requirement for offers of profit participating loans in 2015 (Klöhn et al. 2016).[44] Because the legislator did not want to put an end to crowdinvesting, it also introduced a specific crowdinvesting exemption, under which firms could continue to offer profit participating loans to the crowd under the following conditions:[45]

- The investments must be offered exclusively on a crowdinvesting platform. Thus, the exception to the prospectus requirement does not extend to issuers making direct offerings to the crowd.
- The crowdinvesting platform must be subject to regulatory oversight either under the laws implementing MiFID or under the (much more rudimentary) rules of the Trade Regulation Act (*Gewerbeordnung*). It especially must be obliged to monitor the subscription limit described below.
- The aggregate value of the offer must not exceed EUR 2.5 million. The law does not specify a time period during which multiple offerings by the same issuer will be aggregated when calculating the 2.5-million-limit.

Even when the offering is exempted from the prospectus requirement, the issuer must prepare a so-called investment information sheet

(*Vermögensinformationsblatt, VIB*) which must contain the most essential information about the investment. The issuer must submit the investment information sheet to the German Federal Financial Supervisory Authority (*Bundesanstalt für Finanzdienstleistungsaufsicht, BaFin*) and make it available to every potential investor.[46] The investment information sheet must contain a highlighted warning notice on its first page stating: "The purchase of this investment is associated with significant risks and can result in a total loss of the money invested."[47] Every investor must confirm that he or she understood the warning in writing or in an equivalent digital form, for example digital signature.[48]

10.4.3.2 Portal Regulation

As start-ups offer investment contracts not covered by MiFID, German crowdinvesting platforms do not fall into the regulatory scope of this directive. Hence, their activities are not governed by the German law implementing MiFID and they are not overseen by the federal securities regulator BaFin. Instead they fall under the regulatory reach of the Trade Regulation Act (*Gewerbeordnung*), an act not specific to securities issues which also contains some rudimentary organizational and conduct of business rules for financial intermediaries who are acting outside the reach of MiFID. For the same reason, no capital regulatory requirements apply to crowdinvesting platforms in Germany. Instead, they are required to obtain professional liability insurance under the Trade Regulation Act.[49]

10.4.3.3 Investor Access

The exemption from the prospectus requirement is granted on the condition that investors stay within certain subscription limits (for a comparison of the German and US regulation, see Bradford 2015b).[50] Unlike the UK, German law only limits the amount that an investor may invest in one issuer (single-issuer limit), but not the amount that an investor may invest in the entire crowdinvesting market (aggregate limit). The exact amount of the subscription limit depends on the investor's freely available assets and monthly net income:

- If the investor provides a statement that he or she has freely available assets of at least EUR 100,000, he or she can invest up to a maximum of EUR 10,000 in an issuer.
- If the investor does not have that amount of assets, the limit is twice the investor's monthly net income, but in any case not more than EUR 10,000.
- In all other cases (i.e. particularly if the investor does not provide the statement on assets and income), the investor is limited to a maximum investment of EUR 1000.

Crowdinvesting platforms have a duty to monitor that investors stay within the subscription limits, they may however rely on the investor's information.[51]

10.4.4 Comparative Summary

As stated before, the UK and Germany offer two almost antagonistic crowdinvesting regulatory regimes:

- UK law offers the maximum exemption from the securities prospectus requirement allowed by the Prospectus Directive (the 5-million-limit) while the German legislator only offers the minimum exemption required by the Prospectus Directive (the 100,000-limit).
- In the UK, crowdfunding platforms broker transferable (non-readily realizable) securities, while in Germany they broker investment contracts not covered by the Prospectus Directive.
- In the UK, crowdfunding platforms are subject to the standard MiFID regime implemented in the FSMA and the FCA's Conduct of Business Handbook, while in Germany they are only subject to some rudimentary provisions of the Trade Regulation Act.
- In the UK, crowdfunding platforms are regulated by FCA, that is the national Financial Markets Authority, while in Germany they are

overseen by the trade offices which have no specific expertise in the financial markets sector.

10.5 Crowdinvesting Contracts and (Other) Market-Based Safeguards

10.5.1 Overview

As shown above there is no EU regulation which specifically addresses crowdinvesting and the scope of application of EU securities laws governing securities offers to the public and financial intermediation is limited. Furthermore, we have seen that there is a tremendous variety in crowdinvesting regulation regimes in the member states, as exemplified by the two almost antagonistic regulatory landscapes of the UK and Germany. All this might call for the European legislator to step in and create a level playing field by passing detailed new rules. Such call, however, might turn out to be premature. It has been pointed out in early economic scholarship on securities regulation that issuers might have an incentive to disclose all information relevant to investors without any legal obligation, simply because without such disclosure investors would "assume the worst" and put their money into other ventures (Stigler 1964; cf. Grossman 1981; Milgrom 1981). Also, even in the absence of any legal obligation crowdinvesting platforms might have incentives to provide investors with good investment opportunities by virtue of simple reputation mechanisms (see, e.g. Klein and Leffler 1981; Shapiro 1983; with regard to crowdfunding Wilson and Testoni 2014, 10). Thus, before calling for more detailed regulation, one should try to assess to what extent such reputational and market mechanisms seem to be at work.

10.5.2 The Crucial Role of Crowdinvesting Platforms

When making this assessment, crowdinvesting platforms seem to be of particular importance (on the role of portals see Anand 2014, sub IV.; Heminway 2013). They are the only repeat players in the crowdinvesting market acting as intermediaries between start-ups and investors. However, they are much more than investment brokers. They fulfill three additional functions (see also Heminway 2013, 181 et seq.):

- They are *gatekeepers*, because they decide which start-ups can run crowdfunding campaigns on their platforms.
- They are *information intermediaries*, because they reach out to start-ups and tell them what information they must provide to investors. Also, they usually channel communications between investors and businesses in an investor-relations portal.
- Finally, they are *drafters of investment contracts*; they choose what types of investment contracts start-ups offer to the crowd, and they design the details of those contracts.

Crowdinvesting platforms' profits depend on the amount of funds that they manage to raise (Belleflamme et al. 2015). Increasingly, platforms also participate in the future success of the companies, for example on the basis of carried interest provisions (on the importance of aligning the portal's with investors' interests, see Anand 2014, sub IV.). Still, the bulk of their profits does not depend on the ultimate success of the venture but on the success of the fundraising campaign. Accordingly, platforms compete to broker fundings. Moreover, the crowdinvesting market has characteristics that are typical of network economies (Klöhn et al. 2018; cf. also Viotto 2015, 38). The more investments a crowdinvesting platform brokers, the more attractive the portal is for future campaigns and investments (Klöhn et al. 2018). Accordingly, successful crowdinvesting platforms can increase their profits even if the market volume remains stable (Klöhn et al. 2018). By the same token, it becomes increasingly difficult for new crowdinvesting platforms to enter the market (Klöhn et al. 2018).

There are three plausible scenarios regarding the implications of competition between crowdinvesting platforms (Klöhn et al. 2018):[52]

- *Race to the top*: In the first scenario competition will lead platforms to develop optimal financing agreements. These contracts consist of provisions on which companies and investors would agree if they were rational, fully informed, and could negotiate without transaction costs (Klöhn et al. 2018).

- *Race to the bottom*: In the second scenario, platforms will create the laxest contracts possible to attract start-ups and exploit investors. This scenario is most likely if there are only a small number of companies on the crowdinvesting market and a large number of potential investors "chasing deals" (Klöhn et al. 2018).
- *No race at all or a race to nowhere in particular*: In the final scenario, contractual provisions will not change at all or only due to exogenous factors (tax law, regulations, etc.). Platforms might also simply follow the market leader by copying its contracts and thereby stifle the urge to innovate (Klöhn et al. 2018).

There are good arguments in favor of each of these scenarios (Klöhn et al. 2018). The race to the top scenario is supported by the fact that the crowdinvesting market represents a two-sided market (see Viotto 2015, 38 et seq.). Platforms have to satisfy the demand of both start-ups and investors to be successful. The nature of the companies seeking financing by crowdinvesting supports the race to the bottom scenario. In its seed stage, a start-up essentially consists of an idea which has not been tested in the market. Assessing its true value is a task laden with much uncertainty. Therefore, it is very difficult to distinguish between "good" and "bad" start-ups, that is start-ups with potential for growth and managerial integrity and start-ups with unrealistic ideas and self-enriching management (Klöhn et al. 2018). The final scenario is supported by the present competitive situation of crowdinvesting markets in most European countries, which is a duo- or oligopolistic structure (Klöhn et al. 2018).

One of the major future tasks of law-and-economics scholarship in the field of crowdinvesting is to gather empirical evidence which allows an answer to the question: Which of the aforementioned scenarios is most plausible? As of now there are only a few fact-based studies or hints as to what this answer might be. The first is a study on financial contracting on the German crowdinvesting market (see below Sect. 10.5.3). The second are accounts of other market-based investor protection mechanisms (not related to contract design) that have been developed by crowdfunding platforms, especially in the UK, in the absence of specific legal obligations (see below Sect. 10.5.4).

10.5.3 Crowdinvesting Contracts in Germany

From a financial contracting point of view the German crowdinvesting market is highly interesting. Remember that in Germany start-ups do not offer transferable securities to the crowd (such as stocks and bonds) but subordinated profit participating loans (see above Sect. 10.4.3.1). Originally, these contracts were virtually unregulated. Even after the introduction of a prospectus requirement for offering profit participating loans to the public in 2015 they remain largely unregulated because start-ups make use of the 2.5-million-exemption from that requirement, because platforms brokering such investment are operating outside the scope of MiFID and because these platforms are not overseen by the German financial regulator BaFin but by the local trade offices who have no specific expertise in the field of corporate finance.

The absence of regulation gave German crowdinvesting platforms the opportunity to develop and experiment with new contractual designs. In a recent study Klöhn et al. (2016b) provide an overview of the contractual terms which are currently being used as well as the development of those terms. The most important results can be summarized as follows:

1. There is a tremendous dynamic in the market. From the beginning of crowdinvesting in 2012 until today investment contracts have undergone significant changes on every platform that has stayed in the market.
2. In some respects, contract development follows the classical pattern known from other markets with an oligopolistic structure, that is runner-up firms have changed their standard contracts and adopted clauses used by the market leader. Nevertheless, platforms do not seem to just stick to these standards[53] but keep revising their contracts and experimenting with innovative ideas.
3. So, while there is evidence that crowdinvesting platforms are actually using contractual design to compete, it is less clear whether this is a

race to the top or a race to the bottom. The relatively few insolvencies of start-ups funded by crowdinvesting as well as estimates on the firm survival, which show a higher survival rate of crowd-funded start-ups compared with German start-ups in general (Hornuf and Schmitt 2016a), might support the race to the top thesis. On the other hand, compared to the earnings of venture capital funds, absolute returns in crowdinvesting seem to be low (Hornuf and Schmitt 2016a). In particular, to date, there have been only a few exit opportunities for crowd investors.

10.5.4 Other Market-Based Safeguards in Europe

Crowdinvesting platforms have experimented with several mechanisms beyond investment contract design to reduce the risk of misallocation of funds and of outright fraud (Armour and Enriques 2017). These mechanisms can be divided into three groups: (1) mechanisms to utilize the collective wisdom of crowd investors, (2) mechanism to use VC or angel investor backup and (3) pricing tools.[54]

10.5.4.1 Wisdom of the Crowd

One of the most obvious mechanisms to unleash the wisdom of the crowd,[55] which is commonly used by platforms all over the world, is to initiate discussion about the risks and potential of the investment opportunity on an internet forum hosted by the platforms. Note however, that in its 2015 review on UK crowdinvesting, the FCA reported that negative comments had been deleted from such forums on some sites.[56]

A mechanism along the same line, often used in practice not only in the UK but all over Europe, is to let potential investors know not only the aggregate amount of funding pledged by prior investors but also the individual distribution (Armour and Enriques 2017, 43). This might send valuable information to the crowd because the more a single investor pledges, the more careful his or her due diligence will have been (Armour and Enriques 2017, 43). Along this line, a study of German crowdinvesting platforms finds that, where such information is made available, large investments by a single investor are positively correlated with the number of subsequent investments later the same day (Hornuf and Schwienbacher 2017a).

Finally, crowdinvesting platforms have experimented with restricting investor access to individuals which are expected to be particularly sophisticated or at least well-aware of the risks of crowdinvesting (for empirical evidence on the correlation between the minimum investment and investor sophistication, see Hornuf and Schmitt 2016b). In Germany, the crowdinvesting platform Innovestment started with a minimum investment per individual of EUR 1000 but later abolished this requirement, possibly due to competitive pressure by other platforms using much lower investment limits (the two leading platforms Companisto and Seedmatch use investment limits of EUR 5 and EUR 250 respectively). Just recently, however, Innovestment announced to raise the minimum investment requirement to EUR 1000 again. In the US, AngelMD is an investment platform which allows only medical professionals to invest in medical start-ups (Armour and Enriques 2017, 44).

10.5.4.2 Angel Investor or VC Backup

Crowdinvesting platforms' pay is usually tied largely to fundraising success and only to a small extent to ultimate investment success. Therefore, their incentives to screen start-ups before offering them to the crowd might be suboptimal (Armour and Enriques 2017, 45). It is certainly not easy for crowdinvesting platforms to signal the crowd that their screening is reliable. As a possible remedy, platforms have designed models under which members of the crowd invest alongside VC funds or angel investors at the same contractual terms. For example, the UK platform SyndicateRoom, only lists companies that are already backed by professional business angels (Armour and Enriques 2017, 45).[57]

Also, in the UK some platforms have tried to make use of contractual protection devices used by VCs to offer the crowd a more attractive investment. For example, as Armour and Enriques (2017, 46) point out, the platform Seedrs signs investment agreements in its capacity as crowdfunders' nominee. Those agreements furnish investors with pre-emption rights, tag-along rights, and veto regarding important issues, "such as winding-up the company, changing the business of the company, issuing preference shares, transferring assets out of the company, making certain loans, or increasing director salaries beyond an agreed level."[58] These rights are exercised by the platform as nominee on investors' behalf.[59]

10.5.4.3 Pricing Tools

Start-ups are extremely difficult to price. Given the far from perfect incentives of crowdinvesting platforms to ensure that start-ups are valued at appropriate levels (see above), crowd investors face an exceptionally high adverse selection risk when making their investment decisions (see Armour and Enriques, Chap. 12 sub 12.2.1.; Ibrahim 2015; Hurt 2015, 254). Moreover, most crowdinvesting platforms offer investments at a take-it-or-leave-it price. This exacerbates the danger of herding among crowd investors because on the platform websites investors can only observe decisions to make an investment as opposed to decisions to abstain from making an investment (Armour and Enriques 2017, 12 et seq.; Wilson and Testoni 2014, 7).

Some platforms have experimented with alternative pricing models. For example, the German crowdinvesting platform Innovestment started with an ambitious auction mechanism designed by an economics Ph.D. candidate writing his thesis about auction theory (see Hornuf and Neuenkirch 2017 for details on the auction mechanism and empirical evidence on the characteristics which influence pricing; on the correlation between portal design and investor types see Hornuf and Schmitt 2016b). In the UK, Crowdcube[60] provides a "price review" mechanism, which relies on the bargaining power of investors willing to buy a relatively large stake in the company (see Armour and Enriques 2017, 49 et seq. for details).

10.6 Outlook

So what should the EU do? Any section about the regulatory perspectives in Europe must start with the realization that a full-blown harmonization of the laws governing crowdinvesting is, at least for the next ten years, simply not feasible. As the German experience shows, such harmonization would require extending the European term of "financial instruments" (as within the meaning of MiFID) or "transferable securities" (as within the meaning of the Prospectus Directive) to any investment contract regardless of its exact legal structure, that is to adopt a concept of "financial instruments" or "transferable securities" similar to the concept of "security" which is predominant in the US. This would be a huge step. It would significantly extend the reach of European securities regulation to previously unregulated areas and markets. The potential side effects of such step are almost impossible to assess. Furthermore, there are several (at least on a national level) powerful interest groups whose constituents rely on finance provided by investments not governed by EU regulation (take the Federal Association of Cooperatives in Germany) and who would no doubt strongly oppose such regulation. Crowdinvesting is simply not important enough to convince any decision maker in Brussels or Luxembourg to take this step.

Given this—rather sobering—fact, one must realize that any attempt to regulate crowdinvesting on the EU level will be limited to financial-instruments-based or securities-based crowdinvesting. Market participants will be able to avoid such regulation by designing investment contracts not covered by EU regulation, such as subordinated profit participating loans in Germany. The most important implication is that stricter regulatory requirements in the area covered by European law (securities and financial instruments) will increase issuers' and platforms' incentives to avoid such regulation by designing investment contracts not covered by EU law.

Taking into consideration that crowdinvesting platforms seem to be experimenting with contractual clauses and other market-based solutions to protect investors (see above Sects. 10.5.3 and 10.5.4), the best option seems to be to not further regulate the market but to actually do the opposite and liberate the market in order to create a level playing field for securities-based and non-securities-based crowdinvesting.

- The first step towards such level playing field must be a reform of the small offerings exemption in the Prospectus Directive. The proposal for a new Prospectus Regulation goes into the right direction and creates a mandatory exemption for offers of a consideration below EUR 1,000,000 (as of today this limit is EUR 100,000).[61] It prevents member states from imposing disclosure requirements which would constitute a disproportionate or unnecessary burden in relation to such offers and thus increase fragmentation of the internal market. This is the right approach, but the European legislator should go further and exempt any securities offer to the public with a consideration below EUR 2.5 million from the prospectus requirement. This proposal is also supported by a recent study by Hornuf and Schwienbacher (2017b), which indicates that exemptions from the prospectus requirement should be more extensive in countries with smaller angel and venture capital markets—like it is the case in (continental) Europe—as smaller firms seeking seed or early-stage capital raise inefficiently low amounts of money when the exemptions are restrictive.

- The second step could be tailored exemptions from MiFID's organizational and conduct-of-business requirements to lower market entry barriers for crowdfunding platforms and to give crowdfunding platforms more latitude to develop market-based investor protection tools. For example, it is highly doubtful that the appropriateness test required by MiFID has any significant effect on crowd investor protection in the UK. Instead, EU law could require MiFID crowdinvesting platforms to adopt investor protection measures specifically tailored to the dangers of crowdinvesting (e.g. herding) if it seems probable that such mechanisms would not be introduced by the platforms due to reputational and/or market pressure.

Notes

1. European Commission, Communication from the Commission to the European Parliament, the Council, the European Economic and Social Committee and the Committee of the Regions, Action Plan on Building a Capital Markets Union, COM (2015) 468 final, 30.9.2015.
2. http://ec.europa.eu/finance/general-policy/crowdfunding/index_en.htm.

3. Agendas, minutes, and meeting documents are available at: http://ec.europa.eu/finance/general-policy/crowdfunding/index_en.htm.
4. European Commission, Green Paper, Long Term Financing of the European Economy, COM (2013) 150 final, 25.3.2013.
5. European Commission, Communication from the Commission to the European Parliament, the Council, the European Economic and Social Committee and the Committee of the Regions, Unleashing the potential of Crowdfunding in the European Union, COM (2014) 172 final, 27.3.2014 (for a discussion of the Directives mentioned in the Communication as having potential impact on crowdfunding, see Gabison 2015 at pp. 376 et seq.). The European Supervisory Authorities (ESAs) have also analyzed the crowdfunding market and its regulation and issued opinions and advices within their respective areas of responsibility. In the field of crowdinvesting the European Securities Markets Authority (ESMA) published an opinion and an advice on December 18, 2014 (ESMA, Opinion on Investment-based crowdfunding of 18.12.2014, https://www.esma.europa.eu/sites/default/files/library/2015/11/2014-1378_opinion_on_investment-based_crowdfunding.pdf; ESMA, Advice on Investment-based crowdfunding of 18.12.2014, https://www.esma.europa.eu/sites/default/files/library/2015/11/2014-1560_advice_on_investment-based_crowdfunding.pdf.). The European Banking Authority (EBA) published an opinion on crowdlending EBA, Opinion of the European Banking Authority on lending-based crowdfunding, 26.02.2015, EBA/Op/2015/03, https://www.eba.europa.eu/documents/10180/983359/EBA-Op-2015-03+(EBA+Opinion+on+lending+based+Crowdfunding).pdf.
6. European Commission, Commission Staff Working Document, Crowdfunding in the Capital Market Union, SWD(2016) 154 final, 3.5.2016.
7. European Commission, Commission Staff Working Document, Crowdfunding in the Capital Market Union, SWD(2016) 154 final, 3.5.2016, at p. 30.
8. European Commission, Commission Staff Working Document, Crowdfunding in the Capital Market Union, SWD(2016) 154 final, 3.5.2016, at p. 31.
9. European Commission, Commission Staff Working Document, Crowdfunding in the Capital Market Union, SWD(2016) 154 final, 3.5.2016, at p. 31.

10. European Commission, Commission Staff Working Document, Crowdfunding in the Capital Market Union, SWD(2016) 154 final, 3.5.2016, at p. 31.
11. European Parliament resolution of July 9, 2015 on Building a Capital Markets Union (2015/2634(RSP)), para. 47.
12. European Parliament resolution of January 19, 2016 on stocktaking and challenges of the EU Financial Services Regulation: impact and the way forward towards a more efficient and effective EU framework for Financial Regulation and a Capital Markets Union (2015/2106(INI)), para. 22.
13. For an overview of the regulation of crowdfunding in a global context, see Pekmezovic/Walker 2016 at pp. 397–445.
14. For an overview of the "major", "emerging", and "frontier" markets of crowdinvesting outside the US, see Dehner and Kong (2014), p. 420 et seq.
15. Directive 2011/83/EU of the European Parliament and of the Council of October 25, 2011 on consumer rights, amending Council Directive 93/13/EEC and Directive 1999/44/EC of the European Parliament and of the Council, and repealing Council Directive 85/577/EEC and Directive 97/7/EC of the European Parliament and of the Council (Consumer Rights Directive), OJ (EU) No. L 304 of 22.11.2011, pp. 64–88.
16. http://eurocrowd.org/about-us/code-of-conduct-2/.
17. Directive 2003/71/EC of the European Parliament and of the Council of November 4, 2003 on the prospectus to be published when securities are offered to the public or admitted to trading and amending Directive 2001/34/EC, OJ (EU) No. L 345 of 31.12.2003, p. 64.
18. Commission regulation (EC) No 809/2004 of April 29, 2004 implementing Directive 2003/71/EC of the European Parliament and of the Council as regards information contained in prospectuses as well as the format, incorporation by reference, and publication of such prospectuses and dissemination of advertisements, OJ (EU) No L 149 of 30.4.2004, p. 3.
19. As amended by Directive 2010/73/EU of the European Parliament and of the Council of November 24, 2010 amending Directives 2003/71/EC on the prospectus to be published when securities are offered to the public or admitted to trading and 2004/109/EC on the harmonisation of transparency requirements in relation to information about issuers whose securities are admitted to trading on a regulated market, OJ (EU) No. L 327 of 11.12.2010, pp. 1–12.

20. For the US concept see SEC v. Howey Co. 328 U.S. 293 (1946), compare, with regard to crowdfunding, e.g. Hurt (2015), p. 235 et seq.
21. Directive 2014/65/EU of the European Parliament and of the Council of May 15, 2014 on markets in financial instruments and amending Directive 2002/92/EC and Directive 2011/61/EU, OJ No L 173 of 12.6.2014, p. 39.
22. The terminology refers to the Lamfalussy Process, a legislative procedure under which EU securities regulation is passed. For an overview *see Walla* (2013), pp. 27–36.
23. For the obligations of crowdfunding portals regarding the provision of information and their liability under US law, see Bradford (2015a).
24. Directive 2013/36/EU of the European Parliament and of the Council of June 26, 2013 on access to the activity of credit institutions and the prudential supervision of credit institutions and investment firms, amending Directive 2002/87/EC and repealing Directives 2006/48/EC and 2006/49/EC, OJ No 176 of 27.6.2013, p. 338.
25. Regulation (EU) No 575/2013 of the European Parliament and of the Council of June 26, 2013 on prudential requirements for credit institutions and investment firms and amending Regulation (EU) No 648/2012, OJ (EU) No L 176 of 27.6.2013, p. 1.
26. Directive 2005/60/EC of the European Parliament and of the Council of October 26, 2005 on the prevention of the use of the financial system for the purpose of money laundering and terrorist financing, OJ (EU) No L 309 of 25.11.2005, p. 15.
27. Directive 2015/2366 of the European Parliament and of the Council of November 25, 2015 on payment services in the internal market, amending Directives 2002/65/EC, 2009/110/EC and 2013/36/EU and Regulation (EU) No 1093/2010, and repealing Directive 2007/64/EC, OJ (EU) No L 337 of 23.12.2015, p. 35.
28. Directive 2002/65/EC of the European Parliament and of the Council of September 23, 2002 concerning the distance marketing of consumer financial services and amending Council Directive 90/619/EEC and Directives 97/7/EC and 98/27/EC, OJ (EU) No L 271 of 9.10.2002, p. 16.
29. Regulation (EU) 2016/679 of the European Parliament and of the Council of April 27, 2016 on the protection of natural persons with regard to the processing of personal data and on the free movement of such data, and repealing Directive 95/46/EC (General Data Protection Regulation), OJ (EU) No. L 119 of 4.5.2016, p. 1.

30. European Commission, Commission Staff Working Document, Crowdfunding in the Capital Market Union, SWD(2016) 154 final, 3.5.2016.
31. Section 85(5)(a), Schedule 11A, para 9 FSMA 2000.
32. Section 21 FSMA 2000.
33. Section 19 FSMA 2000.
34. FCA, The FCA's regulatory approach to crowdfunding over the internet, and the promotion of non-readily realisable securities by other media, PS14/4, March 2014. For an overview of the FCA's regulation, see Ridley (2016) at p. 65 et seq.
35. FCA, A review of the regulatory regime for crowdfunding and the promotion of non-readily realisable securities by other media, February 2015.
36. FCA, Call for input to the post-implementation review of the FCA's crowdfunding rules, July 2016; FCA, Feedback Statement, Interim feedback to the call for the post-implementation review of the FCA's crowdfunding rules, FS 16/13, December 2016.
37. FCA, Conduct of Business Sourcebook, 4.2.1R.
38. FCA, Conduct of Business Sourcebook, 4.7.7(3), 4.7.8(2), 10.2.
39. FCA, A review of the regulatory regime for crowdfunding and the promotion of non-readily realisable securities by other media, February 2015, para. 50 (emphasis added).
40. FCA, Conduct of Business Sourcebook, 4.7.7(2), 4.7.9–4.7.10.; see also FCA, The FCA's regulatory approach to crowdfunding over the internet, and the promotion of non-readily realisable securities by other media, PS14/4, March 2014, at p. 35 et seq.
41. FCA, Conduct of Business Sourcebook, 4.7.10.
42. § 3(1)(1) No. 5 Wertpapierprospektgesetz.
43. § 2(3) No. 3 lit. b) Vermögensanlagengesetz.
44. Small Investor Protection Act (*Kleinanlegerschutzgesetz, KASG*) of July 3, 2015, BGBl. I 2015, p. 1114 ff.
45. § 2a Vermögensanlagengesetz.
46. §§ 13, 14 Vermögensanlagengesetz.
47. § 13(6) Vermögensanlagengesetz.
48. § 15(3) Vermögensanlagengesetz.
49. § 34f(2) No. 3 Gewerbeordnung.
50. § 2a(3) Vermögensanlagengesetz. There is an exception from this requirement for investors who are corporate entities.

51. See § 16(4) Finanzanlagenvermittlungsverordnung, FinVermV and § 31(6) Wertpapierhandelsgesetz.
52. On regulatory competition on the level of national regulators and potential regulatory options, see Pekmezovic and Walker (2016), p. 446 et seq.
53. The two market leaders—measured by the amounts of funds raised—are the crowdinvesting platforms Companisto and Seedmatch.
54. Along the same line Armour and Enriques (2017), p. 42: (1) mechanisms that try to leverage more effectively the collective wisdom of the crowd, by reducing the possibility of inappropriate herding, (2) adaptation of contractual protection devices used by VCs and angel investors, (3) attempts to make more use of customized versions of investor protection mechanisms used in traditional IPO markets.
55. For first evidence on the wisdom of the crowd with regard to funding decisions, see Mollick and Nanda (2016).
56. FCA, A review of the regulatory regime for crowdfunding and the promotion of non-readily realisable securities by other media, February 2015, para. 51.
57. https://www.syndicateroom.com/about-us/about-syndicateroom.aspx.
58. https://www.seedrs.com/learn/blog/investors/trends-insights/small-investors-equity-crowdfunding.
59. https://www.seedrs.com/learn/blog/investors/trends-insights/small-investors-equity-crowdfunding.
60. For empirical data on the crowdfunding campaigns on CrowdCube in 2014, see Gabison (2015), p. 403 et seq.
61. Council of the European Union, Regulation of the European Parliament and the Council on the prospectus to be published when securities are offered to the public or admitted to trading, Confirmation of the final compromise text with a view to agreement, 2015/0268 /COD), 16.12.2016.

References

Anand, Anita I. 2014. Is Crowdfunding Bad for Investors? *Canadian Business Law Journal* 55: 215–229.

Armour, John, and Luca Enriques. 2017. *The Promise and Perils of Crowdfunding: Between Corporate Finance and Consumer Contracts*. Working Paper (on file with the author).

Belleflamme, Paul, Nesrine Omrani, and Martin Peitz. 2015. The Economics of Crowdfunding Platforms. *Information Economics and Policy* 33: 11–28.

Bradford, Steven. 2015a. Shooting the Messenger: The Liability of Crowdfunding Intermediaries for the Fraud of Others. *University of Cincinnati Law Review* 83: 371–411.

———. 2015b. Regulating Investment Crowdfunding: Small Business Capital Formation and Investor Protection. *Zeitschrift für Bankrecht und Bankwirtschaft/Journal of Banking Law and Banking* 27: 376–382.

Dehner, Joseph J., and Jin Kong. 2014. Equity-Based Crowdfunding Outside the USA. *University of Cincinnati Law Review* 83: 413–443.

Gabison, Garry A. 2015. Equity Crowdfunding: All Regulated but Not Equal. *DePaul Business & Commercial Law Journal* 13: 359–409.

Grossman, Sanford J. 1981. The Informational Role of Warranties and Private Disclosure About Product Quality. *The Journal of Law & Economics* 24: 461–483.

Heminway, Joan MacLeod. 2013. The New Intermediary on the Block: Funding Portals under the Crowdfund Act. *UC Davis Business Law Journal* 13: 177–205.

———. 2014. How Congress Killed Investment Crowdfunding: A Tale of Political Pressure, Hasty Decisions, and Inexpert Judgments that Begs for a Happy Ending. *Kentucky Law Journal* 102: 865–889.

Hornuf, L., and M. Neuenkirch. 2017. Pricing Shares in Equity Crowdfunding. *Small Business Economics* 48: 795–811.

Hornuf, Lars, and Matthias Schmitt. 2016a. Success and Failure in Equity Crowdfunding. *CESifo DICE Report* 14: 16–22.

———. 2016b. Does a Local Bias Exist in Equity Crowdfunding? The Impact of Investor Types and Portal Design. *Max Planck Institute for Innovation & Competition* Research Paper No. 16-07.

Hornuf, Lars, and Armin Schwienbacher. 2016. Crowdinvesting—Angel Investing for the Masses? In *Handbook of Research on Venture Capital: Volume 3. Business Angels*, ed. Hans Landström and Colin Mason, 381–397. Cheltenham, UK: Edward Elgar.

———. 2017a. Market Mechanisms and Funding Dynamics in Equity Crowdfunding. *Journal of Corporate Finance*. http://www.sciencedirect.com/science/article/pii/S0929119916302450. Accessed 20 Feb 2017.

———. 2017b. Should Securities Regulation Promote Equity Crowdfunding. *Small Business Economics* 49: 579–593.

Hurt, A. Christine. 2015. Pricing Disintermediation: Crowdfunding and Online Auction IPOs. *University of Illinois Law Review* 1: 217–262.

Ibrahim, Darian M. 2015. Equity Crowdfunding: A Market for Lemons? *Minnesota Law Review* 100: 561–607.

Klein, Benjamin, and Keith B. Leffler. 1981. The Role of Market Forces in Assuring Contractual Performance. *Journal of Political Economy* 89: 615–641.

Klöhn Lars, Lars Hornuf, and Tobias Schilling. 2018. Financial Contracting in Crowdinvesting—Lessons from the German Market. *German Law Journal.* Forthcoming.

Lars, Klöhn, Lars Hornuf, and Tobias Schilling. 2016. The Regulation of Crowdfunding in the German Small Investor Protection Act: Content, Consequences, Critique, Suggestions. *European Company Law* 13: 56–66.

Milgrom, Paul R. 1981. Good News and Bad News: Representation Theorems and Applications. *The Bell Journal of Economics* 12: 380–391.

Mollick, Ethan, and Ramana Nanda. 2016. Wisdom or Madness? Comparing Crowds with Expert Evaluation in Funding the Arts. *Management Science* 62: 1533–1553.

Pekmezovic, Alma, and Gordon Walker. 2016. The Global Significance of Crowdfunding: Solving the SME Funding Problem and Democratizing Access to Capital. *William & Mary Business Law Review* 7: 347–458.

Ridley, David. 2016. Will New Regulation on Crowdfunding in the United Kingdom and United States Have a Positive Impact and Lead to Crowdfunding Becoming an Established Financing Technique? *Statute Law Review* 37: 57–76.

Shapiro, Carl. 1983. Premiums for High Quality Products as Returns to Reputation. *The Quarterly Journal of Economics* 98: 659–680.

Stigler, George J. 1964. Public Regulation of the Securities Markets. *Journal of Business* 37: 117–142.

Viotto, Jordana. 2015. Competition and Regulation of Crowdfunding Platforms: A Two-Sided Market Approach. *Digiworld Economic Journal* 99: 33–50.

Walla, Fabian. 2013. Process and Strategies of Capital Markets Regulation in Europe. In *European Capital Markets Law*, ed. Rüdiger Veil, 25–43. Oxford: Bloomsbury UK.

Wilson, Karen E., and Marco Testoni. 2014. Improving the Role of Equity Crowdfunding in Europe's Capital Markets. *Bruegel Policy Contribution* 2014 (09): 1–14.

Lars Klöhn holds a professorship for civil and business law at Humboldt University of Berlin. He has published several scholarly articles on corporate, banking, and capital markets law. He is inter alia co-editor of ZBB, a leading German banking and capital markets law journal, and a regular advisor to the German Legislature and the German Ministry of Finance in matters related to capital markets and banking law.

11

Individual Investors' Access to Crowdinvesting: Two Regulatory Models

John Armour and Luca Enriques

11.1 Introduction

In recent years, a new source of finance, "crowdinvesting", has become available to smaller firms, typically start-ups and early-stage ones. It consists of raising capital via the internet from a large number of individuals, each typically contributing a small sum in exchange for an equity interest in the firm. Crowdinvesting is channeled through a web-based portal, which aggregates business plans from fund-seekers and permits potential investors to browse projects on offer.

Crowdinvesting is one of the riskiest asset classes individual investors may access. Issuers in these markets have usually no track record. Because the market is relatively new, that is also true for the online platforms which may in theory act as gatekeepers and develop a reputation for screening good investment opportunities. And, unless alternative

J. Armour (✉) • L. Enriques
Faculty of Law, University of Oxford, Oxford, UK

D. Cumming, L. Hornuf (eds.), *The Economics of Crowdfunding*,
https://doi.org/10.1007/978-3-319-66119-3_11

information aggregation mechanisms are developed, there is a high risk that individuals will make investment decisions based on what other individuals have done before them (i.e., "herding") rather than on a collective, uncoordinated effort to understand the merits of the investment, such as can be seen in IPO markets (via the bookbuilding process) and in secondary equity markets.

Given the small amount of capital typically raised by a firm pursuing a crowdinvesting call, this mode of fundraising is only likely to be viable if the rigor of "ordinary" securities regulations is relaxed. With issuers aiming to raise a few hundred thousand dollars on average,[1] the compliance costs of fully applicable securities regulations would otherwise swallow too large a chunk of the money raised (Pope 2011). Hence, the choice by many jurisdictions of providing for exemptions and special, more lenient rules for crowdinvesting (Weinstein 2013).

The US and European jurisdictions have approached policymaking in this area from opposite starting points. To make crowdinvesting viable in the US, exemptions and relaxations of existing rules had to be devised anew. The US Congress expressed desire to facilitate crowdinvesting with the JOBS (Jump-Start Our Business Startups) Act of 2012: first, this Act made crowdinvesting available as a source of capital for US businesses by removing obstacles to the setup of crowdinvesting platforms limiting access to accredited investors (i.e., high net worth individuals who are presumed capable of understanding the risks, or failing that, of affording access to professional advice). Several such platforms now exist: the largest four among such restricted-access platforms (EquityNet, Angelist, Fundable, and Crowdfunder) are estimated to have raised together more than USD 575 million in 2014 (Massolution 2015). Then, in October 2015, the Securities and Exchange Commission introduced rules facilitating the operation of crowdfunding platforms for retail investors, fundraising from whom had previously required compliance with the rules for general offerings (Securities and Exchange Commission 2015).

In Europe, the framework was of course less uniform, given the lower degree of uniformity in securities regulation. But Member States could provide for (partial) exemptions from MiFID rules on investment firms and investment services and also dispense issuers from complying with the disclosure rules in the Prospectus Directive, because of its exemption for small offerings.

As a result, crowdinvesting via (exempt) public offerings has been burgeoning in Europe for both retail and professional investors, while in the US it has until very recently been relegated to platforms only accepting accredited investors as funders. It is presently too early to tell whether the new SEC rules for retail crowdinvesting will lower the burdens of securities regulation enough to allow platforms open to retail investors to thrive.

This chapter first identifies the features that make crowdinvesting particularly risky for individual investors (Sect. 11.2). Next, it describes the regulatory framework in two main jurisdictions (the US and the UK) which approached the phenomenon from a different status quo (Sect. 11.3). Finally, it offers some tentative thoughts on how, and how strictly, to regulate crowdinvesting (Sect. 11.4).

11.2 The Perils of Crowdinvesting

Crowdinvesting is one of the riskiest (non-leveraged) investment classes a retail investor can access. Not only is the typical funded firm a start-up or an early-stage business which, as such, presents the three central problems of financing (uncertainty, information asymmetry, and opportunism in the form of agency costs) in an extreme form (Gilson 2010, 901). It is also the case that the usual mechanisms by which retail investors are protected before and after they decide to invest are unavailable in the crowdinvesting setting. To understand the extent of the risk they run, it is worth highlighting how crowdinvesting compares, in terms of risks for retail investors, with investing in an IPO. Before doing that, however, it is worth asking whether, in the presence of other forms of early-stage financing, like angel investing, venture capital ("VC"), and other forms of crowdfunding, none of which particularly lends itself to the exploitation of financial backers, crowdinvesting is doomed to attract bad-quality start-ups, that savvy investors would always refuse to fund.

11.2.1 Adverse Selection?

While going public can be a natural move for successful companies, as it provides liquidity for existing and prospective investors, some have expressed the concern that only "lemons" will resort to crowdinvesting (Dorff 2014, 496–497).

First, where the VC industry is well developed and angel investor networks are available, "good" start-ups should have no problem finding backing from such financiers. Assuming that VCs and angel investors do their job well, that is, that they will indeed finance all projects deserving funding, only those projects that are not worth financing will be left to seek crowdinvesting (Hurt 2015). Or, similarly, if "good" start-ups make their pitch on a crowdinvesting platform, angel investors and VCs may "cherry pick" them, thanks to their specialized knowledge of the field compared to the crowd, and fund them entirely after having the offering removed from the platform, so that investors will only have access to the worst projects (Ibrahim 2015).

A second concern is that innovative start-ups' success will most often rely on keeping information about the venture secret, lest larger-shoulder competitors exploit the idea behind it and deliver the innovation first and/or more effectively (Ley and Weaven 2011, 96–97). Crowdinvesting requires an entrepreneur to publicize sensitive information about his product (as opposed to conveying such information to selected individuals like angel investors and VCs) at a much earlier stage than is typical for an IPO: the risk that the innovative value of the idea will be destroyed by disclosing it is thus much greater. Hence, again, the risk that only "bad" projects that deserve no funding will enter the crowdinvesting market.

Finally, if that is not an issue, one may wonder why, then, an entrepreneur would not choose reward crowdfunding rather than crowdinvesting, given that the former will not require the entrepreneur to share in the venture's profits with the crowdfunders and also has the advantage of providing the entrepreneur with valuable information about demand for his product (Armour and Enriques 2017).

None of these concerns, however, is so serious as to warrant the conclusion that the crowdinvesting market is bound to be a market for "lemons". To start with, angel investor networks and VCs may be very active in (some areas of) the US and in some other high-tech clusters. Both angel investors and, to a lesser degree, VCs tend to invest in ventures that are based in the same geographic area (Wong et al. 2009, 227–228; Ibrahim 2010, 730): especially with the prospect of more intense border controls on immigration in some of the most developed countries, we cannot expect all talented entrepreneurs in the world to migrate to where VCs and angel investors operate. In many countries outside the US, these professional investors networks are much less well-developed and external finance much harder for start-ups to access (Hornuf and Schwienbacher 2017).

In addition, even start-ups in the country where angel investor and VC markets are most well-developed have experienced gaps in the financing cycle. As Oranburg (2015) has documented, a number of start-ups have no problem finding angel investors who will fund their early seed stage, but may run out of cash before they are large enough and at a sufficiently mature stage of product development to attract VCs. At this interim stage in which it is especially difficult to further tap angel investors, who generally prefer to engage in first rounds of financing with other start-ups than pouring more money in one they have previously funded. Crowdinvesting may well bridge the financing gap between early-stage and VC financing.

Second, cherry-picking on crowdinvesting platforms by angels and VCs seems unlikely to become a frequent phenomenon. Both of these players typically receive a much larger number of investment proposals than they accept (Morrissette 2007, 59) and, as mentioned already, tend to invest in ventures based in the same geographical area. Entrepreneurs based in those areas will either have proposed their investment to VCs and angel investors before entering the crowdinvesting markets or will simply be uninterested in those sources of capital.

In fact, there might be various reasons why founders may prefer the crowdinvesting market to angels (and VCs). To start with, VCs and angel investors provide not only capital but also business and strategy advice, for which they will get compensated, however implicitly, in the form of a higher return on their investments and correspondingly, a higher cost of capital for the founders (Ibrahim 2015). An experienced serial entrepreneur, or one with an extremely simple business idea (think of an app or a video game), may simply not need those services. Further, there are strings, whether visible or invisible, attached to the involvement of VCs and, to a lesser degree, angel investors. Venture capital firms routinely negotiate a number of governance rights which limit the entrepreneur's freedom of action and may even put them in control (Fried and Ganor 2006). Angel investors, while relying as often on informal as on formal mechanisms, still heavily monitor ex post the ventures they fund, thereby reducing entrepreneurs' freedom of action (Ibrahim 2008, 1431–1433).[2] Crowdinvesting allows entrepreneurs to obtain funding with hardly any strings attached. It may also avoid the risks inherent to staged financing, which is typical of VC investing, and precisely that VCs will take a less positive view of the venture at stage 2 than at stage 1, not because any new negative information has emerged about the venture but simply because the market as a whole has become less "hot" or optimistic (Nanda and Rhodes-Kropf 2013): the crowd's lack of financial sophistication, together with the hype which may go together with crowdinvesting in a booming technology market, may help the entrepreneur secure enough capital to rule out the financing risk stemming from the staged financing constraint.

In addition to that, while feedback on the product from the crowdfunding community may be more common in the reward than in the crowdinvesting setting, one cannot rule out that interactions with crowdinvestors help the entrepreneur improve the product, the production process, or more likely corporate finance and managerial aspects of the venture. Similarly, crowdinvesting may be an effective marketing tool itself both to find financiers in a later round and to create product awareness (Belleflamme et al. 2015, 40–41).

The risk that competitors appropriate the entrepreneurial idea by taking advantage of information disclosed on the crowdinvesting platform is real. But, while emulation by competitors thanks to crowdinvesting disclosures may be a concern for some projects, some business ideas may be described in the pitch without giving away information that competitors can profit from (Agrawal et al. 2014) or may be difficult to replicate, for example because their success may critically be linked to the founder's personality or unique skillset (Hornuf and Schwienbacher 2016).

Finally, reward crowdfunding cannot be used for each and any entrepreneurial project: Sergei Brin and Larry Page could have never "presold" their search engine or the related services. In addition to advertising-based business models, any business-to-business venture would also be an unlikely candidate for reward crowdfunding. And even business-to-consumer ventures may find it hard to raise sufficient capital via reward crowdfunding if a lot of capital is required to fund the business (Belleflamme et al. 2014).

To conclude on this point, the idea that crowdinvesting will only attract lemons (i.e., fraudsters and low-quality, negative NPV projects) seems unpersuasive.[3] For sure, crowdinvesting will not cater to each and every kind of venture, but there is no reason not to think that entrepreneurs will make use of it for good projects as well.

11.2.2 Market Pricing and the Risk of Herding

The big challenge with investing in an innovative start-up is how to know what to pay. There is no market for the firm's product—indeed, in most cases there is not even (yet) a product—and so profitability forecasts are at best guesstimates of likely production costs and market size. In the case of a traditional IPO, however, this challenge is met by aggregating the assessments of as many different sophisticated investors as possible, through the mechanism of market pricing. The initial IPO will follow a bookbuilding process: an investment bank will set the price based on informed investors' estimates of the likely value of the securities. Retail investors can then free ride on sophisticated investors' informed choices.

After the IPO, secondary market trading acts to aggregate investors' assessments of the price relevance of publicly available information into the market price extremely rapidly. This makes the market price the best available estimate of the securities' value, based on publicly available information. Ongoing disclosure obligations for public companies ensure that the set of publicly available information supports informed pricing. A liquid and informationally efficient secondary market, in turn, makes investment in the primary market, ex ante, less risky.

In the case of crowdinvesting, it is very uncommon, albeit not unheard of (Hornuf and Neuenkirch 2017), to use a bookbuilding process or any auction mechanism akin to that. The issuer directly targets retail investors. Platforms typically give investors access to information about the company's (self-produced) valuation, its business plan, the target amount, and the percentage of equity it represents based on the valuation; in addition to that, information is provided about how much funding the crowd has already committed, and how many (and, unless they prefer anonymity, which) investors have already committed to funding (or declared an intention to fund). Theory suggests that, rather than serving to aggregate information, the sequential arrival of investors is likely to engender herding. In an ordinary secondary market, investors assess their own valuation of the security against that reflected in the market price, which adjusts depending on demand. In the crowdinvesting setting, where a secondary market does not exist or is highly illiquid, the price typically does not change in response to demand. Investors therefore draw inferences about the price from the level of observed demand. Put intuitively: "if lots of others have invested, they must think this is a good opportunity, at this price". An investor who lacks the information necessary to assess the quality of the project might then trust the "wisdom" evidenced by the decisions of the investing crowd.

The problem is that most of the other investors might equally be basing their investment on what everyone else has done. In addition, studies of early investment in crowdfunded projects report that the initial investors are disproportionately likely to be friends and family of the founders (Agrawal et al. 2010). This likely injects an element of bias into the initial signal of support. Success may be a consequence not of attracting "knowledgeable" investors at the outset, but rather of founders being part of a large social network (Colombo et al. 2015).

11.2.3 Reputation

The very nature of the projects as start-ups means that, in most cases, no reputation can be pledged to investors. Nor are there any gatekeepers who can pledge their own reputation to overcome this constraint as effectively as underwriters or securities lawyers in ordinary IPOs on public equity markets (Coffee 2006). It is, again, the absence of a secondary market that creates a long time lag between crowdfunders' investment and an objective, albeit imperfect, assessment of the offering's pricing and available disclosure. In other words, while informed traders, securities analysts, and private and public enforcers of securities regulations provide an immediate, or at least timely, feedback on the IPO's quality, no such mechanism can work out as expediently for crowdinvesting offerings. Therefore, the room for opportunism on the part of the offerors (and the platforms themselves) at the offering stage is much wider. Of course, like reputational intermediaries generally, in the long run platforms stand to gain more from establishing a record of good-quality offerings on their portals. But the presence of fringe operators taking advantage of the crowdfunding hype is a reasonable concern.

11.2.4 Governance

Those who invest in an IPO do so in the shadow of a framework of corporate law rules, stock exchange listing requirements, corporate governance best practices, and market and legal institutions that together reduce the risk of ex post expropriation on the part of those who retain or obtain control over the company (Black 2001). While such direct and indirect protections vary across jurisdictions and industries, and also widely diverge in their effectiveness depending on a company's ownership structure, it is a truism that the higher visibility that comes from having a stock exchange listing, from being subject to mandatory disclosure rules, and from having daily trading on the shares reduces the risk of expropriation. By contrast, a non-listed start-up will be under no such scrutiny other than, if at all, by the crowd and the crowdinvesting platform. Whether and to what extent contractual solutions are offered that can substitute for the absence of all those protections (including corporate law protections, given the tendency of all jurisdictions to provide for more flexible rules in the absence of a listing) will crucially depend on whether the platform acting on behalf of the investing crowd will bargain for such protections.

Financiers of ventures that are similar to crowdfunded ones in terms of uncertainty, information asymmetry, and opportunism risk typically obtain joint or effective control of the company and its future financing decisions as a condition for their investment. In fact, as noticed before, one of the reasons why crowdinvesting may be appealing to entrepreneurs is that they retain a much higher degree of control over their firm than after letting an angel investor or a VC in. Correspondingly, crowdinvestors run a much higher risk of ex post opportunism, especially as regards the dilution of their equity claims in successive financing rounds. While even shareholders in a listed corporation run the risk of dilution once the listed corporation taps capital markets again, such a risk is arguably much lower where a secondary market exists that at least provides a yardstick for the pricing of the newly issued shares. Similarly, in the absence of a secondary market, crowdfunders will also have a much harder time finding a buyer for the rights to subscribe new shares, even assuming (which may well not be the case) that they are entitled to those rights and that, if so, they are allowed to sell them.

11.3 Regulatory Treatment of Crowdinvesting: The UK and the US Approaches

This raises a stark policy question: should securities laws be relaxed for crowdinvesting? Advocates make two key points. First, start-up firms are good for the economy. They are disproportionately associated with innovation (as measured by patent applications and R&D spend) and job creation (Hall 2011; Kogan et al. 2012). Hence relaxations of securities law rules that apply to other firms in favor of start-ups may generate social benefits.

In response to this, others point out that securities laws exist to protect investors. Relaxing the rules in relation to start-ups—arguably the riskiest types of issuer out there—would become a magnet for those willing to part gullible investors from their money, with predictably sour consequences (Hazen 2014). The "dot-com bubble" showed that even with the benefit of securities laws, small investors could be led astray spectacularly; arguably, matters can only be worse if those protections are not in place.

As an outcome of this tension, and the political risks that any choice in this area entails (either stifle crowdinvesting, denying investors the opportunity to finance the next Google, or make "fraudinvesting" feasible, exposing individual investors to losses from unscrupulous promoters), it is perhaps unsurprising that the pre-existing regime for offerings of this kind dictates how strict regulations are that are specifically targeted to crowdinvesting.

To illustrate, we compare the regulation of crowdinvesting in two jurisdictions, the UK and the US, that started out as polar opposites in this area. In the US, no such offering could be made to the public without compliance with burdensome disclosure regulations—that is, an initial prospectus and then continuing disclosure. The costs of compliance with such obligations acted as a *de facto* prohibition on crowdinvesting. Meanwhile, European securities laws permitted Member States to apply a "small offering exemption". Pursuant to this, the UK imposed no real disclosure burden on crowdinvesting. At the same time, crowdinvesting platforms were considered investment services providers in both jurisdictions and both, though with a time lag between the two, chose to provide for special, less burdensome rules for platforms specializing in the crowdinvesting business.[4]

11.3.1 The UK Framework

The EU legal framework, to which the UK is still bound until "Brexit" becomes effective, has always contained an exemption from prospectus requirements for small offerings. That exemption has proved instrumental to make crowdinvesting offerings possible within the EU.

More precisely, the EU Prospectus Directive does not apply to offerings of less than EUR 5 million in a 12-month period,[5] thus allowing Member States, if they see fit, to leave smaller offerings (including via crowdinvesting campaigns) exempt from prospectus requirements. The Prospectus Directive also explicitly prohibits prospectus rules from applying below offerings of EUR 100,000 in a 12-month period. The UK has followed the directive and implemented the EUR 5 million offering size limit.[6]

At the same time, if the securities offered on the crowdinvesting platform qualify as "financial instruments",[7] which is usually the case, then, under the framework set out in the Markets in Financial Instruments Directive ("MiFID"),[8] crowdinvesting portals need to be authorized as performing investment services or activities, because they usually engage at the very least in the business of receiving and transmitting crowdfunders' orders relating to financial instruments (European Securities and Markets Authority 2014, 16).[9] In particular, according to ESMA, crowdinvesting platforms are required to conduct an assessment of whether the investment is appropriate for the investor (id., 14–15).

Within this framework of European rules, the UK's Financial Conduct Authority ("FCA") has established a flexible regime for crowdinvesting platforms. Section 19 of the Financial Services and Markets Act 2000 (as amended) requires crowdinvesting intermediaries to be authorized by the FCA if they conduct regulated activities. Activities that crowdinvesting platforms may only undertake with such authorization include arranging deals in investments[10] and carrying out financial promotions. In particular, financial promotions, defined as "invitation[s] or inducement[s] to engage in investment activity",[11] clearly encompass crowdinvesting offerings.

Under MiFID, all financial promotions must be "fair, clear and not misleading".[12] In 2013, the FCA introduced specific consumer protection rules governing the sale of crowdinvesting securities (Financial Conduct Authority 2014). The main elements of these rules are restrictions on the persons to whom crowdinvesting offerings of non-readily realizable securities may be offered and a requirement that the crowdinvesting platform assess whether the product is appropriate for the client.[13] In practice, this assessment is conducted by means of a simple multiple choice questionnaire carried out as part of the investor's process of signing up for an account with the platform. Platforms provide "investment guides" which investors are encouraged to study as a means of preparing to take these tests.[14]

Such securities may only be offered to certain sophisticated investors or to retail investors who certify that they have not invested, and will not invest, more than 10% of their net assets (excluding the value of their home) in non-readily realizable securities.

11.3.2 The US: The Long-Awaited Crowdfunding Exemption

Under Title III of the JOBS Act,[15] the US Congress provided for a small offering exemption for crowdinvesting and directed the SEC to implement a framework of rules to govern such offerings. While the JOBS Act required the SEC to have crowdinvesting rules in place by the end of 2012, it was not until October 2013 that its "Regulation Crowdfunding" was proposed.[16] These proved contentious, and as a result it was October 2015 before the SEC adopted its final crowdinvesting regulations, which eventually came into force on May 16, 2016.

Title III of the JOBS Act added a new Section 4(a)(6) to the US Securities Act of 1933,[17] which provides an exemption from registration of a crowdinvesting offering under the 1933 Act if certain conditions are met. These conditions include a limit on the amount of capital raised of USD 1 million per 12-month period, limits on the amount a single investor may invest per issuer (rather than in the asset class as a whole) based on his or her income and net worth,[18] a requirement that investors understand the risks of crowdinvesting, and a requirement that transactions are conducted through an intermediary registered with the SEC as either a broker or a new type of regulated entity called a "funding portal".

Regulation Crowdfunding also requires that only a single intermediary is used for a crowdinvesting offering, and that all information in relation to the offering is available "online only" in order to ensure that the collective opinion of the crowd is equally available to all potential investors.[19]

Section 4(a)(b) of the Securities Act requires crowdinvesting issuers to file certain specified disclosures with the SEC and provide these to potential investors and the crowdinvesting platform. Such required disclosures include information on the issuer's directors, officers, and principal shareholders,[20] a description of its business and business plan,[21] the purpose and intended use of proceeds of the offering,[22] the price of the securities or the method for determining the price,[23] the target offering amount, the deadline to reach it, regular progress updates,[24] and a description of the ownership and capital structure of the issuer as well as any risk factors related to the offering.[25] Further, crowdinvesting issuers must provide a complete set of financial statements prepared in compliance with US GAAP for the last two years or the period since the issuer's inception, whichever is shorter.[26] In each case, these financial statements must be certified by the issuer's CEO. For offerings of more than USD 100,000, they must also be reviewed by an independent public accountant, who, in the case of offerings of more than USD 500,000, must also audit the statements.[27] The issuer must also provide a narrative discussion of its historical results, liquidity, and capital resources,[28] and must file annual reports with the SEC following a completed crowdinvesting offering.[29]

In addition, the SEC has used its discretion to propose further items that must be disclosed,[30] including the amount of compensation the issuer is paying to the intermediary[31] the material terms of any debt finance it has raised,[32] and details of certain related-party transactions.[33]

The investor may not transfer securities issued in a crowdinvesting transaction for a period of one year, with certain limited exceptions such as resales to the issuer or to accredited investors, but are freely transferable thereafter.[34]

To avoid conflicts of interest, brokers and funding portals, as well as their directors, officers, and partners, are prohibited from having (or accepting as payment) any financial interest in any issuer using their services.[35] Regulation Crowdfunding also requires an intermediary to take measures to reduce the risk of fraud in crowdinvesting transactions on its platform. Such measures include having a reasonable basis for believing that the issuer is in compliance with relevant regulations and has established means to keep accurate records of holders of the securities it offers.[36] The intermediary must deny access to the platform for issuers that it believes may present a potential fraud risk.

Crowdfunding investors may bring actions against issuers for material misstatements or omissions in the offering documents,[37] and the SEC has indicated that "it appears likely" that crowdinvesting intermediaries would be treated as issuers under the statute's liability provision.[38] The SEC has not clarified its position in its final rules indicating that the determination of an "issuer" liability for intermediaries will depend on the specific circumstances of the matter in question.[39] Intermediaries have an incentive to conduct due diligence on potential issuers before deciding whether to allow them to list their securities for sale on their platform.

The SEC's own estimates of the costs associated with a crowdinvesting offering suggest that the framework established by Regulation Crowdfunding may be unappealing for potential issuers seeking to raise smaller amounts. The fixed costs for required filings for offerings up to USD 100,000 were estimated at USD 2,500 and intermediaries were expected to charge between 5 and 15% of the amount raised, which means that fees for an offering seeking to raise USD 100,000 may be as high as 17.5% of the capital raised.[40] This may make smaller crowdinvesting offerings less attractive to investors.[41]

Issuers may therefore consider other exemptions from registration under the Securities Act. For example, following amendments pursuant to Section 201(a) of the JOBS Act, Rule 506(c) under the Securities Act now allows offerings (of unlimited size) to use general solicitation and advertising, as long as all purchasers are accredited investors,[42] a regulatory innovation that has contributed to the success of crowdinvesting platforms only accessible to such investor class (Ibrahim 2015).

An additional limit to crowdinvesting stems from the US regulation of investment companies (Oranburg 2015, 443).[43] If the practice prevailing among angel investor syndicates were to be followed also in the context of crowdinvesting, investors would not directly hold shares in the crowdfunded venture, but rather hold certificates in a vehicle which in turn would hold those shares. However, for such a vehicle not to be subject to the burdensome regulatory requirements of the Investment Companies Act of 1940, the vehicle must have no more than 100 beneficial owners.[44] Hence, it might be difficult to combine investment from a genuine crowd, in which each individual contributes small amounts, with an effective tool to minimize the costs of interactions between the entrepreneur and the crowd.

Table 11.1 summarizes the regulations of crowdinvesting in the US and the UK and, in addition, provides information about their cross-border aspects.

Table 11.1 US and UK crowdinvesting regulations—summary

	UK	US
Size thresholds	EUR 5M	USD 1M
Portals subject to authorization	Yes	Yes
Mandatory disclosure	Non-itemized	Itemized
Financial reporting requirements	No	Yes
Appropriateness filter	Yes	Yes
Limits to retail investors	Yes, per asset class	Yes, per issuer
Resale restrictions	No	Yes
Periodic disclosure obligations for issuers	No	Yes
Collective investment rules apply to crowdinvesting vehicle, when present	No	Yes
Open to foreign issuers	Yes	No
Open to foreign investors	Yes	Yes
Open to foreign portals	Yes, subject to MiFID rules	Yes, subject to conditions

11.4 The Fine Line Between Throwing the Baby out with the Bathwater and Giving Fraudsters Free Rein

In Sect. 11.3, we described the regulatory framework on crowdinvesting in the US and the UK. In a companion paper, we show how, both in the US (for offerings reserved to accredited investors) and in Europe, crowdinvesting platforms are experimenting with solutions to avoid adverse selection problems and ensure a minimum quality of the offerings, at the very least in terms of self-imposed disclosure requirements (Armour and Enriques 2017). Market experimentation may provide support for a "wait-and-see", minimalist approach to the regulation of the sector. A minimal-intervention approach, like the UK's, would still aim to ensure that potential investors understand the risks of crowdinvesting, for example by conditioning their access to the platform upon correct completion of a questionnaire.[45] The requirement, common to both the US and the UK, that retail investors may only invest a limited proportion of their income or net worth into crowdinvesting also seems a sensible restriction on retail investor participation in the market.

More risk-averse (or market-mistrusting) policymakers may be less persuaded by a laissez-faire, experimentation-friendly regulatory environment, and impose obligations on fundraisers and platforms more similar to those that apply to securities offers and investment (broker-dealer) services providers under "regular" securities regulations: the menu would include a list of items to be disclosed, a general antifraud provision with liability rules favoring plaintiffs, a public enforcement apparatus, and conduct of business rules for platforms, possibly making them subject to strict liability. This appears to be US policymakers' approach to crowdinvesting regulation, the high fixed costs of which entail the risk of precluding retail investors' access to crowdinvesting altogether by freezing supply.

The differing policy choices of the UK and the US as respects crowdinvesting appear to be path dependent. The UK's openness to this innovative form of alternative finance derives from pre-existing rules that made smaller offerings, such as crowdfunding ones, exempt from offerings rules. In contrast, the more cautious approach in the US can be traced to the previously applicable and prohibitively costly regulatory environment under the Securities Act.

In the US, supply of crowdinvesting opportunities will be curbed by the continued imposition of disclosure rules which, though less onerous than the general disclosure regime, nevertheless still impose high compliance costs. In the UK, there is no other restriction to supply than the platforms' willingness to screen issuers for quality with a view to establishing reputational capital and issuers' and platforms' liability in case of financial promotions that are not "fair, clear and not misleading". Only time will tell which system will work best to facilitate effective capital formation via crowdinvesting in the long run. Yet, given the highly dynamic and competitive features of the market for crowdinvesting platforms, one common sense policy suggestion can be made: regulations in this area should have a sunset clause, thereby signaling policymakers' commitment to revise rules once the phenomenon is better known or has evolved in a way that could not be possibly predicted.

Notes

1. The figure for the UK's most popular platform is GBP 440,242 (USD 559,855). See https://www.crowdcube.com/infographic (accessed on December 5, 2016).

2. Angels' investing styles vary significantly: while the overall picture is one of less formal arrangements than in the case of VCs, still some angels adopt the same protective measures that are common in VC investment contracts. See Ibrahim (2008, 1420–1425).
3. The available empirical evidence on the incidence of fraud in reward crowdfunding platforms shows that it is a contained phenomenon. Cumming et al. (2016) find that actual or suspected fraud occurred in 0.01%of initiated projects per year. One may well question, though, whether that is a good predictor of the incidence of fraud on crowdinvesting platforms.
4. See SEC, Crowdfunding, 78 Fed. Reg. 66,428, 66,458 n. 309 (to be codified in scattered parts of 17 C.F.R.); Financial Conduct Authority (2013).
5. Article 1(2)(h) Prospectus Directive [2003] O.J. L 345/64 (as amended) (the "Prospectus Directive").
6. Financial Services and Markets Act 2000 ("FSMA"), Section 85(5)(a), Schedule 11A, para 9.
7. Annex I, Section C, of MiFID 2 defines financial instruments to include transferable securities. Transferable securities are defined in Art. 4(1)(44) to include securities negotiable on the capital market, such as shares in companies.
8. Markets in Financial Instruments Directive [2004] O.J. L 145/1 ("MiFID").
9. MiFID allowed member states to carve out an exemption for crowdinvesting platforms under Article 3, and at least two member states have apparently done so. Id., p. 19, para 57. Such an exemption is premised on the platform not holding client funds or securities, not providing any investment service except the reception and transmission of orders, and transmit such orders only to other authorized firms. Art. 3 MiFID. While this exemption remains in MiFID 2, a new Art. 3(2) therein requires member states to apply to them rules and regulations equivalent to MiFID 2 in many respects, including conditions for authorization and supervision and conduct of business obligations.
10. Art. 25, The Financial Services and Markets Act 2000 (Regulated Activities) Order 2001, SI 2001/554 (available at http://www.legislation.gov.uk/uksi/2001/544/article/25/made).
11. FSMA 2000 s. 21.
12. FCA's Conduct of Business Sourcebook ("COBS") 4.2.1R., implementing Art. 19(2) MiFID (now Art. 24(3) MiFID II).

13. COBS 4.7.7R. Clients could also be advised under COBS 4.7.8R, so that the suitability of the crowdfunding is assessed by the firm or another authorized firm, although that would likely be uncommon in the case of crowdfunding.
14. The tests are not onerous. Typical questions might be of the following form: "Most early-stage and many growth-focussed businesses: (a) succeed; (b) break even; (c) fail." (Taken from sign-up questionnaire at Seedrs, a UK platform: see https://www.seedrs.com/signup/investor-profile/quiz).
15. Jumpstart Our Business Startups Act, Pub L. No. 112–106, 126 Stat. 306 (2012) (the "JOBS Act").
16. Proposed Rule: Crowdfunding, 78 Fed. Reg. 66,428, November 5, 2013.
17. 15 U.S.C. 77a et seq. (the "Securities Act").
18. Under 17 CFR § 227.100(2), the maximum investment for an investor in a single issuer is determined as follows. If the investor has both annual income and net worth of less than USD 100,000, a limit of USD 2,000 or 5% of annual income or net worth, whichever is greater, applies. If either the investor's annual income or net worth exceeds USD 100,000, a limit of 10% of annual income or net worth, whichever is greater, but not to exceed USD 100,000, applies. (The JOBS Act actually stipulated these limits, but did so in a logically inconsistent way, which required the SEC to clarify its position in its final Regulation Crowdfunding).
19. 17 CFR § 227.100, 17 CFR § 227.203.
20. Section 4A(b)(1)(B) of the Securities Act, 17 CFR § 227.201(b), 17 CFR § 227.201(m)(2).
21. Section 4A(b)(1)(C) of the Securities Act, 17 CFR § 227.201(d).
22. Section 4A(b)(1)(E) of the Securities Act, 17 CFR § 227.201(i).
23. Section 4A(b)(1)(G) of the Securities Act, 17 CFR § 227.201(m)(4).
24. Section 4A(b)(1)(F) of the Securities Act, 17 CFR § 227.201(g).
25. Section 4A(b)(1)(H) of the Securities Act, 17 CFR § 227.201(m).
26. Section 4A(b)(1)(D) of the Securities Act, 17 CFR § 227.201(t).
27. Ibid.
28. Section 4A(b)(1)(D) of the Securities Act, 17 CFR § 227.201(s).
29. Section 4A(b)(4) of the Securities Act, 17 CFR § 227.202.
30. The SEC was given discretion under Section 4A(b)(1)(I) of the Securities Act to require additional disclosure for the protection of investors and in the public interest.

31. 17 CFR § 227.201(o)(1).
32. 17 CFR § 227.201(p).
33. 17 CFR § 227.201(m)(5).
34. Section 4(a)(3) of the Securities Act, 17 CFR § 227.501.
35. Section 4A(a)(11) of the Securities Act, 17 CFR § 227.300.
36. Section 4A(a)(5) of the Securities Act, 17 CFR § 227.301. The intermediary is entitled to rely on representations from the issuer, absent knowledge, or indications to the contrary.
37. Section 4A(c) of the Securities Act.
38. Proposed Rule: Crowdfunding (n. 16), 66,499.
39. Crowdfunding, Final Rule, 80 Federal Register 71,387, 71,478.
40. Crowdfunding, Final Rule, 80 Fed. Reg. 71,387, 71,500. Estimates by SeedInvest, a crowdfunding platform, are even higher: if one raises one million dollars via Title III crowdfunding, the cost of the offering will be USD 250,000. See https://www.seedinvest.com/blog/jobs-act/crowdsourcing-title-iii-crowdfunding-cost-model.
41. For example, in the case of an issuer raising USD 100,000 under Regulation Crowdfunding with fees in the region of USD 17,500, the equity actually contributed to the issuer's operations would be USD 82,500 and it would need to increase in value by USD 17,500/USD 82,500, or 21.2%, before the value of issuer's equity would reach the valuation of USD 100,000 where equity investors would break even.
42. Section 201(a) Jumpstart Our Business Startups Act, Pub. L. No. 112-106, 126 Stat. 306 (2012) (codified in 15 U.S.C. §77d). "Accredited investor" is defined in Rule 501 under the Securities Act, 17 CFR §230.501, to include among others any corporation with assets over USD 5million and any individual with either a net worth exceeding USD 1 million or an income above USD 200,000 in the two most recent years and a reasonable expectation of reaching the same income in the current year.
43. Within the EU (and therefore, currently, in the UK) an investment vehicle acting as the crowdinvestors' nominee would seem not to qualify as an Alternative Investment Fund as defined in the Alternative Investment Fund Management Directive. According to this Directive, Alternative Investment Funds are defined as "collective investment undertakings, including investment compartments thereof, which: (1) raise capital from a number of investors, with a view to investing it in accordance with a defined investment policy for the benefit of those investors; and (2) do not require authorisation pursuant to Article 5 of Directive

2009/65/EC (the UCITS Directive) (Article 4(1)(a))". While ESMA's guidelines clarify that it is enough to raise capital from more than *one* investor for capital raising to be from a "number of" them, they also define the term "defined investment policy" in a way that appears to be inconsistent with the mere purchase and holding of securities issued by an individual company in order to exercise the related rights on behalf of investors. See ESMA (2013, 7). Consistent with this interpretation, examples exist of European crowdfunding platforms that use investment vehicles that are not registered as AIFs (see Armour and Enriques 2017).
44. 15 U.S. Code § 80a–3(c)(1).
45. See above, n 14.

References

Agrawal, Ajay, Christian Catalini, and Avi Goldfarb. 2010. *Entrepreneurial Finance and the Flat-World Hypothesis: Evidence from Crowd-Funding Entrepreneurs in the Arts*. NET Institute Working Paper No. 10-08.

———. 2014. Some Simple Economics of Crowdfunding. *Innovation Policy and the Economy* 14: 63–97.

Armour, John, and Luca Enriques. 2017. The Promise and Perils of Crowdfunding. Between Corporate Finance and Consumer Contracts. *Modern Law Review* (forthcoming).

Belleflamme, Paul, Thomas Lambert, and Armin Schwienbacher. 2014. Crowdfunding: Tapping the Right Crowd. *Journal of Business Venturing* 29: 585–609.

Belleflamme, Paul, Nessrine Omrani, and Martin Peitz. 2015. The Economics of Crowdfunding Platforms. *Information Economics and Policy* 33: 11–28.

Black, Bernard S. 2001. The Legal and Institutional Preconditions for Strong Securities Markets. *UCLA Law Review* 48: 781–855.

Coffee, John C. 2006. *Gatekeepers: The Professions and Corporate Governance*. Oxford: Oxford University Press on Demand.

Colombo, Massimo G., Chiara Franzoni, and Cristina Rossi-Lamastra. 2015. Internal Social Capital and the Attraction of Early Contributions in Crowdfunding. *Entrepreneurship Theory and Practice* 39: 75–100.

Cumming, Douglas J., Lars Hornuf, Moein Karami, and Denis Schweizer. 2016. Disentangling Crowdfunding from Fraudfunding. *Social Science Research Network*. https://ssrn.com/abstract=2828919. Accessed 20 Feb 2017.

Dorff, Michael B. 2014. The Siren Call of Equity Crowdfunding. *Journal of Corporate Law* 39: 493–524.

European Securities. 2014. Opinion: Investment-Based Crowdfunding. http://www.esma.europa.eu/system/files/2014-1378_opinion_on_investment-based_crowdfunding.pdf. Accessed 20 Feb 2017.

European Securities and Markets Authority. 2013. Guidelines on Key Concepts of the AIFMD. https://www.esma.europa.eu/sites/default/files/library/2015/11/2013-611_guidelines_on_key_concepts_of_the_aifmd_-_en.pdf. Last modified 13 Aug 2013.

Financial Conduct Authority. 2013. The FCA's Regulatory Approach to Crowdfunding (and Similar Activities). www.fca.org.uk/static/documents/consultation-papers/cp13-13.pdf. Last modified Oct 2013.

———. 2014. Policy Statement 14/4, The FCA's Regulatory Approach to Crowdfunding Over the Internet, and the Promotion of Non-Readily Realisable Securities by Other Media: Feedback to CP13/13 and Final Rules. http://www.fca.org.uk/static/documents/policy-statements/ps14-04.pdf. Last modified Mar 2014.

Fried, Jesse M., and Mira Ganor. 2006. Agency Costs of Venture Capital Control in Startups. *New York University Law Review* 81: 967–1025.

Gilson, Ronald J. 2010. Locating Innovation: The Endogeneity of Technology, Organizational Structure, and Financial Contracting. *Columbia Law Review* 110: 885–917.

Hall, Bronwyn H. 2011. Innovation and Productivity. *National Bureau of Economic Research*. http://www.nber.org/papers/w17178.pdf. Accessed 20 Feb 2017.

Hazen, Thomas Lee. 2014. Crowdfunding or Fraudfunding? Social Networks and the Securities Laws—Why the Specially Tailored Exemption Must Be Conditioned on Meaningful Disclosure. *North Carolina Law Review* 90: 1735–1770.

Hornuf, L., and M. Neuenkirch. 2017. Pricing Shares in Equity Crowdfunding. *Small Business Economics* 48: 795–811.

Hornuf, Lars, and Armin Schwienbacher. 2016. Crowdinvesting—Angel Investing for the Masses? In *Handbook of Research on Venture Capital*, ed. C. Mason and H. Landström, vol. 3, 381–397. Cheltenham: Edward Elgar Publishing.

———. 2017. Should Securities Regulation Promote Crowdinvesting. *Small Business Economics* 49: 579–593.

Hurt, Christine. 2015. Pricing Disintermediation: Crowdfunding and Online Auction IPOs. *University of Illinois Law Review*: 217–261.

Ibrahim, Darian M. 2008. The (Not So) Puzzling Behavior of Angel Investors. *Vanderbilt Law Review* 61: 1405–1452.

———. 2010. Financing the Next Silicon Valley. *Washington University Law Review* 87: 717–762.

———. 2015. Equity Crowdfunding: A Market for Lemons? *Minnesota Law Review* 100: 561–607.

Kogan, Leonid, Dimitris Papanikolaou, Amit Seru, and Noah Stoffman. 2012. Technological Innovation, Resource Allocation, and Growth. *National Bureau of Economic Research*. http://www.nber.org/papers/w17769.pdf. Accessed 20 Feb 2017.

Ley, Andy, and Scott Weaven. 2011. Exploring Agency Dynamics of Crowdfunding in Start-Up Capital Financing. *Academy of Entrepreneurship Journal* 17: 85–110.

Massolution. 2015. *2015CF. The Crowdfund Industry Report*. http://reports.crowdsourcing.org/index.php?route=product/product&product_id=54. Accessed 7 Mar 2017.

Morrissette, Stephen G. 2007. A Profile of Angel Investors. *Journal of Private Equity* 10: 52–66.

Nanda, Ramana, and Matthew Rhodes-Kropf. 2013. Investment Cycles and Startup Innovation. *Journal of Financial Economics* 110: 403–418.

Oranburg, Seth C. 2015. Bridgefunding: Crowdfunding and the Market for Entrepreneurial Finance. *Cornell Journal of Law and Public Policy* 15: 397–452.

Pope, Nikki D. 2011. Crowdfunding Microstartups: It's Time for the Securities and Exchange Commission to Approve a Small Offering Exemption. *University of Pennsylvania Journal of Business Law* 13: 973–1002.

Securities and Exchange Commission. 2015. SEC Adopts Rules to Permit Crowdfunding-Proposes Amendments to Existing Rules to Facilitate Intrastate and Regional Securities Offerings. October 30. https://www.sec.gov/news/pressrelease/2015-249.html. Accessed 07 Mar 2017.

Weinstein, Ross S. 2013. Crowdfunding in the U.S. and Abroad: What to Expect When You're Expecting. *Cornell International Law Journal* 46: 427–453.

Wong, Andrew, Mihir Bhatia, and Zachary Freeman. 2009. Angel Finance: The Other Venture Capital. *Strategic Change* 18: 221–230.

John Armour is Professor of Law and Finance at Oxford University and a Fellow of the British Academy and the ECGI. He has held visiting posts at the University of Chicago, Columbia Law School, the University of Frankfurt, the Max Planck Institute in Hamburg, the University of Pennsylvania, and Sydney University Law School. Armour has published widely in the fields of corporate law and financial regulation. His books include *Principles of Financial Regulation* (OUP, 2016) and *The Anatomy of Corporate Law* (OUP, 3rd ed. 2017). He is an Executive Editor of the *Journal of Corporate Law Studies* and the *Journal of Law, Finance and Accounting*.

Luca Enriques is the Allen & Overy Professor of Corporate Law at the Faculty of Law of Oxford University and a Fellow of the ECGI. He is a coauthor of *The Anatomy of Corporate Law* and of *Principles of Financial Regulation*. He has published several articles in major European and US reviews and journals, including the *Journal of Economic Perspectives*, the *Cornell Law Review*, and the *Harvard Business Law Review*. He has held visiting positions at the University of Cambridge, IDC Hertzliya, Harvard Law School, and other universities and he has been commissioner at the Italian S.E.C. (Consob) between 2007 and 2012.

Index[1]

[1] Note: Page numbers followed by 'n' refer to notes.

D. Cumming, L. Hornuf (eds.), *The Economics of Crowdfunding*, https://doi.org/10.1007/978-3-319-66119-3

The manufacturer's authorised representative in the EU is Springer Nature Customer Service Centre GmbH, Europaplatz 3, 69115 Heidelberg, Germany. If you have any concerns regarding our products, please contact ProductSafety@springernature.com

Printed and bound by CPI Group (UK) Ltd, Croydon, CR0 4YY
30/09/2026
02225653-0010